EUROPEAN INDUSTRIAL
ORGANISATION

PROBLEMS OF ECONOMIC INTEGRATION

General Editor: GEORGE W. McKENZIE

PUBLISHED

European Industrial Organisation
Alexis P. Jacquemin, University of Louvain, and Henry W. de Jong,
   Netherlands School of Business

The Economics of the Euro-Currency System
George W. McKenzie, University of Southampton

Trade Preferences for Developing Countries
Tracy Murray, Graduate School of Business Administration,
   New York University

International Economics of Pollution
Ingo Walter, Graduate School of Business Administration,
   New York University

FORTHCOMING

Economic Interdependence
Sven W. Arndt, University of California at Santa Cruz

International Capital Flows
David T. Llewellyn, Loughborough University

European Industrial Organisation

ALEXIS P. JACQUEMIN

University of Louvain

and

HENRY W. DE JONG

Netherlands School of Business

M

First published 1977 by
THE MACMILLAN PRESS LTD
London and Basingstoke
Associated companies in New York Dublin
Melbourne Johannesburg and Madras

ISBN 0 333 17902 1 (hard cover)
0 333 21102 2 (paper cover)

Typeset in IBM Baskerville by
Preface Ltd
Salisbury, Wilts
Printed and bound in Great Britain by
Redwood Burn Limited
Trowbridge & Esher

Contents

General Editor's Preface

Since the Second World War, the economies of Europe, North America, Japan and the developing world have become increasingly interdependent. This has taken place at various levels. On the one hand we have seen the formation and growth of a formal organisation, the European Economic Community, whose aim is to strengthen existing political and economic ties amongst its members. But interdependence is not solely the result of legal treaties; it is also the outcome of economic innovation and evolution. The growth of the multinational corporation, the development of the Euro-currency system and the rapid growth of international trade are but examples of the trend.

Yet the resulting closer ties among nations have been a mixed blessing. It is no longer possible for governments to formulate national objectives in isolation from activity in the rest of the world. Monetary, fiscal, anti-trust and social policies now have widespread implications beyond national frontiers. How to cope with the complex implications of the current petroleum price developments is but an example of the sort of problem arising in an interdependent world.

Despite its obvious importance most economics textbooks give only cursory attention to international economic interdependence. The purpose of this series is to fill this gap by providing critical surveys and analyses of specific types of economic linkages among nations. It is thus hoped that the volumes will appeal not only to students, researchers and government bodies working in the field of international economics but also to those dealing with the problems of industrial organisation, monetary economics and other aspects of public policy which have traditionally been studied from a narrow, nationalistic viewpoint.

Department of Economics   GEORGE W. McKENZIE
Southampton University

Preface

Most textbooks on industrial economics are written by American scholars for American audiences. Accordingly the issues treated and evidence offered are those generated by the structure and functioning of North American markets. It could be maintained that the classic concepts and theories elaborated in this context can be applied usefully in explaining the operation of other industrialised economies such as the European one.

However, we have felt that since industrial economics is concerned with the structure and functioning of markets in the real world, it would be too simplistic to transfer this general framework on to the European industrial scene without any adaptation. At present, the Common Market is a well established institution with its proper nature, strengths and weaknesses; data on it is becoming available and common fields of concern are arising; common options in matters of industrial and competition policy are being determined. For all these reasons we think it indispensable to take into account the particular characteristics of Europe, both with respect to the relative importance attached to the subjects studied and the available theories, as well as concerning the empirical analyses undertaken and the institutional context. Otherwise the explanatory power of the industrial-economics approach would be rendered much less effective.

It is not our intention to present a handbook covering all the matters that come under the heading of 'industrial organisation'; there already exist some excellent Anglo-American textbooks that serve this purpose. Our aim is to construct a synthesis of what seems to us to be the main poles of reflection with regard to European industry today. However, the book does follow the traditional outline of industrial-organisation texts. Thus, in the following pages, we review successively:

(i) the set of market structures and their evolution over time (Chapters 2–4);
(ii) the relationship between structure and performance (Chapter 5);
(iii) the goals and behaviour of business firms (Chapter 6); and
(iv) anti-trust and industrial policies (Chapters 7 and 8).

We have tried to bring out the characteristics of the European

approach and the manner in which it contrasts with but also
resembles the North-American scene. Thus, for example, we insist
particularly on the behaviour of firms which is likely to mould the
still floating structures of the Common Market; we stress the way in
which firms are financially controlled and the role of holding companies; we discuss the calling into question of economies organised
according to the capitalistic mode in favour of labour management of
various kinds; and, finally, we analyse the conflicts arising between
European anti-trust policies and industrial policies resulting from the
co-ordination of activity and the various forms of planning agreement
between industry and the state.

As a result this book is primarily designed as a treatise on the main
topics in industrial organisation and public policy for European
students who have already mastered a solid course in microeconomic
theory; it could also be considered as a useful complementary text
for American students in industrial economics. Finally, we should
like to think that the book might attract an audience of economists
and businessmen who wish to obtain a wider view of European
industrial economics.

This work, however, is only a first step towards a better understanding of European industrial economics, which is still strongly
heterogeneous, in a state of constant change and for which comparable data are difficult to obtain.

Several imperfections in the manuscript were corrected in time by
the 'visible hand' of good friends. We wish to express our gratitude to
Kenneth George (Cardiff University) and William Adams (University
of Michigan), who voiced both general and detailed criticisms most
of which have been taken into account. We are also indebted to
Alfred Steinherr (University of Louvain), who made several valuable
suggestions and, not least, to Caroline Joll (Cardiff University), who
undertook the arduous task of improving the English text, mean-
while suggesting substantial changes. Finally, our thanks are due to
Anne Sibille of the European Institute for Advanced Studies in
Management (Brussels) whose task it was to type a perpetually
changing manuscript. Of course the responsibility for any errors or
ambiguities which remain has to be totally imputed to the authors.

ALEXIS P. JACQUEMIN
HENRY W. DE JONG

1

Industrial Organisation in a European Perspective

COMPETITION AND INDUSTRIAL ORGANISATION

It has become traditional to criticise the perfect-competition model, from the point of view of both its normative implications and its explanatory value. However, the model remains a useful starting-point. It provides us with a standard of comparison which permits us to examine some of the most prominent characteristics of our modern industrial economy.

Such a comparison will be made by means of a classificatory scheme, which forms one of the paradigms of industrial-organisation studies: the structure, conduct and performance of the market.

The structure of the market is understood to comprise a set of relatively stable industrial characteristics which affect the conduct of the firms operating in that market: the number of sellers and buyers, the nature of the product or service, the amount of knowledge and information at the disposal of market participants, the greater or lesser mobility of sellers and buyers.

Market behaviour of firms includes the various policies followed by the firm, from its pricing policies to its research and development endeavours, including, amongst others, concerted and collusionary policies.

Market performance concerns the results achieved by the firms. These include profit margins, growth, degree of capacity utilisation, product quality, and so on. These results are considered to be the outcome of the various combinations of structure and behaviour.

It therefore seems useful to make a comparison between the perfectly competitive model and observed reality with the aid of this broad general scheme of classification.

Market structure

Comparing reality with the perfect-competition model's assumption of numerous, small decision centres, linked to the postulate of a convex production set, it is immediately obvious that in the economy as well as in most sectors of production or distribution there are large

firms with important market shares. The explanation of this phenomenon of concentration, both on the level of the economy as a
whole and on the level of the industrial sector or market, is one of
the main themes of this book.

The assumption of product homogeneity contained in the model
must give way to the recognition that product differentiation is well
developed. While the model assumes given consumer preferences at
any point in time, industrial-organisation analysis has to inquire into
their formation and evolution over time.

Perfect competition also assumes free entry and free exit to and
from an industry in such a way that profit margins are eroded. But in
the real world there are important barriers to entry and exit, both of
an institutional nature and of technological or commercial origin.

The static nature of the perfect-competition model, with its simul-
taneous actions and reactions of firms, is a serious flaw. For competition is a dynamic process, implying a continuous change in the
data, and it is impossible to understand the concept on the basis of
an assumption that the determinants remain constant. The equilibrium position theoretically reached by the market cannot be verified
in reality and what is observed is probably no more than some kind
of statistical regularity.

Perfect knowledge or perfect information is not usually present;
the firm is confronted by situations of risk and uncertainty. Information may be non-existent, unobtainable, or may only be acquired
after a search process. Uncertainty is at the heart of the competitive
process: it affects entrepreneurial decisions and behaviour
profoundly, and thus also affects short-run equilibrium. What kind of
equilibrium (if any) is reached in a given market depends heavily on
the amount and type of information at the disposal of market
participants.

Goals and behaviour of the firm

Traditionally the goal of the firm is understood to be profit maximisation. But this hypothesis has been contested from two sides. On
the one hand, it is said that the large firm is not an organisation with
a unique objective, but a complex whole, in which various — often
conflicting — goals are pursued. A group of managers exercises
authority within the firm; in theory they maximise profits on behalf
of the owners, who are normally shareholders.

But these managerial directors have to satisfy other groups as well.
Employees, trade unions, customers and government agencies have

their own desires, which they are to a certain extent free to pursue, given the separation of ownership and control in the firm. Instead of profit maximisation this would result in maximisation of a utility function including various goals. The role of profit is, in such models, limited to acting as one of several objectives or as a constraint to be satisfied. Such behaviour would be made possible by the existence of imperfect market structures and the prevalence of 'soft' forms of competition or a complete absence thereof.

On the other hand, according to authors belonging to the behaviourist school, there is no optimising behaviour, whatever the goals may be. Each individual tries to achieve a certain threshold in the realisation of his aspirations. If this threshold is reached, he turns to other objectives, where the satisficing threshold has not yet been achieved.

If it is not reached he revises his level of aspiration and related strategies. As is said to be the case of many European companies, 'satisficing', or striving after sufficient profits instead of maximising them, could then be viewed as a decline in the 'animal spirits' of business behaviour, as Joan Robinson calls it.

In established static theory the firm is supposed to adapt itself to market conditions. Change is treated as an exogeneous factor, so that market conduct is determined by the structure of the system and the role of management is secondary. Goals are to be realised by means of a set of policies which faces a number of constraints such as human and financial resources, internal organisation and structural market conditions. The management has to exploit its knowledge of the level and elasticity of demand, production functions and costs in such a way that the best position is continuously attained. From time to time adjustments are necessary, and so the firm is pushed along its expansion path by means of external forces.

In reality, the firm does not merely adapt itself to short-term changes, but its actions also modify the evolution of the sector(s) in which it operates. As Schumpeter wrote: 'the best way to realistically visualise industrial strategy is to observe the conduct of new organisations . . . who introduce new products or new processes . . . or who reorganise a part or the whole of an industry'.[1] A good deal of modern industrial analysis is therefore devoted to long-term strategies in which market structure is no longer a parameter but a variable. A firm could change concentration in a sector of industry by means of mergers and takeovers; it could erect or increase barriers to entry by means of its price or patent policies, long-term delivery contracts or exclusive distribution agreements; it could increase its product differentiation by means of advertisements and the incurring of selling costs; technological change could be deliberately brought about by research and development. It is only recently that dynamic models have been devised to cope with such phenomena, as we will see.

Market performance

With respect to the performance characteristics of the perfect-competition model there are several well established findings. On the general-equilibrium level there will be an optimal allocation of the given amount of goods produced between consumers and the given amount of factors of production available between producers. The price system will bring about such an outcome. Moreover, it ensures that the marginal rate of transformation between goods supplied by producers will equal the marginal rate of substitution between goods bought by consumers. In such a situation the sales price is equal to marginal cost and no profits will remain in the long run. If monopoly enters the picture all certainty with respect to the Paretian optimum is lost; depending on the nature of the imperfection, there may be insufficient input, selling prices too high, excess production capacity, input prices too low, and so on.

However, it is dangerous to compare the monopolistic and perfectly competitive equilibria. Cost and demand conditions may be radically different. The monopolist might use indivisible equipment, which would assure him very low production costs. His output may be short of that obtained where price equals marginal cost, but such an output might still be higher than under perfect competition. The competitive firms would simply be too small to utilise the larger-scale indivisible equipment.

Second, the comparison should not be limited to monopoly but should also take account of oligopoly, for which there are various models from which it is hard to draw any general conclusions about the consequences of different market failures for efficiency.

Third, the welfare of individuals depends on a much broader range of performance than that taken into account by the perfect-competition model. For example, a perfectly competitive market will probably not undertake sufficient investment in research and development because of high risks and the impossibility of fully appropriating the rewards. Moreover, uncertainty and an attitude of risk aversion on the part of managers may also cast doubt on the results predicted by the theory.

In general, the optimality of the competitive market solution is no longer taken for granted, especially if uncertainty, collective consumption, external effects, social choice and so on are neglected.

However, as we will see, the conclusion that in real life market competition is no longer valuable in steering the economy would be mistaken. In the European Common Market system — as in other mixed economies — the public authorities still assign competition an important function in regulating the system and co-ordinating individuals' decisions.

A EUROPEAN APPROACH TO THE STRUCTURE–CONDUCT–PERFORMANCE PARADIGM

Two general characteristics mark the European approach towards industrial economics.

In the first place, the structure—conduct—performance paradigm can be handled in different ways. The majority of American authors insist on the study of market structure and on the existence of direct connections between structure and actual performance.[2] The role of conduct is minimised in that companies are supposed (a) to have similar goals and (b) to adapt passively to the economic environment.

If S, C and P are the vectors representing structure, conduct and performance respectively, the 'structural' economists write:

$$C = C(S) \text{ and therefore } P = P\ [C(S), S] = \phi(S).$$

Many empirical studies have followed this approach and describe the structure of various industries, their evolution through time and the possible relationships with economic performance. Such studies have filled the empty boxes of traditional microeconomic analysis with some empirical substance.[3]

On the other hand, the majority of European authors have subscribed to the view that conduct is the determining factor in the scheme S–C–P. These authors have emphasised the study of the many possible policies concerning prices, products, cartels, take-overs and mergers which, if followed by firms in similar structural conditions, will cause the firms to record different performance.[4]

It is also recognised that the goals and conduct adopted by firms affect results and even that various types of conduct can change market structures in favour of one or more firms and thereby improve performance in an indirect way.

The preceding expression therefore becomes more complex and could be written:

$$P = f\ (S,C) \quad \text{and} \quad \frac{dS}{dt} = f\ (C,S).$$

Thus the evolution of market structure over time depends on the current structure and the conduct adopted by the firm. The firm and its management thereby regains its role as a driving force in economic development.

The leader of the firm is an entrepreneur in so far as he breaks through repetitive processes in order to establish new and more productive combinations. In doing so, he is no longer the slave of his environment, but exercises an influence on the development of markets; in the long-run these must be forged by wilful actions of producers.[5]

The consequence of this prevailing European view has been a proliferation of general works describing possible strategies but a scarcity of statistical and econometric analysis: the phenomena described have not been measured, either because of a lack of data, or because of their qualitative nature.

A second characteristic of the European approach relates to the expected performance of the competitive system. The virtues of competition have always been considered with some scepticism in European countries characterised by the direct intervention of the state, the role of public enterprises, the 'mixed', 'guided' or 'planned' nature of their national economies. Competition is not seen as a goal but rather as an important means of exercising social control over industry — the most impersonal form; and its maintenance is justified as long as it achieves the set of objectives in a better way than other forms of control, such as more or less detailed public regulation, public ownership of industry or co-operation between the public and the private sectors.

The *First Report on Competition Policy* of the Commission of the European Economic Community declares in the same vein:

Even though the operation of market forces is an irreplaceable factor for progress and the most appropriate means of ensuring the best possible distribution of production factors, situations can nevertheless arise when this by itself is not enough to obtain the required results without too much delay and intolerable social tension. When the decisions of the enterprises themselves do not make it possible for the necessary changes to be made at an acceptable cost in social terms, then recourse to relatively short-term and limited intervention is necessary in order to direct such decisions towards an optimal economic and social result.[6]

In such a climate, it is not surprising that the creation of the European Common Market, with its open boundaries, has meant a profound change. Within the short period of ten years, barriers to free competition, whether consisting of customs duties, import quotas, the right of establishment, and so on, were largely torn down, and the pressure of a few dynamic firms was sufficient to upset the previous equilibria. Since the early 1950s intra-European trade flows have sharply increased, so that internal trade rose to an average share of more than 52 per cent of the total trade of member countries in the early 1970s, or twice as much as in the early 1950s. A vast number of new business establishments have been set up, originating both in member countries and in third countries. Investments have been undertaken to reap the benefits of the expanded market, new products have been launched and whole new industries have made an appearance. Understandably, competition increased, as firms encroached upon each other's traditional markets in an effort to seize the new opportunities. They strove to enlarge market shares, to capture the strategic points of production or distribution, to supply fast-growing new products, to adapt their production processes, to cut costs and to streamline organisation. The means used were the traditional competitive methods such as price-cutting, product variety, advertisements, innovations, and so on. Thus competitive forces have been strengthened to an extent unknown in Europe since the liberalisation movements of the 1860s and 1870s.

This changing international competitive environment brought about large shifts in established positions and in traditional defences. Economic uncertainty increased because the environment was no longer stable.

Of course private business has reacted to regain control of the competitive process, through new cartel agreements, mergers, expansion of multinational and multi-product activities, leading to a reshaping of European industry. Thus a main concern of European authorities has since been to safeguard the dynamism of an enlarged unified market against private restrictive practices.

At the same time, however, there is a resurgence, among the member states and even inside the Commission, of scepticism about the virtues of competition. National governments have increasingly tended to intervene to protect their own national firms and industries, ignoring the regional and industrial policies of the Community as a whole.

This is especially the case with purely 'conservational' aids designed to ensure the survival of industries or undertakings which cannot be expected to cope with national, Community and international competition.[7]

Inconsistencies also arise between European competition policy and the various European structural policies — industrial, agricultural, regional or social — so that today there is shifting balance between a policy of co-operation and co-ordination and competition policy as the main regulator of economic activity.

At this stage we interrupt the analysis to set the scene by giving a brief factual survey of the European economy.

STATISTICAL DIMENSIONS OF THE EUROPEAN ECONOMY

In this section we give a factual survey of the size, internal structure, relative importance and growth of the European Economic Community. By means of these data, the student can become acquainted with the Common Market from the quantitative side. The approach will be divided into two parts: first, attention will be devoted to the macroeconomic aspects, such as population, employment and unemployment, the gross national product and its division between broad sectors, the rate of investment, *per capita* national income and other information of a similar nature; second, we review industrial structure, but only in a very general sense; finally, a short summary of the main institutional arrangements of the E.E.C. is presented so as to clarify the political and legal environment in which the economy operates.

The economy as a whole

Table 1.1 gives the total population of the E.E.C. and its constituent nations. In 1973, the E.E.C. was enlarged by the accession of the United Kingdom, Ireland and Denmark so that formally its population rose from 188 million in 1970 to 257 million in 1973. (For comparative purposes we have added the figures for these three countries since 1950.)

A first aspect is that the weight of the continental countries has increased relative to that of the United Kingdom. For example, the West German population is now 6 million larger than that of the United Kingdom, whereas in 1950 the two were equal, and the French—United Kingdom discrepancy has been halved. Comparing the E.E.C. with some foreign powers (Table 1.2), it also appears that the E.E.C.'s population is comparable to that of the United States and Russia, but much larger than Japan's. Total incomes differ much more as *per capita* incomes diverge widely. Roughly speaking the U.S. total income was one and a quarter times that of the E.E.C., whereas the E.E.C. level was twice that of the Comecon countries, and two and a half times as high as that of Japan.

Table 1.3 gives the totally employed population since 1955. In both the six original and nine current member countries, employment has grown but the rate of increase has been slow, and has

TABLE 1.1

Population in the E.E.C. 1950–73
(in millions, rounded to nearest 100,000)

	West Germany	France	Italy	Netherlands	Belgium/ Luxembourg	E.E.C.(6)	United Kingdom	Ireland	Denmark	E.E.C.
1950	50.3	42.0	46.4	10.2	9.0	157.9	50.3	3.0	4.3	215.5
1955	52.7	43.6	49.2	10.8	9.2	165.5	50.9	2.9	4.4	223.7
1960	55.4	45.7	50.2	11.5	9.4	173.2	52.6	2.8	4.6	233.2
1965	58.6	48.8	52.0	12.3	9.8	181.5	54.3	2.9	4.8	243.5
1970	60.7	50.8	53.7	13.0	10.0	188.2	55.5	3.0	4.9	251.6
1973	62.0	52.1	54.9	13.4	10.1	192.5	56.0	3.1	5.0	256.6

SOURCES: *E.E.C. Social Statistics (1968); Eurostat National Accounts (1973); Eurostat National Accounts (1960–73, 1st quarter 1974).*

TABLE 1.2

Population and total income of some major blocs (1973)

	Population (millions)	Per capita income*	Total income (billion units)*
United States	213	6191	1319
Comecon countries	357	1640	585
of which Russia	250	1700	425
Japan	107	3803	407
E.E.C.	257	4112	1057

*In European units of account at current prices and exchange rates.

SOURCES: E.E.C. *Basic Statistics*; for Russia and Comecon:
United Nations, *Statistical Year Book*.

tended to fall. Stabilisation seems to have been reached in the 1970s.
Comparing Tables 1.2 and 1.3 shows that the share of employed
population in the total population declined: in the six original E.E.C.
countries, it went from 42·4 per cent in 1955 to 39·5 per cent in
1973; in the nine the share declined from 43·6 per cent in 1955 to
40·7 per cent in 1973.

Table 1.3 also brings out the fast rise of the gross national product,
which in money terms rose fivefold in the original six member states
and fourfold in the nine countries. However, if price inflation is
taken into account and the growth of the gross national product is
traced in volume terms, another picture emerges (see Figure 1.1).
If output has risen by some 110 per cent between 1955 and 1973,
and employment (Table 1.3) has increased about 10 per cent, this
suggests that productivity per average employed person in real terms
has risen by some 100 per cent i.e. it has doubled. This is a real
achievement, and one of the big economic questions is to trace how
this has come about. We cannot delve deeply into this problem here
but two factors may be distinguished for the present discussion.

European integration meant an enlargement of the market so that
a greater division of labour, more mechanisation of production processes and larger production units could be achieved under the
pressure of intensified competition. Optimal economic processes had
to be applied, necessitating more capital investment and the utilisation of new and improved technologies. Table 1.4 indicates that gross
capital formation had indeed risen rapidly, in fact more than twofold
in real terms between 1960 and 1973.

On the other hand, the growing *per capita* income (caused by
rising productivity) has shifted consumer expenditure from agricultural products towards industrial goods and services. Accordingly,

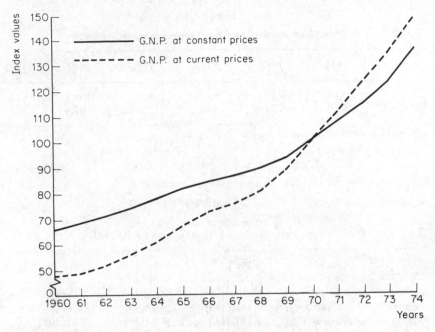

FIGURE 1.1   *Growth-indices of G.N.P. in the Common Market (1970 = 100)*

output and employment in the primary sector (comprising agriculture, horticulture, fisheries, forestry, and so on) increased much less (or even declined) than in the industrial sector, which in turn grew less fast than the services and the government sector. This is demonstrated in Tables 1.5 and 1.6. But, as shown by Table 1.7, there are considerable differences in the contribution to GDP made by the various sectors in different E.E.C. member countries.

TABLE 1.3

Employed population and gross product

| | Employment (millions) | | G.N.P. (billions)* | |
	E.E.C.—6	E.E.C.—9	E.E.C.—6	E.E.C.—9
1955	70.4	97.7	134.2	194.0
1960	74.1	102.0	191.2	271.2
1965	75.1	104.2	310.0	423.6
1970	76.3	104.8	487.0	628.7
1973	76.3	104.7	671.1	836.0

*In European units of account at current prices and exchange rates.

SOURCE: E.E.C. Bureau of Statistics, *National Accounts 1972, 1973.*

TABLE 1.4

Gross fixed capital formation (Volume index 1970 = 100)

	1960	1965	1970	1971	1972	1973
E.E.C.–6	53.7	76.4	100	103.5	107.3	112.5
E.E.C.–9	55.6	77.6	100	103.1	106.9	112.2

SOURCE: Eurostat, *National Accounts.*

TABLE 1.5

Gross domestic product by sector
(market prices; billion units of account, E.E.C.–6)

	1961	1965	1970	1971	1973
Agriculture, etc.	17.1(8)	21.5(7)	26.0(5)	27.0(5)	33.6(5)
Industry	102.7(49)	148.3(49)	235.3(50)	256.5(49)	308.7(47)
Services	71.9(34)	107.1(35)	172.5(36)	192.3(36) }	335.5(50)
State	17.9(9)	28.4(9)	46.2(9)	53.8(10) }	
Total	209.6	305.3	480.0	529.6	677.8
E.E.C.–9				684.1	836.0

NOTE: Percentage share given in parentheses. Figures may not add up to 100 because of rounding.

TABLE 1.6

Employment by sector (in millions, E.E.C.–6)

	1961	%	1965	%	1970	%	1974	%	E.E.C.–9 1972
Agriculture, etc.	14.3	(19.1)	11.9	(15.8)	9.4	(12.3)	7.9	(10)	(9.6)
Industry	31.4	(42.9)	32.6	(43.3)	33.3	(43.7)	32.0	(43.2)	(43.4)
Services	28.9	(38.9)	23.0	(40.9)	25.1	(44.0)	34.2	(46.2)	(46.9)
State	7.1		7.7		8.6				
Total	74.6	100.0	75.1	100.0	76.3	100.0	74.1	100.0	

NOTE: Percentage share given in parentheses.

SOURCE: *E.E.C. National Accounts.*

TABLE 1.7

Division of the gross domestic product
(1972, percentage)

Sectors	Denmark	West Germany	France	Ireland	Italy	Netherlands	Belgium	Luxembourg	United Kingdom
Agriculture	7.7	3.1	6.3	16.9	8.1	5.9	4.3	3.9	2.2
Industry	38.2	51.5	47.1	32.3	41.2	40.5	43.3	41.8	41.6
Services & Government	54.1	45.6	46.6	50.8	50.7	53.6	52.4	54.3	56.2

TABLE 1.8

Foreign trade of major economic areas (1973 in millions of units of account)

	E.E.C.–9	USA	USSR	Japan
Imports ($ million)	171.698	55.296	14.800	30.657
(% of world total)	41.7	13.4	4.3	7.4
Exports ($ million)	167.931	57.053	15.112	29.549
(% of world total)	42.5	14.4	4.1	7.5

NOTE: Both imports and exports of the E.E.C. exclude intra-E.E.C. trade.

SOURCE: Eurostat, *Basic Statistics.*

Ireland and Italy have the largest agricultural sectors, while in Luxembourg and West Germany, the industrial sector contributes more than half the gross domestic product. Denmark and the United Kingdom have strong service and government sectors, although Ireland, Italy and Belgium are not far behind. In the United States, the industrial sector contributes 34 per cent, the agricultural sector 3 per cent and the service sector 63 per cent towards the gross domestic product. The development of the various sectors in the Common Market countries shows a similar pattern: agriculture is declining, industry expanded until the early 1970s but is now stagnating, and the service/government sector is increasing, slowly in the United Kingdom, but quicker in countries such as France and Italy. Finally, the importance of the E.E.C. can also be seen from its foreign-trade figures (Table 1.8). The E.E.C.'s share of world trade is greater than that of any other economic bloc and this shows that European economic welfare is intimately connected with world developments.

Industrial sectors

Even after nearly twenty years of existence of the Common Market, it is not easy to give a general industrial survey of the Community. It is difficult to obtain industrial statistics for the whole Community on a homogeneous basis, and the recent accession of three new member states has complicated matters further. Apart from some general tables we have assembled statistics for individual industries from various sources, which may differ in accuracy, but nevertheless give an idea of the order of magnitudes involved and of the differences in development between countries and between industries.

Table 1.9 gives the development of industrial production during the past ten years. It follows from the table that the 'old' industrial countries (Belgium, the United Kingdom, Luxembourg) have grown

TABLE 1.9

Index of industrial production (1963 = 100)

	1964	1967	1969	1971	1973	1974
Netherlands	110	128	160	188	219	215
Ireland	108	127	153	164	189	196
France	107	121	142	160	183	186
Denmark	112	127	154	159	181	—
West Germany	108	114	144	156	175	171
Italy	101	128	140	145	170	177
Belgium	107	113	131	138	157	163
United Kingdom	100	113	124	127	139	135
Luxembourg	109	116	127	126	147	151
E.E.C.—6	107	119	143	156	178	178
E.E.C.—9	107	118	138	149	168	167

SOURCE: Eurostat, *Basic Statistics.*

less fast than the 'newly' industrialised ones, i.e. those that started large-scale industrialisation in the post-war period, such as the Netherlands, Ireland, France and Denmark (compare with Table 1.7). Italy, which has also become industrialised since the Second World War, has been less successful, particularly in the late 1960s and early 1970s, because of social strife. Also, the country's dual economy is a handicap. On the other hand, such a relatively old industrial economy as the West German one did remarkably well — which suggests that since the war West Germany has at least partially taken over the role of Europe's industrial workshop from the United Kingdom and Belgium. These developments appear still more marked if productivity changes are compared.

Average annual changes in labour productivity may be defined as:

$$\frac{\text{Index of output of year } t}{\text{Employment in year } t} \Bigg/ \frac{\text{Index of output in year } t-1}{\text{Employment in year } t-1}$$

If these rates of labour-productivity changes are calculated for the period 1963—70, the figures shown in Table 1.10 are obtained.

TABLE 1.10

Average annual productivity changes (1963—70)

Netherlands	10.43	Ireland	4.00
West Germany	7.29	United Kingdom	3.86
Denmark	6.43	Luxembourg	2.43
France	6.14	Italy	2.33
Belgium	5.00		

TABLE 1.11

Industrial production of certain industries, 1960–73

		1960	1965	1970	1972–3	Measured in	Index 1970 = 100 1960	Index 1970 = 100 1972–3
Crude iron	E.E.C.—6	54.0	63.2	80.5	89.8	million tons	67	112
	E.E.C.—9	70.1	—	99.6	106.9	million tons	70	107
Crude steel	E.E.C.—6	72.8	86.0	109.2	122.9	million tons	67	113
	E.E.C.—9	97.8	—	138.9	150.1	million tons	70	108
Rolled products	E.E.C.—6	50.8	60.4	79.6	91.7	million tons	64	115
	E.E.C.—9	—	—	101.2	111.5	million tons	—	110
Motor-cars	E.E.C.—6	3.603	5.444	8.015	9.559	million units	54	120
	E.E.C.—9	4.956	7.166	9.656	11.500	million units	51	119
Plastics	E.E.C.—6	—	3.933	9.799	11.338	million tons	—	—
Synthetic fibres	E.E.C.—6	—	419	1.033	1.349	thousand tons	—	136
	E.E.C.—9	—	569	1.375			—	—
Paper and Board	E.E.C.—6	8.565	11.069	15.424	18.056	million tons	55	117
	E.E.C.—9	12.381	15.815	22.077	23.129	million tons	56	105
Woollen yarns	E.E.C.—6	536	538	624	686	thousand tons	87	110
	E.E.C.—9	—	—	888		thousand tons	—	—
Cotton yarns	E.E.C.—6	1.018	1.024	1.044	1.032	thousand tons	98	99
	E.E.C.—9	—	—	—	1.212		—	—
Petroleum	E.E.C.—6	110.3	226.5	391.7	459.8	million tons	26	117
Products (refinery)	E.E.C.—9	152.6	292.8	498.7	578.1	million tons	31	112

SOURCE: *Basic Statistics* (1973–4).

Examination of the data available on the performance of individual industries[8] also reveals wide divergences between sectors. Figures of output (in volume terms) are given in Table 1.11, which shows that the same industries have tended to grow fastest in individual countries as in the original and enlarged Community as a whole. These rapidly growing industries are chemical production, plastics, petroleum refining, and so on. Other more traditional industries such as textiles, leather, clothing, tobacco and food have grown much more slowly.

Such a pattern of industrial growth implies a significant redistribution of the work force, with reduced employment in the extractive industries, textiles, leather, and so on, and the appearance of new employment opportunities in sectors such as chemicals, electronics and information processing. The energy crisis and increased price of raw materials have accentuated this shift, favouring high-technology products and those with high value added. Although the over-all effect of the redistribution of employment has been positive — total industrial employment has increased by over one million in the last twelve years — it is still true that grave social tensions have appeared. These are made more serious by the fact that declining industries tend to be concentrated in certain areas, so that an industrial problem creates a regional problem.

In Table 1.12 the level of annual fixed investment in different industries is compared. The high volume of investment undertaken between 1964 and 1972 is clear from these figures: fixed investment in the original six E.E.C. countries more than doubled. Metal production and chemicals took up to about one-fifth of such investment. Considerable investment has also been going on in the motor-vehicle, engineering and electro-technical industries. The rapid increase in investment in many of these industries may have encouraged the recession which occurred in 1974—75, because firms in several of the major industries over-invested in plant capacity. Thus, in European car manufacturing, production capacity is about 12 million units but output was only 9 million units in 1974 and capacity is only expected to be fully utilised in the middle of the next decade.

The investment figures also show the spectacular growth of some newer sectors such as office machinery and data processing and chemicals. Table 1.12 also raises the suspicion that investment in the United Kingdom, which is the dominant partner within the group of the three new members (EEC—3), has lagged behind in comparison with the original six member states.

Table 1.13 brings this out more clearly. In all seven industries shown on a comparative national basis, U.K. investment is much lower than West German investment; compared with Italy, this was so in four out of seven cases and compared with France in two out of seven cases, whereas investment in two other industries was about equal.

The West German preponderance is especially notable in chemicals, machinery construction, the electro-technical industry and foods.

Dutch industry excels comparatively in chemicals, foods, paper production and electro-technical production. Belgian investment is relatively strong in iron and steel and textile production.

TABLE 1.12

Annual fixed investment in some E.E.C. industries and in total manufacturing industry, 1964—72 (million units of account)

		1964	1968	1972
Total industry	E.E.C.—6	16944	20764	36159
	E.E.C.—3	—	7280	8718
Metal production	E.E.C.—6	1962	1491	4067
and processing	E.E.C.—3	—	337	766
Oil refining	E.E.C.—6	749	864	1439
	E.E.C.—3	—	233	287
Chemicals	E.E.C.—6	1572	2173	3567
	E.E.C.—3	—	588	837
Man-made fibres	E.E.C.—6	178	153	243
	E.E.C.—3	—	60	34
Mechanical engineering	E.E.C.—6	832	1010	1664
	E.E.C.—3	—	398	476
Office machinery and	E.E.C.—6	58	310	628
data processing	E.E.C.—3	—	32	30
Electro-technical industry	E.E.C.—6	788	886	1616
	E.E.C.—3	—	253	355
Motor vehicles and parts	E.E.C.—6	913	977	2027
	E.E.C.—3	—	227	270
Textile industry	E.E.C.—6	670	693	1129
	E.E.C.—3	—	285	280
Paper and paper products	E.E.C.—6	653	859	1172
and publishing	E.E.C.—3	—	300	369

SOURCE: Eurostat, *Statistical Studies and Surveys,* 2 (1974).

Attention should also be drawn towards the extremely high investment in the steel industries of France and Italy, two countries where the construction of coastal plants has proceeded fast in 1972 and in preceding years. Table 1.13 shows heavy cycles in investment expenditure which demonstrates that investment is still the major cause of the economic fluctuations to which a private-enterprise economy is subject.

TABLE 1.13 (*continued*)

Sector	Year	West Germany	France	Italy	Netherlands	Belgium	Luxembourg	Britain	Ireland	Denmark
Food and drinks	1962	587.3	349.3	262.2	152.9	85.0	3.5			
	1964	650.0	409.9	199.8	185.2	91.1	6.4			
	1966	651.5	435.8	301.3	223.3	112.2	7.9			
	1968	996.6	555.4	373.4	224.4	124.4	7.4			
	1970	1221.8	617.2	401.6	241.0	155.7	7.3	645.8	50.2	72.9
	1972							750.7		99.1
Textiles	1962	244.9	182.3	200.2	43.5	1.4				
	1964	239.4	172.3	159.2	47.9	50.8				
	1966	274.5	145.8	146.4	42.6	62.1				
	1968	269.4	130.3	185.3	49.0	58.5				
	1970	422.1	224.2	249.0	59.6	79.9		283.0	20.4	22.2
	1972	396.0	262.9	340.2	44.3	85.5		262.1		18.1
Pulp, paper and cardboard industry	1962	101.9	93.6	68.3	34.2	10.8				
	1964	61.9	71.3	65.6	13.9	19.7				
	1966	95.0	81.5	37.3	16.9	16.7				
	1968	128.8	84.9	107.7	9.9	16.8				
	1970	236.1	74.8	92.3	21.6	26.6		81.6	2.9	12.8
	1972	109.9	75.0	90.5	50.5	34.5		56.6		10.4

SOURCES: Eurostat, *Industrial Statistics*, no. 1 (1968), Bureau voor de Statistiek der Europese, Gemeenschappen, 2, (1972), *Statistische studies en enquêtes*; Eurostat, *Statistical Studies and Surveys*, 2, (1974).

TABLE 1.13

Annual investments in fixed assets in E.E.C. industries (mio units of accounts)

Sector	Year	West Germany	France	Italy	Netherlands	Belgium	Luxembourg	Britain	Ireland	Denmark
Iron and steel industry	1962	520.5	467.9	245.8	59.4	136.5	40.3			
	1964	538.0	241.5	645.3	43.1	106.7	46.3			
	1966	441.5	205.5	245.8	73.8	145.7	28.4			
	1968	252.5	323.3	260.2	138.0	71.4	14.1			
	1970	654.3	377.5	411.7	121.2	222.3	44.1	439.9		
	1972	861.2	917.8	962.8	122.5	185.2	42.2	601.7		
Chemicals	1962	612.4	308.1	349.8	104.6	62.7	0.2			
	1964	695.7	340.8	276.8	196.4	60.9	1.1			
	1966	1098.4	505.4	289.4	346.0	99.5	0.4			
	1968	774.3	457.6	473.9	306.6	153.8	6.8			
	1970	1725.1	625.1	743.0	506.4	221.2	3.0	958.3	6.5	45.5
	1972	1308.6	747.1	863.2	417.5	218.2	12.6	792.0		44.9
Engineering	1962	566.4	222.4	173.1	38.1	23.3	0.5			
	1964	481.1	165.9	107.5	41.2	26.8	0.7			
	1966	496.5	171.8	103.2	47.2	28.1	1.3			
	1968	484.2	225.6	202.4	45.9	50.0	1.4			
	1970	1027.5	230.6	292.5	56.9	52.9	2.1	490.8	2.4	40.6
	1972	966.1	279.1	320.4	47.5	48.5	2.8	445.4		30.1
Electro-technicals	1962	406.4	159.7	105.8	87.7	23.5	0.1			
	1964	371.1	199.7	100.3	96.5	19.7	0.2			
	1966	439.0	229.2	105.6	84.8	24.4	0.4			
	1968	408.9	234.1	134.7	67.1	40.8	0.5			
	1970	896.2	272.2	210.9	155.0	72.2	0.2	306.5	5.5	22.6
	1972	833.5	315.2	292.5	98.9	75.3	0.3	336.7		18.6

continued overleaf

INSTITUTIONAL BACKGROUND

As a conclusion to this first chapter it is useful to review the institutional background to European industrial organisation and also to see how the interplay of institutions and economic forces may affect developments. When the Treaty of Rome was signed in 1957 the European states were still more or less isolated economic unities, even though forces had earlier been set in motion which aimed at liberalisation of trade and payments. The Common Market, following the examples of regional and functional integration set by Benelux (1944) and the European Coal and Steel Community (1952), united the six continental European economies of West Germany, France, Italy, Belgium, Luxembourg and the Netherlands in a programme of integration under which trade barriers for goods and services were abolished, the freedom of movement of production factors was made possible, and firms were enabled to establish themselves freely in other member countries. Thus the six national markets were unified into a free common market where competition (together with other means) was supposed to work pervasively towards the goals of unification, that is an increase in *per capita* incomes and employment and an improvement in the social welfare of the population in all countries of the Community. Obviously such an economic process needed institutions to guide and supervise the steps taken towards achievement of both short- and long-term goals. When, in 1973, three new member states gained admission — the United Kingdom, Ireland and Denmark — the institutions were adapted so that their present-day composition differs from the original one.

The main decision-making process has remained unaltered, however. The E.E.C. Commission and the Council of Ministers provide the day-to-day impetus in the Community's decision-making process. The Commission makes policy proposals after consulting a wide range of experts and interested parties; the Council takes final decisions after consulting the European Parliament and the Economic and Social Committee and after discussion in the Committee of Permanent Representatives. The Court of Justice is the ultimate Court of Appeal.

The *European Commission* is composed of thirteen members — two each from larger states and one from the smaller countries — who are Community statesmen, pledged to act independently in the common interest of the Community.

The Commission is (1) a policy-planning body which initiates Community action; (2) a mediator between governments which steers its policy proposals through the Council and adjusts them if necessary in the light of discussion; (3) an executive, taking many detailed decisions; (4) a watch-dog which can in the last resort take governments or firms to the Court for breaches of Community law.

The Commission reaches its decisions by simple majority vote if necessary, and is collectively answerable to the European Parliament. But each of its members is mainly responsible for one or more of its departments, or directorates-general.

The Commission has nineteen directorates-general and a number of specialised services. Of the directorates-general, two are of special importance to the study of European industrial organisation: D. G. III (Industry and Technology) and D. G. IV (Competition).

The *Council* is composed of nine Ministers, each representing one of the member governments, the actual Ministers of finance, foreign Ministers, etc., depending on the subject under discussion. The Presidency is held for six-month terms in alphabetical order of the member states' names as spelt in their respective languages.

The Council's main role is to decide on Commission proposals. The Commission is present at Council meetings, and if it refuses to alter its proposals the Council can over-rule it only by unanimous vote, so that minorities are protected. In practice, majority voting in the Council is rare; when it takes place, national votes are normally weighted, giving the United Kingdom, France, West Germany and Italy ten votes each, Belgium and the Netherlands five each, Denmark and Ireland three each, and Luxembourg two. Out of this total of fifty-eight votes, forty-one are needed for a majority, which must include the votes of six member states in cases where the Treaty does not require the Commission to make a proposal.

Council meetings are prepared by the Committee of Permanent Representatives (*Coreper*), the member states' 'ambassadors to the Community', with the Commission represented at all levels.

The Council has its own secretariat-general with some 1200 officials of whom one in five are linguistic staff.

The *European Parliament* consists of 198 Members, at present chosen by and from the national parliaments, although the founding treaties envisage that, ultimately, members will be elected by direct universal suffrage throughout the Community. Thirty-six seats are allotted to the United Kingdom, France, West Germany and Italy, fourteen each to Belgium and the Netherlands, ten each to Denmark and Ireland; and six to Luxembourg — but members sit in party groups rather than national delegations. In late 1974 there were fifty Christian Democrats, forty-eight Socialists, twenty-six Liberals, twenty European Conservatives, fifteen Communists and Allies, sixteen Progressive European Democrats and seven Independents. There were sixteen vacant seats.

The Parliament's main task is to monitor the work of the Commission and the Council. It has to be consulted on most Commission proposals before the Council can take a decision on them, and its members can put written and oral questions to both the Commission and the Council. It has a number of standing committees: on Political Affairs; Legal Affairs; Economic and Monetary Affairs; and so on. They hold 'hearings' with representatives of the Commission, national ministers and officials, trade-union and industrial bodies, as well as other public and private groups, and then draw up reports for the plenary session, which may lead the Commission to change its original proposals.

The Commission has to report annually to the European Parliament, which can dismiss it on a two-thirds majority vote of no confidence. The Parliament has no such power over the Council, but it gives its opinion on the Community's annual budget, and from 1975 onwards has had the final say on the 'non-obligatory' parts of it — that is, expenditure other than that directly stemming from Community treaties or Community legislation. Proposals for further gradually increasing the Parliament's powers are before the Council at the time of writing.

The *Court of Justice* is a supreme court of nine independent judges, assisted by four advocates-general, all appointed jointly by the member states for renewable six year terms. Their decisions are taken by simple majority vote, and dissenting opinions are not made public.

The court is the final arbiter on all legal questions under the Community treaties. It deals with disputes between member states and community institutions and firms, individuals or Community officials. It can hear appeals from member states, from the Commission, from the Council, or from any individual, on all of whom its rulings are binding. It thus acts as an international court, a constitutional court, an administrative court, a civil court and a court of appeal. At the request of national courts it can also, and increasingly does, give preliminary rulings on the interpretation of Community law.

National courts are responsible for enforcing Community legislation, but they retain full jurisdiction over criminal and ordinary civil law, which remains the responsibility of the member states. By the end of 1973, more than 1000 cases had been submitted to the Court.

In addition to these Community institutions a greater number of consultative bodies aid the Community's work. The most important of these for our purposes is the *Economic and Social Committee*, which is a 144-member body representing employers' organisations, trade unions and other interests (including consumers) in equal numbers. The Commission and the Council must consult the Economic and Social Committee on all major proposals, and it may also give advice on its own initiative.

The three Community treaties, and especially the E.E.C. Treaty, are chiefly a framework for making and adapting policy through consultation and consensus. When agreement is reached according to the procedures outlined above, proposals are adopted and published in the Community's *Official Journal*. The results may be either:

(1) *Regulations,* or Community laws, legally binding on member countries, and applied directly, like national laws;

(2) *Directives,* equally binding on member states as regards the aim to be achieved, but leaving national authorities to decide how to carry them out;

(3) *Decisions,* binding in every respect on those to whom they are addressed, whether member states, firms or private individuals; or

(4) *Recommendations and Opinions,* which have no binding force.

The Commission, as well as the Council, can issue regulations, directives, decisions, recommendations and opinions on certain subjects such as the day-to-day application of competition or industrial policy.

During recent years, there has been a growing concern about the possibility of maintaining the original nature of the European institutions. A tendency has emerged to treat the Commission as a technocratic organisation, the European Parliament as a consultative body and for the Council to be transformed into an intergovernmental conference, replacing the Parliament in so far as the control of the Commission is concerned. A better European consensus on vital issues, linked with a regeneration of the role of the European Parliament (in itself strengthened through the process of direct elections), becomes a necessity in order to avoid the threat that the European Community may degenerate into a mere customs union.

The role of institutions in industrial organisation

The relationship between institutions and the economic or market process is two-way: on the one hand economic forces are to a large extent responsible for the types of institutions that arise and for the shape they adopt; on the other hand institutions, once formed, direct the operation of the economic process.

This interrelationship is clearly visible in the European market economy as it has evolved since the war. The creation of the

Common Market has spectacularly increased output and exchange among member countries and promoted competition in the dynamic, effective sense. Firms have penetrated each other's markets, prices have come under pressure and general welfare has been enhanced through growth, higher *per capita* incomes and quality improvements. The intensification of competition has put pressure on profit margins, so that a number of firms have had to stop production or reorganise, while others have tried to evade competitive battles by means of agreements, mergers or takeovers, or collusionary behaviour. New institutional arrangements become necessary to retain the tendency among firms to restrict competition. Simply stated, firms could not be allowed to restrain competition in the free European market, after the professed goal of doing away with national or state barriers had been (largely) achieved.

Thus treaty regulations have been brought into play: a tightening up of existing and the creation of new arrangements in order to control company behaviour. The general rules forbidding the restraint of competition have been made more precise, an anti-merger bill has been devised by the E.E.C. Commission, and policy approaches to the problem of adapting industries to changed conditions have been mapped out. We will speak about these various institutional arrangements later on in the book.

The important point to note here is the close connection between the evolving economy and the institutions, which constitute the economic order. The present-day European economy is a mixed economy, in which private ownership of the means of production, private decision-making in production, consumption and exchange, and the market process are still of overriding importance, but governments play an increasingly important role. Thus national and supra-national governments are laying down rules of behaviour in laws, regulations and norms designed either to counteract private restrictions or to promote freedom, stability or equality in the economy. On the other hand the market is increasingly dominated by large institutions and competitive and other firm behaviour is felt to be in need of guidance and control.

Thus, a realistic view of the European market economy should take into account both the economic structure and process and the institutional arrangement and, above all, should trace their mutual influence.

The present book, which is an introduction to the European market economy, confines itself largely to the first two tasks. The third task is not wholly neglected, to be sure, but in a general sense it represents the achievement which industrial-organisation economists should aim at in future years.

CONCLUSION

Industrial organisation is one of the fields of economics which clearly
requires a multidimensional approach. Being concerned with the
structure and the functioning of markets in the real world, it calls
upon not only microeconomic theory but also empirical and institutional analysis. It uses the alternative theories of the firm as well as
statistical investigations to discover the precise relationships between
structure, conduct and performance, and it suggests public policy in
such areas as the promotion of competition through anti-trust laws
and the choice between private and public enterprise.

These theoretical, empirical and institutional dimensions have
some generality for the various industrialised economies. However,
the realistic application of these tools to study the industrial
organisation of a specific economy requires the recognition from the
start of those features of the economy which are most likely to
affect the analysis.

For this reason the first chapter elaborated a distinctly European
framework at the level of:

(i)   the theoretical structure—conduct—performance paradigm;
(ii) the statistical characteristics of the European economy; and
(iii) the institutional background.

A main point which follows from these considerations is that in
the European Community, as compared with North America, the
reliance on competitive market structure for harmonising private
business conduct with the public interest is a new and still very
fragile practice. The progress in promoting competition has owed
much to the high levels of demand and growth rates of the European
economies in recent years, as was previously illustrated; but with
different economic conditions, private and public conduct, which are
crucial determinants of the still unstable European market structure,
could put into question such an impersonal regulator. In the future,
one could expect greater reliance upon the various forms of public
regulation and of planning agreements between industry and the
state.

2

Industrial Concentration

Traditionally, market structure has been characterised by the
following factors:

(i)   the degree of concentration of firms;
(ii) the level and types of barriers to entry;
(iii) the degree of product differentiation; and
(iv) the nature of industry demand, its evolution and elasticity.

The first aspect, concentration, has undoubtedly given rise to the
largest number of studies and to the most vivid controversies. Karl
Marx was the first to integrate this phenomenon into a general theory
of capitalist development.[1] He maintained that the concentration of
capital could be looked at from two points of view:

(a) within the firm, accumulation takes place because surplus-value
derived from variable capital is invested in fixed capital, that is in
material means of production (machinery, buildings, raw materials,
and so on). This process raises the scale of enterprise, but concentration in this sense of accumulation is limited by the growth of fixed
capital in society, which in turn depends on over-all economic
growth.

(b) between firms, centralisation of decision power occurs because
of competition between capitalists. Large firms — which are more
productive because of the process of accumulation and have lower
costs per unit of output — compete small firms out of existence into
merger or liquidation. Centralisation is not limited by the rate of
economic growth but ends only with the establishment of monopoly
positions in particular industries. Small capitalists can persist in
sectors where large-scale methods have not yet penetrated. However,
in the course of capitalist development, on-going centralisation is
inevitable; labour will be shed from the production process to swell
the ranks of the 'industrial reserve army'.

On the other hand, the amount of surplus-value to be earned will
also decline, at least in a relative sense, so that the profit rate will
have a tendency to decline. Both developments will cause increasingly
severe economic crises and the ultimate explosion of the capitalist
regime.

At first, this analysis did not gain an audience among the majority of economists, but since the Great Depression of the 1930s, authors like Chamberlin, Robinson, Schumpeter, Berle and Means have started to investigate concentration and three aspects of concentration have gained a lasting place in economic analysis. First, the concentration of ownership in the economy as a whole poses the problem of the distribution of means of production and of wealth among individuals or families. This requires an analysis of initial endowments, which economic models too often take as given.

Second, one can investigate the concentration of decision-making power over the economy's resources which will be different from the first problem in so far as there exists a separation of ownership and control. Research is therefore undertaken into the role played by financial groups and institutions as well as large enterprises in the over-all economy.

Third, concentration in industrial sectors or markets has been the subject of much inquiry in industrial economics. The distribution of market shares between firms, which determines competitive conditions is studied. This aspect will be analysed in this chapter. However, the growth of multiproduct and multinational enterprises, especially during the second half of the twentieth century, makes it more and more important to devote attention to the problems posed by large firms and conglomerates, and so aggregate or over-all concentration will be examined in Chapter 3.

In this chapter, we will first examine the determinants of size and concentration, secondly examine the statistical measures of concentration, and thirdly discuss the evidence relating to the existing level of concentration and its evolution. The second part of the chapter will then be devoted to an analysis of vertical concentration. The various institutional ways in which concentration can be increased and the main characteristics of the methods used in Europe are presented in the last section of this chapter.

DETERMINANTS OF SIZE AND CONCENTRATION

Several explanations of the concentration process have been given. The main division is between those explanations which focus attention on the deliberate action of firms, so that the concentration process becomes a result of entrepreneurial strategies, and those explanations which consider that the growing role of a small number of large companies is the outcome of chance. From the latter point of view, increased concentration results from the cumulative stochastic occurrence of a myriad of small events. The

law of proportionate effect summarises this by attributing the
differences in concentration to the underlying probability of equal
percentage rates of growth by firms of all sizes disturbed by
random influences. We first discuss the impact of deliberate
behaviour and firm strategy, linked with scale economies, learning
processes, externalities, product life-cycles, capitalistic control of
output and monopoly power, and public policies. Second, we
present the possible role of random processes.

Scale economies and learning processes

The existence of scale economies depends on the characteristics of
the production function pertaining to different industries. This can
be written as $Y = Y(K, L)$, in which Y = the level of output per unit
of time, K = the amount of capital per unit of time, L = the amount
of labour per unit of time. There are economies of scale* when
increasing K and L each by the constant proportion α will result in a
more than proportional increase in Y:

$$\alpha^k\ Y = f(\alpha K, \alpha L), \text{ with } k > 1.$$

The firm thus has an incentive to expand its production. But if
market demand does not grow, the number of firms has to be
reduced and a monopoly may even result. In Figure 2.1, the long-run
average-cost curve is given. If minimum efficient scale, that is the
smallest scale at which all economies of scales are realised, is OA =
100 units, and if aggregate industry demand is OB = 300 units, the
maximum number of efficient firms in the industry will be three. If
demand were to fall to 100 units there would be a natural monopoly.
   Statistical studies of cost functions in many industries indicate a
downward-sloping *short-term* cost curve, because fixed costs can be
spread over a larger number of units if output increases; however, if
output expansion approaches capacity limits, the cost curve will bend
sharply upwards. The *long-term* average-cost curve is found to be, not

* Let us recall that if $f(\alpha K, \alpha L) = \alpha^k f(K, L)$ for any point (K, L) and for any value of α,
then the function $Y = f(K, L)$ is homogeneous of the kth degree. The case $k = 1$ gives the
linear homogeneous function characterised by the fact that a proportional increase in all
factors leads to a proportional increase in product and leaves the average and, marginal
product of each factor unchanged. It is economically improbable to have a production
function that exhibits homogenity and it is more likely that a firm will experience various
returns to scale.

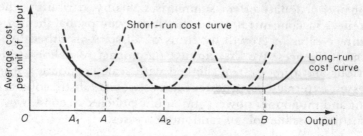

FIGURE 2.1   *Minimum efficient scale*

U-shaped, but L-shaped: beyond a zone of decreasing unit costs, average and marginal long-term unit costs remain constant. The causes of this latter phenomenon are more complex. Several reasons have been mentioned why long-term average costs at a greater output (OA_2) are lower than a smaller output (OA_1):

(1) The division of labour, made possible by a large output, improves the productivity of men and machines, by specialising them according to tasks.

(2) Indivisible equipment gives rise to the principle of multiples: if the firm must combine various indivisible pieces of equipment, it has to choose its minimum level of output according to the least common multiple of the production maxima of the various pieces of equipment. In Europe cars can be assembled efficiently at levels of 60,000 to 80,000 units per year whereas engines may be produced optimally at five or six times that scale and the stamping of engine cover sheets or rear cover sheets may show economies of up to 600,000 to 1,000,000 units. However, if firms can buy parts or components from outside suppliers, the principle of multiples need not apply and efficient operation may be achieved at a much lower level of output.

(3) In industries using three-dimensional apparatus, such as tanks, boilers, vats, pipes, containers, and so on, unit costs fall sharply as size increases because construction costs (up to a point) depend on surface area whereas processed output varies with capacity. The first is a two-dimensional measure, the second a three-dimensional one, and costs per unit depend on the quotient of the two. In such cases engineers apply the '0.6 rule of thumb', that is, the elasticity of cost with respect to output is approximately 0.6.

(4) Another aspect is what Florence calls the 'economies of massed reserves'.[2] In order to protect itself against the breakdown of production a small firm with one piece of equipment has to double its size. Larger firms can economise here by holding a proportionately smaller amount of equipment in reserve.

(5) Apart from the static economies, where unit costs decrease with the rate of output, there are dynamic economies according to which unit costs decrease with the cumulative total volume of production. This concerns *learning processes*: 'practice makes perfect' and the experience can reduce production costs, especially if the product is relatively new. The learning curve is depicted in Figure 2.2.

The corresponding function can be written as

$$z = \beta \, x^{\lambda},$$

where z = the number of hours required to produce the xth unit, x = the total number of units produced, β = the number of hours required to produce the first unit, $-1 < \lambda < 0$, λ being the elasticity of z with respect to x. It is clear that $dz/dx = \lambda(z/x) < 0$: an increase of the total number of units produced reduces the number of hours required to produce an extra unit.

The learning curve should not be confused with the traditional cost function; it connects the points of different production functions to the extent that there is a factor of production which becomes more productive as output increases. The learning curve was first discovered in wartime U.S. aircraft production where unit cost was reduced by about 20 per cent for every doubling of output. This implies an elasticity coefficient of -3.3. Subsequent studies for the electrical, petroleum, steel and paper-producing industries have verified the principle.[3]

(6) Another reason often mentioned for the existence of large firms is technological development. Galbraith in particular has argued (like Veblen half a century before) that the worst enemy of the competitive system is not the left-wing doctrinaire, but the engineer. The march of technology, it is held, will require larger and larger scale and

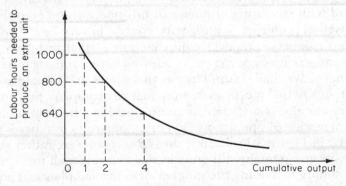

FIGURE 2.2

thus reduce the possibility of having a sufficient number of small firms in a given market.

This conflict between competition and technical efficiency may occur in certain branches of industry such as transatlantic aircraft building or computer manufacturing (hardware), but it is not universal; on the contrary, in many sectors of industry, as Blair has pointed out,[4] the growth of technology has had a decentralising impact — Examples include electricity generation, the processing and application of plastics and the direct reduction process of steel manufacture. In the latter case, mini-steel plants (with an optimal capacity below 500,000 tons) accounted for 34 per cent of total steel investment in the E.E.C. in 1974. Their contribution to total output was some 15 per cent in 1975 and further growth (to some 40 per cent of output) is foreseen for future years.

(7) *Economies of scale* may no longer be attainable from technical units or plants, but exist *on the level of the firm or group*. One can think of central overhead facilities, such as research and development, management, computer services, centralised book-keeping, and so on. A multiplant firm, producing homogeneous goods, can also save substantially by centralisation of inputs on large scale. Large diversified firms can make their purchasing power felt in dealing with specialised suppliers, financial groups may be better able to overcome the imperfections of the capital market, and so on. When discussing European statistics on industrial organisation, we shall see that many European firms are indeed large but with small-scale establishments. This discrepancy can be explained by the way such firms have grown: by means of merger and takeover, centralising management and financial control, but leaving the plants as they were. The most typical case concerns the financial holdings which operate in all countries of the E.E.C.

On the other hand, it may be asked whether *diseconomies of scale* exist beyond a certain size (level *OB* in Figure 2.1). This might be connected with increasing problems of information and co-ordination, as well as problems of budgetary control in very large firms. Such firms risk becoming overly bureaucratic so that technological scale advantages are outweighed by administrative and organisational inefficiencies. We shall return later to this theme and investigate to what extent internal inefficiency may hamper company performance. For the moment it is sufficient to point out that firms can usually extend their scale of operations along flat long-run cost curves (the stretch *AB* in Figure 2.1). Even if the *AB* section were rather short, a company or group might still grow in size and retain all the advantages by simply increasing the number of firms and plants of a size between *A* and *B*. The multiplant firm, producing homogeneous

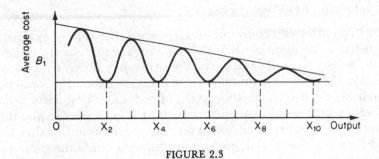

FIGURE 2.3

goods, therefore has a favourable position, especially if transport costs are relatively high. Such a firm can locate its plants in areas of high demand. It will have a 'corkscrew' cost curve[5] depicted in Figure 2.3.

If it is assumed that overhead costs (for example co-ordination costs, research and development costs, purchasing costs, and so on) are proportional to output, the firm can always add a plant of optimal dimensions $(X_2, X_4, X_6, X_8,$ etc.) if demand increases. It will therefore be able to achieve minimum average plant production costs per unit of output whatever its size, while, moreover, its possible extra costs due to the working of the last plant at a sub-optimal rate will be divided over a large output with increasing size, which accounts for the progressively lower peaks of the curve. The curve also explains why small-scale firms (say of OX_2 size) are able to compete successfully with large companies, provided they do not surpass their optimum output level.

Now, the assumption of proportional overhead costs may well be questioned for multiplant firms producing homogeneous goods, since reasons (1), (4) and (5) above would lead one to expect economies with increasing scale. The learning process in particular benefits the leadership of a firm having several plants of a similar type which will be able to compare performances and apply best practice everywhere. The result would be that the points of lowest unit costs $(X_2, X_4, X_6,$ etc.) would lie successively lower.

Doubts can be raised where firms have plants producing diversified output. Here the managerial tasks will be compounded, while the advantages mentioned in the fields of research and development, purchasing, the holding of stocks, and so on, may be small or absent. The solution found to this problem earlier in this century is the adoption of a divisional organisation in which there is a general office made of general executives who allocate resources to a number of quasi-autonomous, fairly self-contained divisions.

Internalisation of external effects

Apart from internal economies of large scale, the role of external effects has to be mentioned.* The basic idea is that, beyond their private money benefits and costs, the firms may be motivated to eliminate external diseconomies or to increase external economies by centralising decisions; another level of production and costs would be achieved, which would enhance over-all profits. For example, the expansion of one firm's chemical research could benefit other firms in a different industry, or, conversely, thermal contamination of a river that affects the production of a neighbouring firm could be better controlled and limited by co-ordinated action.

A similar argument could be developed in the case of firms operating in two distinct but interrelated product markets, the interdependence of the demand functions corresponding to the existence of substitutes or complementary products. An analytical treatment of the argument is given in the appendix to this chapter (pp. 79—82).

In short, it is possible to earn excess profits by co-ordinating price and output decisions among several firms, not only through monopolisation, but more generally by taking into account the effects of decisions on each other's profits.

Product life-cycles

The product cycle concept focuses attention on the various stages through which products pass from birth to death. Somehow or other, the stages of innovation, expansion, maturity and decline are involved, especially in products of technical origin or natural products processed by means of modern methods. Thus, whereas strawberries are not liable to product-cycle developments, mass-produced frozen chickens are, and so, *a forteriori*, are durable consumer goods. Product cycles, which have been extensively observed since the Industrial Revolution,[6] obviously differ as to length, amplitude and economic impact. The main idea, in the context of the present discussion, is that such cycles (or at least the more important ones) show some systematic relationship with structural changes.

If the industry is new and is considered to have a bright future in some vague sense, the potential market will be estimated to be large in relation to actual sales. Consequently, entrepreneurs, including

---

* A special case is when the expansion of the industry might cause a downward shift of every firm's cost curves, so that the industry long-run supply curve could become downward-sloping. Among examples, there is the progressive specialism of firms in producing raw materials and specialised machines, marketing, research, and so on.

new entrants, will build up new capacity to expand output. This may
be done by means of building larger plants and achieving more
mechanised output, or by means of building more plants of the same
size (for example if transport costs are important). Thus there will be
a tendency towards lower absolute and relative concentration.
Vertical integration will often be reduced because more numerous,
independent suppliers can each achieve higher levels of optimum
output (and a reduced cost price), made possible by the growth of
the market. Also, existing firms or firms entering the industry concerned will be inclined to buy inputs instead of making them because
such a policy releases scarce resources which are needed for
expansion. The expansionary policy will not benefit all firms equally.
Some will grow more than others, which may be explained either by
means of the stochastic process, as we shall see, or by reference to
differing entrepreneurial abilities. As expansion proceeds, relative
concentration will tend to increase.

But no product has an indefinite future. Though new applications
for the new product at existing prices may be discovered, or price
reductions may expand the market, the expansion of demand will
sooner or later be curbed. Limits may be of an absolute nature, if
some substitute product, which satisfies consumers better, is
developed, or they may be of a relative nature, so that demand
growth slackens, because new consumer demand turns towards completely different products and only replacement demand has to be
met; thus market saturation develops (see Figure 2.4).

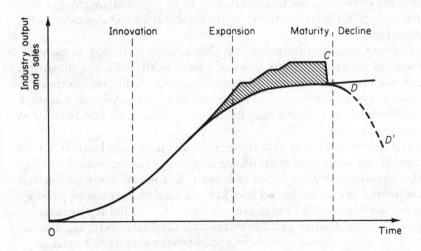

FIGURE 2.4

Entrepreneurs, having expanded capacity in line with previous rates of growth during the expansionary process, now discover that excess capacity arises (capacity-expansion C in Figure 2.4 goes forward stepwise because of an assumed 'lumpiness' of investment) and will try to avoid this by price reductions. The ensuing price battles will inflict losses on the less efficient or less liquid firms, forcing them into liquidation or takeover. Moreover, those firms which hold out will try (a) to conclude cartel agreements to reduce the downward pressure on prices, or (b) to merge with or takeover other firms, or (c) to co-ordinate their behaviour. Whichever form of collusion is chosen depends on a number of factors, such as the existence of competition policy preventing form (a), important economies of scale which favours solution (b), or the prevalence of a few strong independently owned firms (c).

Thus horizontal concentration will increase as industrial growth proceeds. Likewise, there will be a tendency towards vertical integration, for two main reasons: (1) the expansion of the industry will require more resources, so that during maturity, relative scarcities develop and prices of (some) inputs rise. Suppliers will earn rents (related to quality, ability and location) and this puts a premium on the acquisition of such resources by the firms in the industry because it will increase their chances of survival. (2) The reduction in the number of firms as a result of the price squeeze will narrow the sales possibilities for suppliers, who may react by forming vertical agreements with the leading firms in the mature phase.

The industry may continue its slow growth during the rest of the mature phase (path D) in Figure 2.4, as is the case with margarine, or there may follow a decline (path D'), as in rayon filaments, coal furnaces, or oil heating in the Netherlands after the discovery of natural gas.

In some cases, an industry may, because of circumstances, start a new product cycle, on the basis of a previously achieved maturity. A typical example is the oil industry, which until the beginning of the century was a kerosene-producing industry, but proceeded along a new product cycle when first motor-car petrol and then fuel oil were demanded.

The mature phase is also the period during which large financially strong firms with uncertain or unpromising prospects diversify into other industries by means of takeover. As the invention of basically new products cannot be achieved at will and the means of production of a new product cycle are not instantly available for such mature firms, despite extensive research facilities, external diversification is often considered to be the best way out of the mature phase, as we shall see in Chapter 3.

Capitalistic control of output

In contrast to the Marxist theory of concentration, in which internal and external concentration, prompted by technological factors, are an expression of an inherent contradiction in capitalism, recent 'neo-Marxist' studies take a different point of view: 'It is not the steam engine which has given us capitalism; it is capitalism which has engendered the steam engine'.[7] In other words, capitalist organisation is not technically determined, but has been built up to establish the socio-economic power of the capitalist class, and the technological transformations are an induced result.

In this view the transfer of control of output from workers to capitalists takes pride of place. In contrast to Galbraith, it is held that mechanisation could be adopted because handicraft production gave way to large-scale enterprise. The goal of such a concentration of production was not the achievement of technical superiority, but the striving after capitalist profits:

(i) the desire to control output of the weavers, who, if they were not placed under supervision in factories, had a tendency to cheat and sell part of their output themselves;

(ii) to compel the weavers to work longer and more intensively than they would have done had they remained the masters of their tools;

(iii) to appropriate technical inventions in order to extract a maximum profit;

(iv) finally, and above all, to organise production in such a way that the direct producers could not pass by the capitalist.

Monopoly power

Concentration can also be seen as a necessary but insufficient condition for monopoly power. Producers are regrouped in order to facilitate collusion, to reduce the free choice of consumers and to increase their bargaining power. The outcome would be the classical consequences of monopoly: high prices, substantial profits and welfare losses. Stigler has, by means of an oligopoly model, shown that the tendency to collusion is a function of numbers and relative dimensions of sellers, and diminishes rapidly as firm sizes become more equal and their number increases.[8] Inversely, it is held that there is a direct relationship between concentration and cartels: because the costs of collusion are reduced if the number of firms is small. Recently, theorems on the core of an economy have confirmed the significance of the number of firms for competitive equilibrium.[9] Another dimension could be added: the growth of market sales. It is

held that quick-growing markets offer less scope for collusion than
stagnant markets, because under conditions of fast growth independent behaviour is more rewarding and less likely to be detected.

Both views contain a substantial amount of truth and are mainly
complementary. In fast-growing markets (such as artificial fibres in
Europe during the 1960s) even a very small number of large-scale
companies may compete fiercely for a slice of the expanding demand,
whereas relatively stagnant sectors with hundreds of firms have seen
durable cartel agreements (for example textiles); but it remains true
that markets which are slow-moving and moreover contain a small
number of firms are monopolised more thoroughly, permanently and
easily and therefore constitute the bigger problem for public policy.

Role of the public authorities

The last aspect to be dealt with is the role of the authorities and
regulation in the concentration problem. The state often seems to
sustain large firms by its fiscal policy, industrial policy, public contracts and aid for research and development. Examining the U.K.
situation, George writes: 'as far as the government is concerned, it
may be said that a high level of concentration is convenient from the
point of view of planning, whether this be in the form of indicative
planning or of direct government participation in industry'.[10]

Fiscal policy in the form of company taxation encourages the
retention of profits to finance investment and growth, relative to
their distribution, which attracts double taxation, once on corporate
income and once as part of shareholders' personal income. And the
cascading sales tax has favoured vertical integration for a long time;
the adoption of the value-added tax system in the Common Market
has at least theoretically eliminated this incentive to increased
concentration.

Government contracts often benefit big enterprise because of
lower risks of failure and supposedly higher efficiency.[11] This means
that technological progress was systematically encouraged in such big
firms.

Again, commercial policy and import tariffs have often promoted
non-competitive market structures by protecting national industries.
The European trade-liberalisation movement has increasingly undermined such traditional means of protection; however, national states
now have a tendency to intervene directly in order to support their
large businesses, in the form of sectoral or regional aid, financing on
attractive conditions and participatory measures. Even if such intervention is seen as part of a piecemeal type of adaptative economic

policy, it obviously distorts competitive conditions (see Chapter 8 on industrial policy).

Random processes

According to a second perspective, the evolution of market structure, and specifically the level of concentration, is stochastically determined. In other words, statistical forces are supposed to bring about the observed changes. If we assume the law of normal distribution (law of Laplace-Gauss), variations in firm size would be the outcome of a large number of independent causes, with small but cumulative effects. These can be represented by the solid curve in Figure 2.5. The growth of firms is given by the formula $S_t - S_{t-1} = \lambda_t$, where S is the size at time t, S_{t-1} the size at the preceeding period, and λ_t is an independently distributed random variable. This would imply that the probability of changing size by a given absolute amount is the same to small as to large firms. Then small firms would gradually reach the sizes of the larger ones, so that the group would tend to become more equal in size. Reality does not support this theory: the observed size distribution of firms is positively skewed in number terms, as is indicated by the dotted curve in Figure 2.5. The law of proportionate effect, formulated by Gibrat, may explain this phenomenon. It says that, irrespective of size at a given moment, all firms have the same probability of a given proportionate growth. The size variation would then result from a great number of small random factors affecting all sizes of companies in a similar manner, but in a multiplicative fashion. The distribution of companies by size would then appear normal when numerical values are converted into logarithms. Such a distribution is given in Figure 2.6, corresponding to the dotted curve of Figure 2.5, with absolute sizes converted into

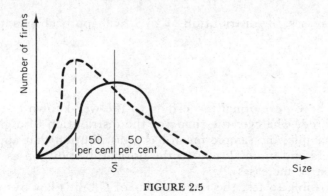

FIGURE 2.5

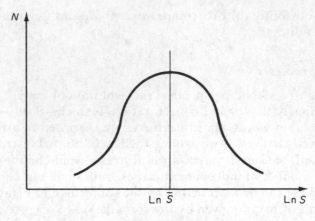

FIGURE 2.6

logarithms. Figure 2.6 shows again a normal distribution, but on a log basis and is therefore called a log-normal distribution.

The growth of the firms is expressed by

$$S_t - S_{t-1} = u_t \times S_{t-1},$$

or

$$\frac{S - S_{t-1}}{S_{t-1}} = u_t.$$

Knowing that u_t, the growth rate, is a whole series of random variables with identical distributions, we may also write:

$$S_t = (1 + u_t)\, S_{t-1} = S_0 (1 + u_i) \times (1 + u) \ldots (1 + u_t).$$

If the percentage increase u_i is small, we obtain approximately:

$$\ln S_t = \ln S_0 + u_1 + u_2 + \ldots + u_t.$$

If t increases, the distribution of $\ln S_t$ will approach asymptotically

$$\sum_{i=1}^{t} u_i$$

and thus becomes normal (according to the well-known central limit theorem whatever the shape of the distribution of a given random sample, the sample mean has a distribution that approximates more and more closely to the normal distribution as the size of the sample increases).

It is possible to test the implications of Gibrat's law by regression analysis. If we define X as the logarithm of size, $X = \ln S$, we can write

$$X_t - \overline{X}_t = \beta(X_{t-1} - \overline{X}_{t-1}) + u,$$

or

$$\sigma_t^2 = \beta^2 \, \sigma_{t-1}^2 + \sigma_u^2,$$

where $\overline{X}$ = the logarithm of average size in the sector, σ^2 = the variance of the logarithm of size, σ_u^2 = the variance of the distribution of the error term, and β = the regression coefficient corresponding to the systematic component.

If the process of growth is probabilistic in the sense defined, small firms will grow at the same proportional rate as large ones, and the dispersion of size in relation to the mean must be the same at both time t and time $t-1$; the value of β will not be significantly different from unity. Including the effect of the residual variance σ_u^2, however, means that there is no regression towards the mean size: an increase in dispersion will result from a growth in t. Thus, excluding the role of entry, the concentration of any given industry would increase over time, due simply to the fact that if the large firm possesses the same probability of a given proportionate growth as the small firm, the logarithmic variance of the distribution of firm sizes about the mean will tend to increase over time.

We shall come back to this conclusion when studying the performance of firms. Let us simply now emphasise that several studies suggest that the observed size distributions often correspond to one or other theoretical distribution, be it the log-normal distribution, the Pareto or the Yule distribution. These results demonstrate the inevitable role of chance and of natural selection in the current industrial configurations and in the relative positions of constituent firms.

STATISTICAL MEASURES OF CONCENTRATION

The interest shown in the degree of horizontal concentration is derived from the importance attached to the role of monopoly power. A good measure of the degree of concentration would vary with the amount of monopoly power in a particular industry. In this sense, it is generally argued that, *ceteris paribus*, an increase in numbers (of firms) intensifies competition, whereas, in reverse, redistribution of market share towards large firms increases market power. Thus both numbers and relative market positions affect concentration; although it is true that no rigorous proof exists that a change in the degree of concentration necessarily implies a proportional change in monopoly power, a link between specific measures of concentration and specific measures of monopoly power has been proposed in the appendix to this chapter (pp. 82–4).

The nature and coherence of concentration measures

Several authors have argued along the above lines, that for a measure of concentration to have sound theoretical support it must meet several conditions.[12] The axiomatic basis usually suggested includes the following postulates:

(1) The measure used must yield an unambiguous ranking of industries by concentration.

(2) The measure should not depend on the absolute size of the market or industry but be a function of the combined market shares of the firms. It can therefore be thought of as a weighted sum of relative shares, in which the weights are related to market shares:

$$C = \sum_i h\,(P_i)\,P_i,$$

in which C is the concentration measure, P_i is the relative share of firm i, with $P_i > 0$, $\sum_i P_i = 1$, and $h(P_i)$ is the weight attributed to the relative share of firm i.

(3) The measure should record an increase in concentration if a firm lower down the size scale loses market share to a firm higher up the scale and vice versa.

(4) The concentration measure must be a decreasing function of the number of firms, in order to correspond to the economic idea that a larger number of firms intensifies competition.

(5) If the market shares of all firms are reduced by any arbitrary factor, then the concentration measure should fall by the same proportion. This condition gives a cardinal property to the measure.

There is no general agreement as to the importance of these requirements. The fact that a measure does not meet all the above conditions does not mean that it is not economically interesting. Therefore we shall use these properties mainly to discuss the virtues and the limitations of existing measures more precisely; and we shall restrict our attention to measures which are used by the European Commission to determine the evolution of concentration in European countries (see the annual *Reports on Competition Policy*).

Types of concentration measure

The concentration ratio measures the share of the market or industry held by the m largest firms ($m = 1, 2, 4, \ldots 8, \ldots 20, \ldots$). It is written

$$C = \sum_{i=1}^{m} P_i, \qquad (i = 1, \ldots m, m + 1, \ldots, n),$$

where the ith firm has rank i in a descending order of classification, where C = the sum of the shares of the m top firms, and where P_i = the share of firm i. If we examine this measure according to the above criteria we find, first of all, that only the m largest firms are taken into account, so that the index refers to a given point of the distribution, and that these firms are as equally important (weights of one).

Problems may arise in using the concentration ratio for inter-industry comparisons. Compare industries A and B in Table 2.1, which may also be represented graphically (Figure 2.7).

TABLE 2.1

	Industry A	Industry B
4 largest firms	60	40
8 largest firms	80	70
12 largest firms	84	90
20 largest firms	90	100
Total number of firms	40	20

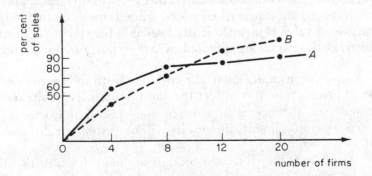

FIGURE 2.7

Here the answer as to which industry is more concentrated will depend on the numerator chosen (number of firms), and this can be immediately detected from the cumulative concentration curves which intersect.

In practice such cases are not very frequent. Empirical studies have found similar results whatever number of firms is used in the numerator, so that the choice of an arbitrary number of firms does not necessarily distort the results.

As to the transfer of market shares, changes outside or inside the group chosen do not affect the formula, but may nevertheless indicate an important change in the competitive situation. A number of further general remarks may be made concerning the difficulties which in fact relate to most measures:

(a) In the case of multiplant firms, concentration at the enterprise level will obviously be higher than at the plant level. Such divergencies can also be measured and may indicate something about the type and the causes of concentration; if technological factors are important, the divergence will be small and vice-versa. In the other direction, it is becoming more and more necessary to ask whether the concept of firm or company should not be replaced by that of the group, that is a set of distinct legal entities controlled by a central economic unit calculating on an over-all basis. Such groups can be studied by means of consolidated balance sheets, but these do not reveal everything. By means of (often minority) shareholdings, interlocking directorships and personal ties, groups are able to control larger amounts of human and financial resources than concentration measures would suggest.

(b) The selection of the variable in which size is expressed affects the results:

(i) If sales are taken as the criterion, the importance of the firm in relation to demand comes out neatly, but vertical integration is not taken into account, as it is when added value is used. Unfortunately data on added value is unsufficiently available for statistical purposes. Moreover, both criteria are affected by price changes which alter money values.

(ii) Employment and financial capital are both indispensable factors of production, but reflect the capital intensity of the sector concerned. For instance, if firm size in mechanised industries is measured by employment, the results will be systematically undervalued.

(iii) Assets, whether fixed or total, pose the problem of the difference between historic and current values, due to changes in the monetary unit, revaluations and depreciations. In a more fundamental sense the link between this type of variable, which is a measure of output capacity, and the firm's market influence is not obvious.

However, statistical studies reveal a high positive correlation between both the degrees of concentration and the measures of size, calculated according to the different variables,[13] though it is important to keep the possibility of different outcomes in mind.

(c) It is necessary to define the *product market* in order to measure concentration. The latter will obviously vary with the breadth of definition: the metal-container or glass-container markets are narrower than the container market in general. Theoretically the degree of substitution in the eyes of the consumer is decisive, but in practice the investigator is constrained by the available industrial classifications, which are not usually made on the basis of the economically relevant concepts. The same product may be classified differently in various countries or at various dates: one may use production processes or raw materials or end-uses as criteria; but industrial classifications usually depend more on supply charac-teristics than on demand considerations.

In the E.E.C. a standardised classification, called 'Nomenclature des industries établies dans les Communautés européennes' (N.I.C.E.) has been developed and was published in its definitive form in 1963. The degree of disaggregation is indicated by the number of digits used, which in the case of the N.I.C.E. is three; this is still fairly aggregated. Thus a one-digit classification would be extractive industry (1), manufacturing industry (2), and so on. A two-digit classification distinguishes the drinks industry (21), tobacco industry (22), textile industry (23), and so on. The three-digit classification has about ninety-four sub-sectors, but even at this level of classifica-tion no real product markets are distinguishable. The U.S. Census goes much further in its Standard Industrial Classification (S.I.C.), which uses a seven-digit classification comprising some 7500 different products. It is generally agreed that a four-digit classification would correspond well with real markets.

(d) Equally important is the *geographical* definition of the market. Concentration tends to be much higher, *ceteris paribus*, in small industries or countries. On the other hand, calculations based on production in a national market would overestimate concentra-tion if any imports were not taken into account. In general the degree of concentration is a diminishing function of market size, i.e. $C = a_0 + a_1 D$, where C is the degree of concentration of the four largest firms, D is market size and the regression coefficient a_1 is less than zero. Therefore the entry of the United Kingdom into the Common Market should, other circumstances being equal, reduce

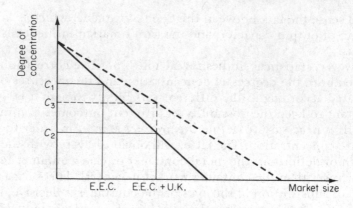

FIGURE 2.8

industrial concentration ($C_2 < C_1$ in Figure 2.8). However, it could be that the extension of the market has other effects, such as an increase in the scale of production and in firm size, in which case the straight line would rotate (or shift) to the right ($C_3 > C_2$ in Figure 2.8). In this case, if firm size rose sufficiently an increase in market size would have no impact on concentration.

In contrast to the concentration rate, various other measures take into account all firms in the sector and differ mainly in the weights given to market shares. Instead of reviewing all the possibilities, it is therefore sufficient to present some of the most representative types. A well-known measure is the *Hirschman—Herfindahl index:*

$$H = \sum_{i=1}^{n} P_i^2,$$

that is the sum of squared market shares of the n firms in the market. This takes account of all firms in the sector, weighted according to relative market share. The smaller the firm, the less it counts.

The maximum value of this index is given by the case of a monopoly where one firm occupies the whole market and H equals unity, while the minimum value, corresponding to a situation where the n firms hold an identical share, will be $1/n$:

$$H = \sum_{i=1}^{n} \left(\frac{1}{n}\right)^2 = \frac{1}{n}.$$

H is therefore an inverse function of the number of firms in the sector. The simplicity of this measure and its link with the oligopoly theory[14] make it very popular.

The more recent *entropy coefficient*

$$E = \sum_{i=1}^{n} P_i . \log \frac{1}{P_i}$$

measures the degree of disorder or uncertainty in a given market. The higher the entropy coefficient, the greater is the uncertainty for a firm of retaining its relationship with any given customer. It is therefore an inverse measure of the degree of concentration. If there is monopoly, the uncertainty is minimal and, because $P_i = 1$, the index is equal to zero. If all market shares are equal, there will, on the contrary, be a maximum of entropy: $P_i = 1/n$ and

$$\sum_{i=1}^{n} \frac{1}{n} \times \log n = \log n.$$

It is clear that both increased equality of market shares and an increase in the number of firms enhances entropy, but the latter factor plays a diminishing role because of the use of logarithms: the addition of an extra firm, when numbers are already large, becomes less significant from a competitive point of view.

The fact that the number of firms affects the entropy measure has led to the use of a relative measure of entropy, that is entropy divided by the maximum value of the coefficient:

$$E_r = \frac{E}{\log n}.$$

This expression shows how the actual degree of dispersion compares to the maximum dispersion possible for a given number of firms.

Finally, the entropy coefficient has a property which favourably distinguishes it from other measures. If the sample which is investigated can be decomposed or disaggregated into several groups (for example firms belonging to different industries, countries, regions, size classes), it is possible to determine the contribution of each group to over-all entropy by breaking down the over-all index into its constituent weighted elements. Thus entropy exists within groups and between groups; and these elements could be added to obtain total entropy. Such a decomposition, which is not possible in the case of other measures, is presented in the appendix to this chapter (pp. 84–5).

Finally, another measure of industrial concentration is the *Linda index*, which is widely used in the statistical studies of the Commission. Let us define:

$$Q_i = \frac{A_i}{i} \bigg/ \frac{A_K - A_i}{K - i},$$

where A_i = the total market share of the top i firms, among the K large firms, A_K = the total market share of the K large firms in the sample, and K may be any number of firms from two to N. Q_i is then the ratio between the average share of the first i firms and the average share of the remaining $K - i$ firms.

The Linda index is defined as:

$$L = \frac{1}{K(K - 1)} \times \sum_{1}^{K-1} Q_i$$

that is, the Linda index is $1/K$ multiplied by the average of the Q_is. The Linda index is designed to measure the degree of inequality between the values of the variable included in a sub-sample of K units and is an answer to a defect of the concentration ratio, that it ignores differences of shares among the largest K firms. It is also intended to define the boundary between the oligopolists within an industry and the other firms. This boundary occurs at the first major discontinuity between values of the variables ranked in descending order and implies that oligopolists can be distinguished in terms of the variable concerned. Linda indices are calculated for the first two firms (K = 2), then the first three (K = 3), and so on, until a minimum value is produced (that is the index for $K + 1$ is greater than that for K firms). At this point the 'oligopolistic arena' is defined.

Apart from the preceding measures there are the classic statistical measures of dispersion. The coefficient of variation is the ratio of the standard deviation σ to the arithmetic mean $\bar{q}$. It is written:

$$V = \frac{\sigma}{\bar{q}} = n \sqrt{\frac{1}{n} \sum_{i=1}^{n} \left(q_i - \frac{1}{n} \right)^2},$$

where

$$\bar{q} = \frac{\sum p_i}{n} = \frac{1}{n}.$$

$\bar{q}$ is in fact, the average market share. This coefficient varies between 0 and $\sqrt{n-1}$; the greater its value, the more important is the inequality of market shares.

The *Gini coefficient* can be understood by reference to the *Lorenz curve*. This graphical representation (Figure 2.9) has on the horizontal axis the cumulated percentage of units (establishments, firms) and on the vertical axis the cumulated percentage of the size variable used (sales, employment, value-added, and so on).

In the case of perfect equality, the observations will be located on the diagonal. The greater the inequality in the distribution, the

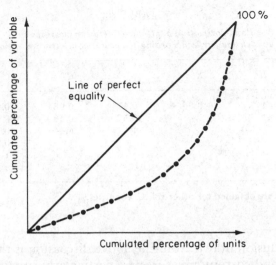

FIGURE 2.9

greater the area between the diagonal and the Lorenz curve. The
formula of the Gini coefficient could then be written:

$$G = \int^{100} \{ x - f(x) \}dx.$$

It may be remarked that the number of firms does not influence
the result, because an industrial sector composed of two firms with
50 per cent of the market each would give the same degree of concentration as a sector composed of 1000 firms each with 0.001 per
cent of the market.

Some authors use the *variance of logarithms* of each firm's activity
(as expressed by sales, assets or employment), but again this index
does not take into account differences in the number of firms and is
therefore a poor candidate to be an adequate concentration measure.

In comparing the several types of measure we perceive that they
require and provide different information. Efforts have been made to
construct formulae which combine the weights of the largest firms
and distribution within the sector. But the results are cumbersome
and do not add much to the separate calculation of the two types of
indices. It seems, moreover, that empirically the indices do tend to
converge. We have calculated the rank-correlation coefficient
between classifications of European manufacturing industries
according to various concentration measures. Table 2.2 confirms a
high correlation, not only between the rankings made by using C_4
and C_8 but also by H and E, while the Gini coefficient leads to a
different rank.

TABLE 2.2

*Rank-correlation coefficients between classifications
of French industries according to various concentration measures**

Measures	H	E	G	C_4	C_8	L_4
H	1	0.86	0.47	0.98	0.96	0.78
E		1	0.52	0.88	0.90	0.61
G			1	0.44	0.35	0.55
C_4				1	0.98	0.77
C_8					1	0.70
L_4						1

*Similar results are obtained for other E.E.C. countries.

The conclusion drawn from the above discussion is that the C, Herfindhal and entropy measures are particularly suitable for empirical studies.

EMPIRICAL ANALYSIS OF EUROPEAN CONCENTRATION

Empirical studies of European concentration are still very rare. We have seen that official data relating to a homogeneous industrial classification (N.I.C.E.) were assembled for the year 1962, but even now there does not exist any systematic and coherent information on the changes since 1962 due to the formation of new firms, changing size of existing firms and disappearance of other companies. In order to make good these *lacunae*, the Commission has set up a large-scale programme of concentration studies, utilising research institutes in member states. The first stage comprises a limited number of sectors (forty-five). There are also some private studies which will be reviewed as well as the official ones.

Let us first underline that it is particularly difficult to handle the problems discussed above of finding a useful measure of concentration in the European context. This is because of the following:

(i) the determination of the geographic market is not easy; in some sectors integration of national markets has come about, in others not. In many industries, tariff barriers have been replaced by non-tariff ones, instituted by the member states (standards, safety measures, subsidies, procedures, and so on). Moreover, firms themselves have created national barriers by product differentiation, or artificially by means of cartel agreements or concerted behaviour (see Chapter 4).

(ii) the determination of the product market is difficult because of the existence of the multiproduct firm which is classified in various industries, so that observations are not independent of each other. This is a general problem which, however, is made worse in Europe through the entanglements of finance, commerce and industry. The great financial and industrial holdings cross both national and sectoral boundaries, often totally undetected because of the family nature of the group. Nationally based sectoral concentration ratios therefore seriously underestimate real economic power and need to be supplemented by qualitative evidence (if available — see Chapter 3).

Plant concentration

Technological economies of scale play a role at plant level. In Table 2.3 some data on estimates of optimal plant scales are

TABLE 2.3

Estimated optimal plant scales in the Common Market (1968)

Article	Type		Per cent of E.E.C. output
Shoes[1]	Leather, simple	4800—5000 units per day	0.2—0.3
Woollen carpets[2]	Machine made, tufted	5,000,000—5,500,000 m.	5.0—6.0
Beer[3]	Pilsener, bottled	100,000—200,000 hectolitres	0.1—0.15
Sugar refining[4]	Beet processing	5000—6000 tons	0.1—0.20
Motor-cars[5] (assembly)	Standard passenger	100,000—300,000 units	1.5—5.0
Steel drums[6]	55 A.G.	625 units per hour	6.0—7.0
Washing machines[7]	Simple, small types	400,000—500,000 units	10.0—11.0
Refrigerators	Simple, small types	500,000—600,000 units	9.0—10.0
Steel	Ingots	3,000,000—4,000,000 tons	3.5—4.5
Nitrogeneous fertilisers[8]		300,000 tons	6.0—7.0

[1] C.F. Pratten and R. Dean, *The Economics of Large-scale Production in British Industry* (Cambridge University Press, 1965) p. 61.

[2] *Volkswirt* (23 February, 1968) p. 44; based on output of largest German producer.

[3] A.G. Hoelen, in a study of the beer market (1960) estimated optimum scale at 60,000 to 80,000 hectolitres.

[4] *Volkswirt* (January 1968); based on output of new Suedzuecker A.G. capacities.

[5] See motor-car study in de Jong, *Hearings on Economic Concentration*, pt 7A (Washington, D.C.: U.S. Government Printing Office, 1968).

[6] Information from the industry.

[7] Pratten and Dean, *Economics of Large-scale Production*, pp. 81—8; Professor Schenck, *Volkswirt* (10 November 1967) calculates a reduction of capital costs per ton to 500 Deutsche Marks at 4,000,000 tons.

[8] C. Boutelier, 'Les causes du mouvement de concentration et de cooperation dans l'industrie chimique du Marche Commun', *Revue du Marche Commun* (December 1967) p. 641.

assembled, based on best-practice plants or newly constructed plants of large companies throughout the economy of the Six. They are taken from company reports or based on company and/or industry information, indicating the sizes of the newest installed plants (or those under construction at the time) by some of the leading firms in the industry. They present only a crude approach, and obviously these optimal sizes were not (and need not be) generally achieved by all firms in the trades at the time. They seem to indicate, however, that in many branches even the application of best-practice technology does not require heavy concentration in the Common Market.[15]

One reason is the evidence of transport costs, which are particularly heavy for large or fragile goods. Transport costs may rise with the size of plant output in order to reach more distant customers; such an increase will be more important if plant size increases in relation to market dimension, for:

(i) it will often become difficult to pass on such costs to selling prices because of local competition;

(ii) the density of consumers declines with increasing distance; and

(iii) the heterogeneity of transport systems (reloading, etc.) will increase.

Thus the effect of transport costs will often reduce optimum plant scale below that optimal to production alone (Figure 2.10). In Figure 2.10, *OA* is the level of output at which lowest unit cost of production is attained, but because of the existence of transport costs *OB* will be the minimum efficient scale (M.E.S.). The minimum efficient plant will be the smaller the faster transport costs increase and the

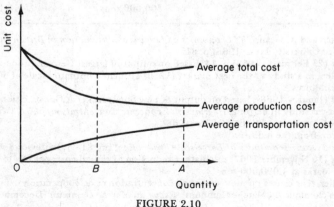

FIGURE 2.10

TABLE 2.4

*Number of plants of minimum optimal size
compatible with domestic consumption*

Industries	United States	Canada	United Kingdom	France	Sweden	West Germany
Drinks	29.0	2.9	10.9	4.5	0.7	16.1
Cigarettes	15.2	1.3	3.3	1.6	0.3	2.8
Construction	451.7	17.4	57.0	56.9	10.4	52.1
Paints	69.8	6.3	9.8	6.6	2.0	8.4
Petroleum	51.6	6.0	8.6	7.7	2.5	9.9
Shoes	523.0	59.2	164.5	128.2	23.0	196.9
Bottles	65.5	7.2	11.1	6.6	1.7	7.9
Cement	59.0	6.6	16.5	21.7	3.5	28.8
Steel	38.9	2.6	6.5	5.5	1.5	10.1
Transport	72.0	5.9	22.8	17.0	3.3	n.i.
Refrigerators	7.1	0.7	1.2	1.7	0.5	2.8
Batteries	53.5	4.6	7.7	12.8	1.4	10.5

slower production costs fall with increased output. A second reason which could explain the existence of plants of smaller than minimum efficient scale is market size: the demand may not be sufficiently large to absorb output from a number of efficient plants and then conflict between productive efficiency and competitive structure becomes apparent. This is what Table 2.4 indicates. Thus for efficient production of refrigerators, there would have to be a quasi-monopoly in the United Kingdom, France and Sweden, while Table 2.3 (p. 51) shows that in the Common Market as a whole there is room for nine to ten producers of efficient size.

Multiple-regression analysis confirms this.* For four countries (France, Sweden, the United Kingdom and West Germany) Scherer

---

* Let us recall that in a simple regression where the dependent variable is related to one independent variable only, the simple correlation coefficient measures the degree of variation in the dependent variable that is associated with variation in the independent variable, relative to the total variation in the dependent variable. The coefficient of determination, R^2, is then the square of the correlation coefficient: it measures the proportion of the variance in the explained variable that is accounted for by the variance of the explanatory variable. In the case of a multiple regression, where two or more explanatory variables are used, the partial coefficients determine the correlation between the dependent variable and each one of the several independent variables, while eliminating the influence of the remaining independent variables; this corresponds to the economic assumption of impounding certain variables in a *ceteris paribus* clause. On the other hand, the multiple-correlation coefficient measures the degree of variation in the dependent variable that is associated with all independent variables in the regression equation taken in combination, and correspondingly the multiple coefficient of determination, R^2, measures the percentage of the variance in the dependent variable that is accounted for by the variance of all explanatory variables in the regression equation taken in combination.[16]

obtains the following relationship:

$$\log X = 1.33 + 0.412 \log PC - 0.293 \log T + 0.902 \log C_3$$
$$\quad\quad\quad (0.149) \quad\quad\quad\quad (0.083) \quad\quad\quad (0.128)$$

$$+ 0.62 \log S$$
$$(0.061)$$

$$R^2 = 0.762 \quad\quad\quad n \text{ (number of observations)} = 45,$$

where X = the relationship between the size of the largest plants, representing 50 per cent of the total employment, and minimum optimal scale, PC = the percentage increase of unit cost of production, T = unit transport costs, S = domestic consumption divided by minimum optimal scale, C = absolute concentration (as measured by the share of the three largest firms).

It seems that both market size (S) and concentration (C) have a significant positive effect on plant size.[17] But other general information contradicts this. Table 2.5 shows that the proportion of plants with less than twenty persons is lowest in the Benelux countries and highest in France and Italy, while the reverse is true of plants with more than 1000 employees.[18] This result is visible in nearly all sectors, even the least expected such as chemicals and electrical construction. However, the paradox resulting from a comparison of Tables 2.4 and 2.5 may be more apparent than real, if in Table 2.4 domestic consumption is calculated in the usual way, that is, as production + imports — exports = apparent domestic consumption, while in Table 2.5 size is established directly by measuring employment. The latter size measure thus includes production for export, which will tend to increase M.E.S. compared with the method used in Table 2.4.

This conclusion is reinforced by the rather broad product groups used in Table 2.4. In reality firms may be importing some of these products and exporting some other types within the same group (the

TABLE 2.5

Distribution of plant size by employment, 1962–3 (percentage)

Country	More than 1000	From 100 to 499	Less than 20
United States	31	31	7
West Germany	28	25	18
The Netherlands	28	14	15
Belgium	25	28	13
France	17	27	25
Japan	16	22	26
Italy	14	22	35

Netherlands pharmaceutical imports are to a large extent composed of bulk-line articles, whereas exports consist of speciality articles). The use of apparent domestic consumption as the denominator in the calculation of M.E.S. would then be misleading.

We therefore consider the results shown in Table 2.5, that the relatively open, low-tariff countries, West Germany and Benelux, had more plants of optimal size than some of the other large countries, to be more convincing than the contrary results of Table 2.4.

Firm concentration

Firm concentration can be approached either by chronological analysis or by cross-sectional analysis of different industries or countries.

The first approach leaves no doubt that although the number of mergers between firms in different member countries is growing much faster, mergers between firms of member countries and those of third countries are still more common (Table 2.6). A large proportion of the mergers takes place in Belgium because of its geographical location. The role of U.S. firms seems to be diminishing (Table 2.7).

Studies of the evolution of concentration in the various European countries indicate that concentration is rising. This is illustrated by Tables 2.8 and 2.9, for the *United Kingdom* and *France* respectively. The U.K. case is particularly striking, even at the two-digit level. For the French manufacturing industries, it appears that both concentration ratios have increased by 2 per cent over the period studied and that this increase has largely occurred between 1965 and 1969.[19]

In the *German* case, a recent study, using a sample of twenty-five industries for the period between 1958 and 1971, concludes that

TABLE 2.6

*Regional distribution of international
mergers in the E.E.C. 1966—73*

	West Germany	France	Italy	Netherlands	Belgium	Luxembourg
1966	22	19	13	16	24	6
1970	24	22	12	13	22	7
1971	22	24	11	12	24	7
1973	16	26	7	13	22	16

SOURCES: E.E.C., *Competition Policy*, Report no. 2 (April 1973) p. 144; and
          E.E.C., *Competition Policy*, Report no. 4 (April 1975) p. 11
          (adapted to the original six members).

TABLE 2.7

Share of member and non-member countries involved
in international mergers in the E.E.C.

	E.E.C.	United Kingdom	United States	Switzerland	Japan	SC†	OC††	Total
1966	50	9	21	5	—	3	4	100
1970	56	10	18	7	1	3	5	100
1971	55	10	17	7	2	4	5	100
1973*	73	—	12	6	2	2	5	100

* The United Kingdom, Denmark and Ireland included in the E.E.C. share.
† SC = Scandinavia.
†† OC = other countries.

fifteen showed an increase in concentration expressed by the share of
the four largest firms and eight showed a decrease.[20] The same study
found that in 1971 all but five industries had a four-firm concentration ratio of more than 40 per cent. This study focused on economically defined markets. A broader study, reported in the Federal
Cartel Office *Report* for 1973, shows that the same tendencies
prevailed in industry at large. Out of eighty branches and sub-
branches, concentration increased between 1962 and 1970 in forty-
six cases and declined in only twenty-five.

TABLE 2.8

Industrial concentration in the United Kingdom

Industry	Percentage of net assets of the industry held by the ten largest firms		Number of firms accounting for 50 per cent and more of the assets of the industry	
	1954	1965	1957	1967
Food	65.7	72.1	7	4
Drinks	41.6	74.9	12	4
Chemicals	81.6	87.7	2	2
Metallurgy	62.8	73.0	6	4
Mechanical construction	33.8	29.0	—	—
Electrical construction	61.4	64.6	5	3
Automobiles	50.1	76.4	5	2

SOURCES: M. A. Utton, 'The Effects of Mergers in Concentration: U.K. Manufacturing
            Industry, 1954–1965; *Journal of Industrial Economics,* no. 1 (November
            1971); Department of Trade and Industry, *A Survey of Mergers 1958–1968*
            (1970).

TABLE 2.9

Unweighted average and sales-weighted average concentration ratios
(share of the 4 largest firms) for 48 two-digit French manufacturing industries

	1961	1963	1965	1967	1969
Unweighted average C_4	25.75	26.21	25.98	26.70	27.88
Weighted average C_4	20.08	20.21	19.42	20.73	22.10

Similar results have been established for other community markets.[21] The drawback of such studies is that they are difficult to compare. For this reason, some years ago the E.E.C. Commission started research on uniform criteria, and the results have been published in the successive reports on *Competition Policy* (I to V). Summarising these findings, it appears that national concentration is rising at an increasing rate and this is also true of the Community as a whole. This was brought out by the Commission's *Third Report on Competition Policy*:

> Of the fifty-five national studies carried out, forty-six individual reports give comparable information on the degree of concentration in 1962 and in 1969. The individual studies cover industries and Member States where levels of concentration are high and low. Thus they can be considered to give a representative sample of Community industry and can provide information on the development of concentration which is of general validity for purposes of statistical comparison.
>
> If we set out, from smallest to largest, the sales proportions in given industries accounted for by the four leading firms in individual industries (if these figures are unavailable, then the employment shares) for the two reference years (1962 and 1969), we obtain the pattern shown [in Figure 2.11]. It shows that the concentration ratios in 1969 (black columns) were substantially higher in virtually all industries than in 1962 (white columns).[22]

While in 1962 the four largest firms already accounted in 28 per cent of cases for 50 per cent or more of the forty-six relevant markets, in 1969 the corresponding proportion of cover had risen to 39 per cent. So that between 1962 and 1969, the number of less-concentrated industries (where the four largest firms accounted for less than 50 per cent of the relevant market) fell by 15 per cent, while the number of highly concentrated industries (where the four largest firms accounted for 50 per cent or more of the market) rose by 38 per cent. The largest rates of increase (67 per cent) are found

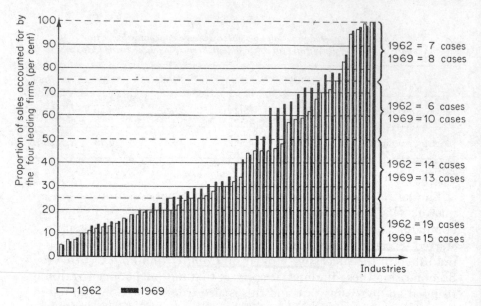

FIGURE 2.11

in the industries where from 50 per cent to less than 75 per cent of the relevant markets were accounted for by the 'top four', and the sharpest decline in concentration (21 per cent) is found in industries where less than 25 per cent was held.

The decline in the number of firms, which is a general conclusion to be drawn from the studies already processed by the Commission in selected industries and countries of the Community, is accompanied by a general rise in the market shares held by the leading firms. Admittedly this does not lead directly to the conclusion that competition is becoming less intense in the Community. However, if this process were to continue uninterrupted, then the workability of competition would be jeopardised in more and more industries.

Cross-sectional comparisons suggest that the most *concentrated sectors are more or less the same in the various countries*, which confirms the influence of technological factors, transcending institutional and economic differences. Horowitz has calculated, using the industrial census results of 1962, the correlation coefficients between concentration (measured by the entropy index) of various industries in different E.E.C. countries.[23] Table 2.10 is the outcome.

The observed correlation indicates that strong similarities exist between the industries of various European countries. However, several factors, such as market size, the importance of international

TABLE 2.10

*Matrix of correlation coefficients between degrees of
entropy in the manufacturing industries of six countries*

	West Germany	France	Italy	The Netherlands	Belgium	Luxembourg
West Germany	0.9021	0.7814	0.8724	0.9619	0.6509
France		0.7829	0.8723	0.9111	0.5787
Italy			0.6892	0.7435	0.5954
The Netherlands				0.9089	0.7567
Belgium					0.7412
Luxembourg					

trade, the share of the public sector and the policies adopted by the authorities, and so on, may distort the comparison. According to Table 2.11, in which the ratios (times 100) with respect to Belgium of paired concentration ratios are presented, the countries with the smallest geographical size would seem to have the highest level of concentration; the central tendency is towards a comparable concentration level in the Netherlands, and towards a lower level in France and Italy.

It is possible to correct for varying market size. In the case of the absolute entropy coefficient we know that it reflects both the number and distribution of the firms in an industry or country. Thus, if for a specific industry the calculated coefficient for France is double that for Belgium, this is compatible with the hypothesis that both countries have analogous production or employment distributions between firms in the industry, but that France has a

TABLE 2.11

*Distribution of ratios (times 100) of the concentration
ratio (four largest companies) of one country to
Belgian concentration ratio, by industry*

Country	Number of industries	Median	Quartiles
The Netherlands	93	100	58–146
France	93	64	43–94
Italy	93	50	33–106

SOURCE: L. Phlips, *Effects of Industrial Concentration* (Amsterdam: North-Holland, 1971) p. 148; see also Jacquemin and Phlips, 'Concentration, Size and Performance of European Firms', in *Markets, Corporate Behaviour and the State,* ed. Jacquemin and de Jong (The Hague: Nyhoff, 1976).

TABLE 2.12

Absolute and relative entropy for twenty one manufacturing industries

Countries	Absolute entropy	Relative entropy
Italy	10.4182	0.7667
France	9.6728	0.7300
West Germany	9.4443	0.7271
The Netherlands	7.7763	0.7395
Belgium	7.5681	0.7267
Luxembourg	4.3666	0.7301

much larger number of firms than Belgium. This could be corrected by using the relative measure of entropy obtained by dividing absolute entropy by the logarithm of the number of firms, which is an approximation of market size.

Thus Table 2.12, comparing absolute and relative entropy, shows the impact of such a calculation. By allowing for number of firms, most of the national differences are eliminated and the Benelux countries seem much less concentrated.

Divergence between plant and firm concentration

As we have seen, the main economies of scale are realised at the plant level; although real enough, they are mixed with diseconomies and monopoly power at the level of the firm. In Europe, concentration often takes the form of an alignment of small, separate units under central financial control. This poses the question of how to measure divergence between the two levels of concentration.

Table 2.13 gives the calculated ratio of firm employment to employment in plants of more than a thousand persons in various countries. These results are confirmed by the calculation of the ratio between the four-firm concentration ratio and the four-plant con-

TABLE 2.13

Degree of divergence between employees in enterprises
and in plants of more than 1000 persons

France	1.92
Italy	1.6
West Germany	1.43
Belgium	1.1
The Netherlands	1.0

TABLE 2.14

The relationship between the concentration ratios of the four largest firms and plants
(average size of four largest firms:average size of four largest plants)

Industry groups*	United Kingdom	West Germany	France
A	2.73 (11)	1.80 (10)	2.32 (10)
B	2.63 (10)	1.43 (10)	1.70 (10)
C	2.40 (10)	1.46 (9)	1.52 (10)
D	2.21 (10)	1.53 (9)	1.44 (10)
Unweighted average	2.50	1.56	1.75
Weighted average for the dimension of the industry (employment)	3.00	1.76	1.87

*The groups are arrangements in descending order of concentration ratios of the industries listed in appendix 2 of K. George and T. Ward, *UK—E.E.C. Industrial Structure*, Working Paper, Department of Economics, University College, Cardiff (1974) p. 56. The number of industries in each group is given in parentheses.

centration ratio (Table 2.14). British, French and Italian industries would seem to be more highly concentrated at firm than at plant level. This indice is confirmed if we recall that a large proportion of plants in these countries are of small size (Table 2.5, p. 54).

On the other hand, West Germany and the Benelux countries have smaller degrees of divergence between plant and firm concentration and the lowest proportion of small plants.

The hypothesis that countries of large geographical extent benefit more frequently from production units of optimal scale can therefore be questioned and the relative 'openness' of economies and the degree of competition may be equally or more important.

VERTICAL INTEGRATION

Concentration in the vertical sense, or vertical integration, is a process or situation in which a firm exercises its activities in two or more industries belonging to various successive stages of the manufacturing process of a product. The process can be divided into forward and backward integration, according to whether the integration is with supplier firms or with customer firms.

Determinants

The many determinants of vertical integration can be grouped under one general heading: since external markets and intra-firm transactions are alternative means of completing a given set of transactions,

then, if the costs of the market are higher than the one of the
internal organisation, profitability requires that transactions be
performed internally and governed by administrative processes
insteau of the market. This proposition holds whether the integration
takes the form of a merger, a takeover, a long-term delivery contract
or some other form. As Arrow has emphasised, why should integration occur at all if the costs of recourse to the market are zero?[24]
The next question is then: what are the factors which cause these
costs?

In many continuous processes technological interdependence creates
economies of scale which can be realised if production is vertically
integrated. The classic example is the melting down of iron in blast
furnaces, where, if there is an adjacent steel-rolling or forging mill,
there is no need for the steel ingots to be reheated. Similar examples
may be found in chemical and petroleum engineering, paper making,
jam manufacturing (the so-called 'in-line packaging') and other
industries. Thus in such cases the market is eliminated by technological considerations.

It has been held that in an expanding industry specialisation rather
than integration becomes imperative if scale economies are to be
achieved in the various stages of production. On the other hand, it
could also be argued that, in an expanding industry, the economic
tensions of excess demand will be transmitted to factor markets.
The firm will then experience supply difficulties and will have an
incentive to manufacture inputs on its own premises. This apparent
paradox can, we believe, be partially resolved by reference to the
concept of the product cycle (see Chapters 3 and 4).

A second explanation is the existence of *market imperfections*;
instead of acquiring inputs at non-competitive prices, the firm will
prefer to make them itself. Threatening to take over one's own
supply or distribution may be an efficacious way of making other
firms offer better terms. Such situations may develop not only as a
result of monopolistic controls but also if fluctuations and uncertainty threaten the stability and security of supply or distribution.

This leads to a third factor influencing the decision to integrate:
the *risks connected with market operations*. The problem of waiting,
bottlenecks, irregular quantities supplied or bad adaptation of supply
to demand are bound up with what is called 'moral risks'. Suppose a
computer component is manufactured at uncertain cost. The producer of the component is willing to assume this risk, on the conditions that a risk premium is added to the delivery price. If the buyer
considers this too high, he can buy the apparatus (including the
connected risks) and bear the consequences himself. In this case, the
producer has no incentive to minimise risk or the costs connected

with risk and he may reallocate his resources towards the fulfilment
of those contracts which do involve risk.

If the buyer could control the process of component manufacture,
or at least have sufficient knowledge of it, he would be able to avoid
such 'moral risks', but normally he cannot. Thus there is an incentive
on his part to integrate vertically. This argument is reinforced if
several successive stages of production are involved, for then the costs
of communication and negotiation are multiplied.

The competitive effects of vertical integration are mixed. On
certain assumptions this type of concentration improves competitive
effectiveness and leads to a welfare gain for the consumer. This
occurs with two monopolies in successive stages of production, if
one of the monopolists considers his input price as given by the
other. The case has been thoroughly discussed by various authors
and is not very important in practice, so we limit discussion to Figure
2.12.

The monopoly price will necessarily be higher than marginal cost,
so that the amount produced and the price charged to the consumer
will be lower in the case of an integrated monopoly than if the two
monopolists operate independently (or, for that matter, if the
second monopolist is also a monopsonist, so that there is a bilateral
monopoly).

If we suppose that the intermediate monopolist can impose his
price on the final producer, the former will maximise his profit by
fixing price p_1, corresponding to the amount q_1. This price becomes
the cost to the producer of the final good, which, in its turn, will sell
q_1 at price p_2. If both firms are integrated, the consumer price will
be reduced to p_3 and the quantity sold will be q_3. This more
favourable outcome, even if the cost curves do not change as a result

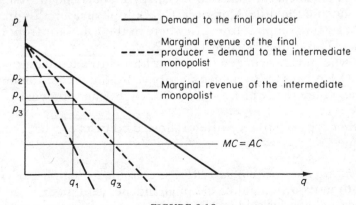

FIGURE 2.12

of integration, depends on the slope of the final demand curve,
which will always be more elastic than that of the demand curve
confronting the intermediate producer.

The practical unimportance of this case follows from the assumptions: two pure monopolists operating in successive stages of production under static conditions. If looser monopoly positions are
admitted (a dominant supplier with some small competitors), or if a
growing market is assumed, the result is no longer uniquely
determined. In reality each producer will retain a certain amount of
bargaining power so that the second monopolist need not simply
accept the price p_1. Moreover, the cost curves are likely to be
changed as a result of integration. They may go down if economies
are achieved, or go up if the larger combination experiences a loss of
flexibility, management problems or friction in its internal com-
munications. Also, the outcome will only be favourable in the
welfare sense if cost savings due to integration are passed on to
consumers.

An *integrated firm* which achieves some measure of market power
in one or more of its stages of production *can employ various
strategies to reduce actual or potential competition.* One such
strategy is the exclusion of competitors from sources of supply or
retail outlets controlled by the integrated firm.

In 1972, the E.E.C. Commission condemned such an action on the
part of the American Commercial Solvents Corporation (C.S.C.) and
its Italian subsidiary, the Istituto Chemioterapico Italiano (I.C.I.) on
the basis of Article 86, which forbids the abuse of a dominant
position. C.S.C. has a world monopoly in the production and sale of
a chemical which is an essential ingredient of a drug to combat
tuberculosis. C.S.C. ordered its subsidiary I.C.I., which initially only
distributed the chemical, to start manufacturing the drug and to stop
selling the chemical substance to Z.O.J.A., an independent Italian
firm producing the drug. Moreover, C.S.C. took measures to prevent
Z.O.J.A. getting supplies from elsewhere in the E.E.C. or from third
countries. This is illustrated in Figure 2.13.

Thus when I.C.I. switched from distributing to manufacturing this
drug, Z.O.J.A. was only enabled to survive by the E.E.C. Commission
issuing an injunction which forced I.C.I. to resume supplying
Z.O.J.A.

Another type of strategy often followed consists of what is called
price-squeezing:

(a) *The simple price squeeze.* If A is a dominant supplier of a good
used both in its own plant X and in an independent plant Y, and if
the processed good is sold on the market by the sales organisations V

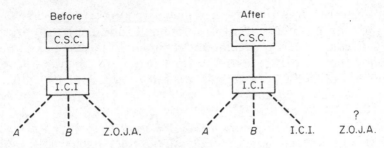

FIGURE 2.13

and S (belonging to or working respectively for X and Y), then A may be able to squeeze Y out of existence. A will sell to Y its inputs at a high price, and will sell the final product cheaply through V, which is a direct competitor of S. In such cases, the independent companies Y and S will be subsidising their own failure (see Figure 2.14). An example was the Aluminium Corporation of America, which sold its aluminium ingots dear to independent processors and subsidised sheet sales to the final consumer.

(b) *The complementary price squeeze.* This system can be used if durable goods have components which need renewal at irregular and uncertain intervals. A motor-car firm in a dominant position can charge high prices for components unobtainable from other producers, as long as the prices dealers charge for replacements can be controlled and a high degree of vertical integration exists, so that volume production of components can be achieved.

(c) *The differential price squeeze.* If components' manufacturers have a market-dominating position, they can charge low prices to

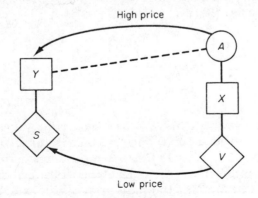

FIGURE 2.14

large customers (with whom they may have long-term contracts) for
deliveries of new items for incorporation in goods, and high prices to
individual customers for replacement purposes. To some extent, such
a policy may encourage assembly firms to integrate backwards, or
stimulate competition in the manufacture of components if the
techniques can be mastered.

(d) *The reversed differential price squeeze.* According to the
reversed differential price squeeze, sales to the next stage of production occur at high prices, but customers in the free market are supplied at low prices. Dealers or distributors in the subsequent stage of
production will be hurt, but the policy may nevertheless be advantageous for the supplier if surplus capacity or temporary excess
stocks have to be disposed of. The classic example is the sale of
surplus oil supplies to non-brand dealers during the 1960s, which
benefited the oil companies, which were able to run their refineries
at a higher level of capacity utilisation than would otherwise have
been possible or to dispose of temporary surplus stocks. Brand ·
dealers tied to the oil companies but responsible for their own
financial results were hurt in varying degrees.

The above strategies may restrain not only actual competitors but
also reduce potential competition by erecting barriers to entry. A
firm considering entry in such a vertically integrated market would
have to set up operations in two stages at the same time, which raises
capital requirements and increases risk (see Chapter 4).

Statistical measures

Various measures of vertical integration have been proposed.
Adelman has suggested the ratio of the sum of value added (V.A.)
to the sum of sales (S):[25]

$$C_{V1} = \frac{\sum\limits_{i=1}^{n} V.A.}{\sum\limits_{i=1}^{n} S}.$$

The more integrated a firm is, the higher is its value added compared to sales, and in the extreme case numerator and denominator
will be equal, so that $C_V = 1$. Conversely, the less activities are
integrated, the more transactions take place between firms, and the
lower the value of C_V. But the measure has serious deficiencies, as
is illustrated by a numerical example.

Suppose there are three firms: A produces raw materials which are an input for B's manufactured goods, which C distributes. Each firm contributes one-third of total value added by the industry. Table 2.15 can be constructed. If the manufacturer absorbs the primary producer (backward integration), the index increases from 0.5 to 1; on the other hand, if the manufacturer absorbs the distributor (forward integration), the index becomes 0.67. The measure gives different results, depending on which stage integration is measured at. It is therefore less an indicator of concentration than of the stage of production or distribution and cannot be used to compare integration between firms in different stages of production. This is shown if mergers are considered: both mergers, ($A+B$ and $B+C$), the one a forward integration, the other a backward integration, bring about an increase in vertical concentration, but apparently to an unequal degree. On the other hand, the complete merger, $A+B+C$, brings about the same increase in concentration as the merger $A+B$.

TABLE 2.15

	A	B	C	Total	$A+B$	$B+C$	$A+B+C$
Value added	100	100	100	300	200	200	300
Sales	100	200	300	600	200	300	300
C_V	1	0.5	0.33	0.5	1	0.67	1

This measure therefore reflects the direction rather than the level of integration, and does not sufficiently take into account the number of integrated stages. Moreover, independent of the level of vertical integration, the measure will be higher for firms or industries whose production has the greater value added (for example higher for watch-making than for metal processing), or the higher their profits. Also, fluctuations in prices and costs will have divergent effects on the numerator and denominator.

A second measure is the ratio between the value of stocks (I) and sales (S):

$$C_{V2} = \frac{\sum\limits_{i=1}^{n} I}{\sum\limits_{i=1}^{n} S}.$$

The rationale behind this measure is that increasing the number of stages of production undertaken by a firm will raise I. But again there are various criticisms: (1) the importance of stocks in relation to sales may change for other reasons than changes in market structure — for example, the introduction of computers or more efficient warehousing facilities may enable rationalisation of stockholding; (2) the value of the measure will vary according to whether the stocks held are of low-value raw materials or high-value intermediate goods; and (3) once again price fluctuations will affect the outcome.

Barnes has proposed a measure to show how much a firm in a given stage of production or distribution depends upon the market.[26] In the case of a paper manufacturer, for example, the measure would be the ratio of the manufacturer's own output of pulp to his total input. In the case of complete integration, this measure would equal unity. There is an obvious link between such a measure and the Leontief input—output analysis. Unfortunately data are often hard to come by. Also, if the ratio is expressed in monetary values, the transfer prices used between the various establishments of the same firm may diverge from the prevailing market prices, and this discrepancy will influence the result. Nevertheless, this approach comes closest to direct measurement of the choice which confronts the firm in considering vertical integration: whether to undertake its own production and/or distribution or to have recourse to external markets with their attendant costs and benefits.

ROUTES TO INCREASED CONCENTRATION IN EUROPE

In a given market a rise in the degree of concentration depends on the rate of growth of the various firms. This may take different forms.

There are in principle two ways of growth: *internal* and *external*. The first consists of a better utilisation of all resources belonging to the firm and above all on its investment policy and the ways it is financed: either through retained profits, or by means of an appeal to the capital market, or by bank credit of a long-run nature, as in West Germany. The second leads to a closer association between two or more firms, from the simple liaison to a complete merger, in the economic sense in which two or more firms are brought under central control.

Comparing the two, external growth presents some advantages from the point of view of the firm:

(i) external growth through acquisition or merger relates to existing assets and may be a quicker mode of achieving profitability than the building up of assets by means of a long drawn-out investment process;

(ii) if the acquired firm is a competitor, external growth increases the market share of the acquirer, without the creation of additional capacity for which there may be no market demand;

(iii) external growth may be a means of acquiring human or material resources for which there is no market or a very imperfect one.

But there may be drawbacks too:

(i) the human problems, connected with the deterioration of the firm's working climate, following upon a merger or acquisition, may be acute — there may be managerial conflicts, personnel releases, reorganisations and reclassifications which may create internal uncertainty and reduce the efficiency of the productive resources;

(ii) integration of the separate units, central economic calculation and definition of goals take time to accomplish;

(iii) the valuation of other companies is often full of pitfalls, notwithstanding the progress made in financial analysis;

(iv) last, but not least, on the European level there are numerous difficulties in the administrative, legal and fiscal fields connected with the existence of separate national regulations.

Various theoretical models have proposed criteria to determine an acquisition price below which the purchase of another firm should be replaced by internal investment. This limit price corresponds to the sum of anticipated profits, which is equal or superior to the profitability of an alternative investment. However, if specific factors, such as the acquisition of unique resources, or the achievement of synergy, as well as uncertainty, enter the calculations, there will clearly be divergencies in both the objective determination and the subjective perception of the expected profits.

The institutional modes of external growth can be divided into two groups: those leading to tight-knit associations and those which remain loose-knit associations, such as cartels or trade associations.

Tight-knit associations

A merger in the legal sense assembles two companies in one and the same legal structure. Such a merger may be achieved between companies which disappear altogether, or by means of the absorption of one of them. In the first case a new company is formed and the shares of the disappearing firms are exchanged against those of the new company. In the second case the transfer of assets to the absorbing company is effected against payment of money or shares to the shareholders of the absorbed firm.

A merger usually leads to important restructuring, from the

composition of the managerial board to the range of products offered, even if it is initially announced that nothing will change. Such restructurings are connected with the goals of concentration operations: an extension and consolidation of the market share, reorganisation of the industrial structure of a declining market, and so on.

The European merger encounters two principal obstacles: *institutional* and *psychological.* On the one hand, the company laws of the various member states are different, ranging from those which do not recognise such a type of operation to those with strict legal control. A merger in the legal sense occurs if two or more legal persons 'merge' into one. Their rights and obligations are joined and one or more of the legal persons ceases to exist. In the Netherlands such legal mergers are impossible; what occurs is that separate legal entities are subjected to centralised financial control. In West Germany, on the other hand, the legal merger in the above sense is subject to strictly prescribed procedures.

The E.E.C. Commission has submitted a proposal to co-ordinate national regulations, envisaging as community goals adequate shareholder information, the consultation of labour and the protection of creditors. The proposed Council regulation concerning the statutes of the European limited corporation is mainly a legal instrument to promote international mergers. The European corporation could only be constituted by two or more member-state corporations through merger, the creation of a holding company or the setting up of a joint subsidiary. It would have a single statute, easier to work with than the different harmonised statutes.

The fiscal rules concerning mergers are also an important institutional obstacle. The fiscal cost of such an operation is considered to be the total or partial liquidation of the company to the benefit of the foreign unit which is constituted. The liquidating company would have to pay taxes on the difference between the current and book values of its assets, which might be considerable. The Commission has therefore proposed a regulation to eliminate those costs. Only at the moment of its effective realisation, that is if the merged company is liquidated, would this surplus value be taxed, not on the occasion of the merger itself. The profits of the merged company may be taxed either in the countries where they were earned, or on a universal basis (i.e. its total profits) in the country where it is incorporated, with the deduction of taxes paid in other member states, as the company chooses.

On the other hand, there are important socio-psychological barriers to mergers at the public as well as the private level. The main reason which often lies behind all such barriers seems to be nationalistic sentiments, especially discernable in the larger European countries. Cases where these sentiments came to the fore may or may not be important. Some spectacular cases were, for example, the intended takeover of Citroen by Fiat, which was stopped by the French government, and the formation, on the instigation of the German government, of a national oil company. In the private sector, when the Hoogovens—Hoesch combination was formed, the unions objected to the shifting of the central office out of West Germany.

Furthermore, according to Mazzolini, two important obstacles to transnational mergers are 'strategic inertia' and 'human problems'.[27] Strategic inertia essentially refers to the fact that the possibility of transnational consolidation does not receive adequate attention from the corporate strategists of European firms. The human problems are represented by the management's reluctance to implement change per se, European management being strongly attached to its working methods and environment, and by unfamiliarity with, as well as misconceptions about, their foreign counterparts.

As long as these obstacles remain important, the number of European mergers will be limited, and alternative forms of increasing concentration will be preferred. However, within each of the national European states there has been a spectacular increase in the number of mergers, undertaken disproportionately frequently by large companies.[28]

Takeover is one of the most frequent modes of increasing concentration in Europe; it consists of one company acquiring a number of shares in another company, while leaving its distinct legal structure and organisation intact. Such an acquisition may serve either a financial or an industrial goal, whether it is effected by means of a transfer of shares in a once-for-all private deal, or the gradual purchase of shares on the stock exchange, or a takeover bid.

If one company possesses more than half of the capital of another, one speaks of the 'mother' or 'parent' company and its subsidiary. An important reason for setting up subsidiaries is to regroup activities while maintaining decentralised decision-taking; the decentralisation may be required for reasons of geographical distance, nationality, new activities or the spreading of risks. In the case of joint subsidiaries or joint ventures, that is companies owned by two or more independent mother companies but managed collectively, the risk-pooling aspect is particularly important because the aim is to reduce individual commitments while achieving a goal which would be difficult to pursue alone. That may be so because the required technology, commercial or local knowledge may be exclusive or costly and the joining of forces may be the only way to get the venture started. It may also be the case that joint ventures serve the goal of restricting competition, especially potential competition in a new field of activities.

A group of companies which is under central economic control is an important but complex structure of a primarily economic nature, existing in almost every European country. The means of control may be majority or minority shareholders, interlocking directorships and other personal liaisons, and so on, and the structure may show various stages: holdings with subsidiaries, or holdings with sub-holdings with their own subsidiaries which may be leading a relatively independent existence. The group may maximise its over-all interests or those of a dominant company within the group.

(a) In the first case the over-all profit could surpass the algebraic sum of the profits of the individual companies.* To achieve this, it would, for example, be necessary to reduce output, sales or profits of one of the participating companies in order to enhance more than proportionally the results of another company. Such a global strategy would also require an over-all policy of profit distribution, this being probably unequal. By means of continuous internal reallocation of resources, the group would be able to maximise its achievements.

(b) In the second case, the interest of the group as a whole is identified with that of a dominant company. In such a case the maximum result of this latter company could be gained, not by means of a better allocation of resources within the group as a whole, but through the exploitation of the subsidiary companies by the dominant one. The leading company makes the others part with their assets or products at prices below true values, lends out monetary capital at high interest rates or, conversely, uses up liquid means at very low rates of compensation, retains all or a major share of the profits of subsidiaries in its own business, and so on. This behaviour is against the interests not only of the minority shareholders but also of any creditors of the subsidiary companies and of employees whose companies have to expand and is in general against the public interest as such speculative activities do not create wealth.

The aforementioned proposal concerning the statute of the European company also has a chapter devoted to groups. The aim of this proposal is to facilitate the operation of economic groups, while taking into account both the economic necessity of central manage-ment and the justified claims of minority shareholders and creditors. When a company is incorporated with the E.E.C. it would adopt the

---

*Two examples are the internalisation of external effects and the case of synergy. See below, pp. 79—81 and 94—6.

status of a 'European company', and would be subject to national
laws only in a subsidiary sense. Minority shareholders in dependent
companies would be offered the choice between straight compensation (purchase of their shares) or the exchange of their shares for
those of the dominant company. Creditors would be assured that the
European company had full responsibility for the obligations of
dependent companies. On the other hand, the dominant company
would have the right to direct instructions to the managers of
subsidiary companies.

Legal methods of setting up concentrated structures are still being
formulated in Europe but this does not mean that nothing
economically significant has been achieved so far. Business has found
ways to achieve indirectly what could not be obtained straightfor-
wardly. Three such types of structure are worth mentioning:

(1) *The international holding*. The Dutch holding company A, with
its operating company C, which incorporates all producing companies,
jointly sets up with a German company B a German company D. A
and B each have 50 per cent of the shares and the companies' boards
are composed on a basis of parity. All the operating activities of both
companies B and C are brought under the control of D, which legally
stays a German company. This occurred in the Fokker–Vereinigte
Flugzeug Werke case.

(2) *The double international holding company*. If both the Dutch
company A and the German company B make the same product and
both companies incorporate their interests in the field into separate
companies C and D, respectively established in West Germany and the
Netherlands, they can take cross participations of 50 per cent in
both companies. Also, the boards can be composed on a parity level.
In such cases, the absence of a central company prevents the legal
compensation of profits and losses. This pattern was chosen in the
cases of Agfa–Gevaert and Siemens–Philips.

(3) *The group with parity contracts*. A British and a Dutch company
conclude a contract stipulating the following:

  (i)   a uniform and equal composition of the governing boards;
  (ii) business management according to identical principles;
  (iii) the parallel distribution of dividends, with profit compensation between the parent companies.

This is the 'Unilever' construction found in the pre-war period and
connecting Unilever Limited (the United Kingdom) and Unilever
N.V. (the Netherlands), which also has preferential shares with
nomination rights. Legally this pattern can only be followed in the
Netherlands and the United Kingdom.

However, notwithstanding the feasibility, such patterns do complicate real economic, legal and technical integration.

Cartels and other loose-knit associations

Finally, there are *associations of firms* formed on the basis of contractual or verbal agreements. The participants are legally on a par and are evidently willing to co-operate. Among such agreements are *cartels.* Cartel agreements have been a frequent and long-standing phenomenon in Europe.

Firms joining a cartel agreement agree to act jointly in certain respects. Cartels do not establish centralisation of decision-taking except to some extent in cases of sales syndicates or joint selling agencies. The reason for including cartels in our treatment is that they often lead to fully-fledged mergers, especially if cartels are formally forbidden by competition-policy legislation.

Cartels, according to a classic definition by Liefmann, represent 'the contractual cooperation of independent companies in similar activities with the goal to influence the market in a monopolistic way'.[29] But only if an appreciable percentage of the market is controlled are cartels able to exert a dominating influence. The 'outsider problem', that is the undercutting of the cartel's prices by a non-aligned rival, always lurks in the background and can be dealt with:

(i)   by economic warfare (for example the waging of a price war);
(ii) by purchasing intruding companies;
(iii) by admitting them to the cartel;
(iv) by exclusive dealing, possibly coupled with boycotts, with companies in preceding or following stages of production.

Very often there is also an 'insider problem', that is a successful cartel will undermine its own foundations through the over-expansion of participating companies, or the giving of secret rebates or other advantages in order to secure business.

The outsider and insider problems explain the pronounced instability of many cartels. Even though cartels are not concentrations in the strict sense of the word, they may substantially reduce the number of independent sellers in a given market. Many cartels arise because the competition between companies has become so fierce that their profitability or even their existence is endangered. There is therefore some truth in the famous pronounciation of the nineteenth-century German economist, Kleinwächter, that 'cartels are the children of adversity'. Not all cartels are equally long-lived or equally successful, however. The main factors which condition cartelisation are the following:

(1) Demand for the product concerned needs to be relatively
inelastic with respect to price changes. Thus a cartel fixing a higher
price will not lead to important substitution nor to a large reduction
in the amount demanded and the price elasticity of demand is below
unity. In the same sense, a cartel fixing quotas will be the most
successful if production restrictions are accompanied by more than
proportional price increases. As this condition is more likely to be
fulfilled in well-established mature sectors than in young, rapidly
growing ones, successful cartels are a much more frequent occurrence
there. A case in point was the electric-light-bulb cartel; this was
rather ineffective at the beginning of the century, when a rapidly
growing demand and technical revolutions (carbon-wired, metal-
wired and gas-filled lamps) occurred, whereas during the 1930s the
cartel successfully reduced the burning hours of the bulbs.

(2) Supply of the good also has to be relatively insensitive to price
changes, at least in the long run. If physical output conditions,
technological circumstances or heavy capital investments restrict an
expansion of industry supply, the cartel partners will be in a stronger
position. In the short run it may be an advantage to the cartel
partners if they can elastically adapt supply to fluctuations in
demand, so that no excessive price rises or waiting periods for supplies
arise which might induce outsiders to step into the market. Both
these circumstances indicate that the cartel will be the stronger the
more it is composed of a small number of large, financially powerful
companies which are protected from outside competition by means
of entry barriers and flexibility of reaction to demand changes.

(3) The third condition is that firms in that market must be able
to agree, which means that transaction and control costs will not be
too high. The greater the number of firms in the market, the heavier
these costs will be. The creation and the functioning of a central sales
organisation that takes charge of all supplies and fixes prices, handles
orders, conditions, and so on, could then become difficult.

Each type of cartel can be distinguished according to its lower or
higher grade of organisation. The higher-organised cartels have a joint
syndicate, or sales agency, very often in the form of an independent
company,* which is the legal European company form, adopted
respectively in the Netherlands, West Germany, and the French-
speaking countries, comparable to the public and private corporations of the Anglo-Saxon countries.

*Naamloze Vennootschap (N.V.), Aktiengesellschaft (A.G.), or Société Anonieme (S.A.)
and Besloten Vennootschap (B.V.), Gesellschaft mit Beschränvter Haftung (G.m.b.H.),
Société à responsabilité limité (S.a.r.L.).

Companies participating in a more highly organised form of cartel conclude independent agreements with the syndicate, nowadays of a non-exclusive nature in order to comply with cartel policy rules (see Chapter 7). Thus a syndicate is usually a strong form of cartel and approaches in fact, though not in theory, a full merger. This is also the case because syndicates, by centralising sales, break the contact which the individual companies have with their markets, so that, *ceteris paribus*, their decisions in the fields of production, investment and research also cease to be independent.

The advantages claimed for the syndicates are the following:

(i) a better adaptation of supply to demand, by means of temporal and spatial restriction of types of goods supplied and a bringing together of fragmented sources of supply; and

(ii) cost saving through rationalisation.

The experience of the German Federal Cartel office has shown that these claims are often overrated. Freight savings are usually unimpressive, and took second place after customer preferences and unused quotas. Rationalisation results have been small, and a tendency to quote premiums (difference between syndicate price and competitive price) was apparent.[30]

A specific form of collaboration between firms is the economic interest group, created in France as a legal structure by the ordonnance of 23 September 1967. Such a *groupement d'intérêt économique* (G.I.E.) is intermediate between a company and an association. It may be composed of physical and legal persons and may be constituted, by simply signing an agreement, without any exchange of shareholdings. It is not allowed to have as its goal striving after profits to be distributed between members.

On the European level, the Commission proposed in 1974 to set up 'European cooperation groups', intended to complete or prolong the activities of member companies belonging to different member states.[31] Such a formula would facilitate international co-operation, which is now made difficult by the absence of a statute for the European corporation. The group would not be entitled to appeal to the general public for funds. Member companies would remain individually responsible for the group's undertakings. An essential economic part is that the group facilitates a member firm's access to certain facilities (research, commercial or accounting) without increasing its size. Thus one may describe it both as a way of achieving a limited degree of concentration or of restraining the quest for size.

To conclude, let us underline that other forms of contractual relationship, such as co-operation, concession, specialisation or sub-contracting, areas likely to give rise to domination and economic subordination as to actual acquisitions; it would therefore be mistaken to regulate those types of relationship in which the dominance of one firm by another is most obvious.

Finally, the legal forms of vertical integration are substantially the same as those used in horizontal concentration.

An important role is played by sub-contracting and by exclusive dealing agreements. The types may be combined if exclusivity clauses are inserted into a sub-contracting agreement. Such types of agreement are mid-way between total integration, as effected by a merger, and free market dealings; they therefore correspond to 'quasi-integration'. Sub-contracting can be defined as the industrial practice by which a firm which has received an order retains responsibility for the customer but in fact has the order wholly or partially executed by another firm.

The vertical-integration aspect is introduced by various clauses instructing the sub-contractor to behave in certain ways (choice of investment, materials or men). Very often the sub-contractor gets into a subordinate position, because the contract may be revoked and new tenders requested, while his commitment to production processes, machinery and employees will be fixed for a given period.

He may then be compelled to quote unprofitably low prices or even work at a loss. Quasi-integration may thus promote concentration of economic power, because sub-contractors are often dependent on a single dominant customer for a substantial part of their business.

In the Common Market, several proposals have been made to set up sub-contracting exchanges, which would centralise and handle supply and demand for such contracts. These markets would reorganise such types of business, harmonise investment policies, evade the playing-off of firms against one another and equalise prices for the same types of work.

In distribution, several types of contract are encountered: the sales agreement without obligation in which distribution is undertaken by an independent firm; or the commercial agency, which is a subsidiary of the producer, which continues to own the goods; or the franchise, which gives the retailer the right to exploit a brand, a name, a product or a way of selling in return for a percentage of his sales.

A widespread type of agreement is the exclusive agency, by which a firm assures the distributor the exclusive right to distribute goods in a particular area, for a given period, under its supervision. Normally with such contracts the conceding firm wants the managerial behaviour of the concessionary to be integrated with its own commercial operations, in exchange for the granting of a monopoly position. It should be clear that exclusivity will have a stronger economic impact the nearer the distributors are to optimum size and the less substitutes for the product are available.

Within the Common Market, exclusive distribution was a priority topic when competition policy with respect to agreements was formulated. The Common Market was in effect split up into separate markets by means of absolute territorial protection granted to sellers — which made it impossible for sellers in other territories to export to the protected area. The prevention of so-called 'parallel imports' ran counter to the aims of European integration and provided producers and sellers with a way of exploiting their market power. Large price differences came about. (For some examples, see Chapter 7, the section on restrictive practices policy.) Consequently, such practices were vigorously attacked by the Commission, which since 1962 has dealt with more than 30,000 contracts.

CONCLUSION

In this chapter the concept, methods and factors influencing industrial concentration have been discussed. Concentration plays a pivotal role in market-theory studies, providing as it were an entrance to the whole field. Most of the features in market economies are somehow or another related to concentration, as the rest of the book will demonstrate. It is a fact of life that in the integrated European economy, as it is already the case in the United States, big business is achieving a dominant position both in sectoral markets (as was shown in this chapter) and in the economy as a whole (as the next chapter will point out). Behind this phenomenon of concentrated industry are such pervasive factors as technological developments and the market strategy of firms. In this way industrial concentration is linked both with wider environmental forces of the present-day world and with behaviouristic characteristics of the leaders of the firms which operate in the market. In both senses developments in the United States and in European economies run strikingly parallel.

Differences remain, however, which should keep us from drawing hasty parallels or conclusions. For one thing, even though the European industrial structure may well become as homogeneous as the American through the process of economic and political integration, several factors tend to maintain various forms of segmentation between national markets so that an analysis of industrial concentration at the national level has still some relevance. In this context it appears that the largest plant sizes in European countries are generally lower than those in the United States: this does not seem to result from smaller market size but from the deliberate choice of multiplant operations linked by some loose holding-company structures at the expense of plant size; and, as is well known, concentration at this level is associated with much more questionable scale economies.

As advances are made in creating more homogeneous economic conditions in Europe, the statistical apparatus for measuring concentration and relating it to conduct and performance criteria becomes largely inadequate as it is basically orientated towards national goals and standards. This seriously hampers European studies from being carried out in the same way as is done in the United States. On top of this, European governments and parliaments are not yet sufficiently willing to promote 'openness' in publications relating to structural and policy questions and are not yet inclined to set up high standards of disclosure for the firms operating in their territories. This of course retards and hinders whatever initiatives may come from the E.E.C. Commission. The combination of these aforementioned factors makes the field of industrial organisation a difficult one since researchers often have to start from scratch. In comparison, in the United States (and to a lesser extent in the United Kingdom) one can fall back on a wide array of published material. However, every year brings some progress in this regard, so that gradually a fund of knowledge is being created in order to bring structural features into a truly European perspective.

APPENDIX

Internalisation of external effects as a determinant of concentration

In Chapter 1 we argued that, apart from internal economies of scale, co-ordination of the policies of firms which are interdependent through their cost functions (externalities in production) or their demand functions (complementary products or substitutes) could increase profits and lead to concentration.

A simple analytical treatment shows how this effect comes about. In the first case, the total cost functions of firms 1 and 2, illustrating the existence of externalities in production, are as follows:

$$C_1 = 5q_1 + 0.1q_1^2 - 0.1q_2^2$$

and

$$C_2 = 7q_2 + 0.2q_2^2 + 0.025q_1^2$$

where q_1 = quantity produced by firm 1 and q_2 = quantity produced by firm 2. The ruling market price is assumed to stay at 15. Firm 1 is assumed to cause external diseconomies to firm 2, in the sense that an increase in the production of firm 1 increases the costs of firm 2; thus

$$\frac{\delta C_2}{\delta q_1} > 0.$$

Firm 2 causes external economies to firm 1; that is

$$\frac{\delta C_1}{\delta q_2} < 0.$$

If both firms remain independent, they will try to maximise individual profits; thus

$$\Pi_1 = 15q_1 - 5q_1 - 0.1q_1^2 + 0.1q_2^2 \tag{2.1}$$

and $\Pi_2 = 15q_2 - 7q_2 - 0.2q_2^2 - 0.025q_1^2$ (2.2)

The first-order conditions for achieving maximum profits are

$$\frac{\delta \Pi_2}{\delta q_2} = 0, \frac{\delta \Pi_1}{\delta q_1} = 0,$$

so that $q_1 = 50$, $q_2 = 20$, $\Pi_1 = 290$ and $\Pi_2 = 17.5$.

Both firms maximise their profits with respect to the variable which they control, even though the level of profits depends on the level of production of the other firm. If, on the other hand, the firms were to co-ordinate their decisions, they would maximise joint profits:

$$\Pi = 15(q_1 + q_2) - 0.125q_1^2 - 5q_1 - 0.1q_2^2 - 7q_2 \tag{2.3}$$

First-order conditions require that

$$\frac{\delta \Pi}{\delta q_1} = 15 - 0.25q_1 - 5 = 0$$

and

$$\frac{\delta \Pi}{\delta q_2} = 15 - 0.2q_2 - 7 = 0,$$

which implies $q_1 = 40$, $q_2 = 40$ and $\Pi = 360$. Thus the joint profits are higher than the sum of profits earned by the two firms maximising profits separately. Moreover, the firm which caused external diseconomies has a lower level of output ($40 < 50$), while the firm giving rise to economies has seen its output rise ($40 > 20$).

Therefore, as long as $\delta C_2/\delta q_1 \neq 0$ and $\delta C_1/\delta q_2 \neq 0$, there is a certain price which one firm is prepared to pay to acquire the other one. There will be an advantage in merging the two firms, in order to internalise the external effects, which does not require public subsidies or taxes. A similar argument showing the advantage of maximising joint profits instead of individual profits could be developed in the second case given above, when two monopolists operate in distinct but related product markets, so that the demand functions are as follows:

$$q_1 = f_1 \ (p_1, p_2), q_2 = f_2 \ (p_2, p_1).$$

It is easily shown how the policies are changed by maximising the joint profit function,

$$\Pi = \Pi_1 + \Pi_2 = p_1 \ q_1 \ (p_1, p_2) + p_2 q_2 \ (p_1, p_2)$$

$$- C_1 \ \{q_1 \ (p_1, p_2)\} - C_2 \ \{q_2 \ (p_1, p_2)\},$$

instead of maximising individual profits,

$$\Pi_1 = p_1 \ q_1 - C_1 \ (q_1)$$

and

$$\Pi_2 = p_2 \ q_2 - C_2 \ (q_2).$$

For example, if the products are substitutes $\partial q_2 / \partial p_1 > 0$, the first-order condition for maximising the individual profit of firm 1 is

$$\frac{d\Pi_1}{dp_1} = \frac{dR_1}{dp_1} - \frac{dC_1}{dq_1} \times \frac{dq_1}{dp_1} = 0,$$

where $R_1 = p_1 \ q_1$. By contrast, a necessary condition for maximising the joint profit is written as follows:

$$\frac{\partial \Pi}{\partial p_1} = \frac{\partial R_1}{\partial p_1} - \frac{\partial C_1}{\partial q_1} \times \frac{\partial q_1}{\partial p_1} + \left(p_2 - \frac{\partial C_2}{\partial q_2}\right)\frac{\partial q_2}{\partial p_1} = 0.$$

The fulfilment of this last condition would then imply $d\Pi_1 / dp_1 < 0$, as the last term is itself positive.

Given the second-order conditions, namely the concavity of the profit function, this requires that, once interdependence between the

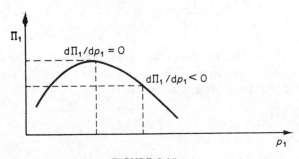

FIGURE 2.15

substitutes is taken into account, the firm will produce less at a
higher price than when maximising individual profit (see Figure
2.15). The inverse result is easily verified for complementary products
$(\partial q_2/\partial p_1 < 0)$.

A link between the concentration ratio and the degree of monopoly

As we have mentioned, there is no general theoretical justification for
thinking that the level of concentration is a good measure of
monopoly power. However, a link has been established in the case of
price-leadership, in which collusion between the k largest firms fixes
a price which is followed by the remaining $n - k$ firms.[32] If market
demand is $Q_m^D = f(p)$, where p = selling price, and the $k > 1$ firms
maximise joint profits, the quantities supplied by the $n - k$ firms are
determined by the following relationship:

$$Q_s^r = g(p).$$

If the market is assumed always to be in equilibrium, the demand
function for the k largest firms is given by

$$Q_k^D = Q_m^D - Q_r^S = f(p) - g(p).$$

The first derivative with respect to price is

$$\frac{dQ_k^Q}{dp} = \frac{\delta Q_m^D}{\delta p} - \frac{\delta Q_r^S}{\delta p} = f'(p) - g'(p).$$

In terms of elasticity,

$$\frac{dQ_k^D}{dp} \times \frac{p}{Q_k^D} = \frac{\partial Q_m^D}{\partial p} \times \frac{p}{Q_k^D} \times \frac{Q_m^D}{Q_m^D} - \frac{\delta Q_r^S}{\delta p} \times \frac{p}{Q_k^D} \times \frac{Q_r^S}{Q_r^S}.$$

It follows that

$$\epsilon_k = \epsilon_m \times \frac{Q_m^D}{Q_k^D} - \theta_r \times \frac{Q_r^S}{Q_k^D} = \epsilon_m \times \frac{f(p)}{Q_k^D} - \theta_r \times \frac{g(p)}{Q_k^D}, \qquad (2.4)$$

where ϵ_m is the elasticity of market demand and θ_r is the elasticity
of supply of the $n - k$ firms. The *degree of monopoly power or
Lerner index* for the k largest firms is

$$\lambda_k = \frac{p - c_k}{p},$$

where c_k is the joint marginal cost of the k firms. Such a measure is

based on the divergence between price and marginal cost, a divergence that does not exist in the case of perfect competition.

Furthermore, if it is known that given total revenue $R = p(q) \times q$,
marginal revenue is written as

$$\frac{dR}{dq} = p + q\frac{dp}{dq} = p\left(1 + \frac{q}{p}\frac{dp}{dq}\right) = p\left(1 + \frac{1}{\epsilon}\right).$$

As the typical monopoly equilibrium requires that marginal revenue
equals marginal cost, we have, given the maximisation of joint
profits at every moment,

$$c_k = p\left(1 + \frac{1}{\epsilon}\right).$$

From this last expression, we obtain:

$$\lambda_k = \frac{p - p(1 + 1/\epsilon_k)}{p} = -\frac{1}{\epsilon_k}. \tag{2.5}$$

Expression (2.5) is therefore the inverse of (2.4):

$$\lambda_k = \frac{1}{-\epsilon_m \, Q_m^D/Q_k^D + \theta_r \dfrac{Q_r^S}{Q_k^D}}. \tag{2.6}$$

The concentration ratio for the k largest firm is

$$c_k = \sum_{i=1}^{k} P_i = \frac{Q_k^D}{Q_m^D},$$

where P_i is the market share of firm i. Moreover, knowing that
$Q_r^S = Q_m^D - Q_k^D$, we can write:

$$\frac{Q_r^S}{Q_k^D} = \frac{Q_m^D - Q_k^D}{Q_k^D} = \frac{Q_m^D}{Q_k^D} - 1 = \frac{1}{c_k} - 1 = \frac{1 - c_k}{c_k}.$$

Therefore, (2.6) can be written:

$$\lambda_k = \frac{1}{-\epsilon_m \, 1/c_k + \theta_r \times \{(1 - C_k)/C_k\}}$$

or

$$\lambda_k = \frac{-c_k}{\epsilon_m + \theta_r (c_k - 1)} = \frac{c_k}{\theta_r - \theta_r c_k - \epsilon_m}.$$

This formula shows that a link exists between the monopoly-power measure and the degree of concentration. In the case of the k largest firms we also see that an increase in concentration causes a rise in monopoly power if $\theta_r > 0$ and $\epsilon_m < 0$, which is normally the case:

$$\frac{\partial \lambda_k}{\partial c_k} = \frac{-\left[\epsilon_m + \theta_r (c_k - 1)\right] - \theta_r (-c_k)}{\left[\epsilon_m + \theta_r (c_k - 1)\right]^2} = \frac{\theta_r - \epsilon_m}{D} > 0.$$

The decomposition of the entropy measure of concentration

When comparing the various measures of concentration, we have emphasised that the entropy measure has one exclusive property: it can be disaggregated to show the contribution of each group of firms to total concentration among all firms. Consider a disaggregation of n firms into G groups and let S_g be the set of indices of the gth group ($g = 1, \ldots, G$). The disaggregation of the entropy measure can be written as follows:

$$E = E_0 + \sum_{g=1}^{G} P_g E_g,$$

where $P_g = \sum_i S_g P_i$ is the combined share of the firms in the gth group.

$$E_0 = \sum_{g=1}^{G} P_g \log \frac{1}{P_g}$$

is the entropy between the G groups; and

$$E = \sum_{i \in S_g} \frac{P_i}{P_g} \log \frac{P_g}{P_i}$$

is a weighted average of the entropy within each group. And finally:

$$\sum_{g=1}^{G} P_g E_g$$

is the total entropy within all groups. The decomposition process itself is best understood if we write:

$$E = \sum_{i=1}^{n} P_i \log \frac{1}{P_i} = \sum_{g=1}^{G} \left(\sum_{i \in S_g} P_i \log \frac{1}{P_i} \right).$$

It is clear that $\log 1/P_i = \log P_g/P_i + \log 1/P_g$. Hence:

$$E = \sum_{g=1}^{G} \left[\sum_{i \in S_g} \frac{P_g}{P_g} P_i \left(\log \frac{P_g}{P_i} + \log \frac{1}{P_g} \right) \right].$$

Given E_g as above, we have:

$$E = \sum_{g=1}^{G} \left(\sum_{i \in S_g} \frac{P_g}{P_g} P_i \log \frac{P_g}{P_i} \right) + \sum_{g=1}^{G} \left(\sum_{i \in S_g} \frac{P_g}{P_g} P_i \log \frac{1}{P_g} \right)$$

$$E = \sum_{g=1}^{G} P_g E_g + \sum_{g=1}^{G} \left(\sum_{i \in S_g} P_i \log \frac{1}{P_g} \right)$$

$$E = \sum_{g=1}^{G} P_g E_g + \sum_{g=1}^{G} \left[\log \frac{1}{P_g} \left(\sum_{i \in S_g} P_i \right) \right]$$

$$E = \sum_{g=1}^{G} P_g E_g + \sum_{g=1}^{G} \log \frac{1}{P_g} P_g.$$

Over-all Concentration, Conglomerate Bigness and the Largest European Corporations

It has often been stated that the absolute size of a firm is irrelevant to the question of competition and that there is no or little connection between the aggregate level of concentration and the level of concentration in individual markets; and while concentration ratios within particular industries are accepted as conventional indicators of market power, the use of measures of over-all concentration has been viewed with suspicion. Over-all (or aggregate) concentration is defined as being the proportion of some aggregate of economic activity accounted for by a relatively small number of the largest firms taken together.

Nevertheless, the current trends in the nature of industrial organisation make it imperative that we improve our understanding of over-all concentration: its origins, its evolution and its consequences. The actual degree of diversification by firms and the multiplication of conglomerate mergers give rise to entities which cannot be reduced to the classic one-product firm. In consequence, the concentration of economic power in the hands of these entities is not easily analysed in terms of the traditional approach. The increasing extent of diversification across product and industry lines creates theoretical as well as empirical problems.

On the one hand, microeconomic theory is still very poor in terms of providing verifiable hypotheses of how multi-industry firms behave. On the other hand, the researcher who uses census of manufacturing data on industries must be aware of the fact that parts of a single firm may be included in a number of industries so that the observations are not independent. Those considerations explain the renewed attention being paid to the analysis of the size structure of giant diversified firms and their pattern of growth over time.

Such an interest is not new in Europe. As early as 1958, Houssiaux stated that the over-all economic power exercised by a diversified firm may be greater than the sum of the market power it has in each industry in which it operates, so that one should really study its position in a national or international framework across industries.[1]

But the difficulty is to go beyond vague statements about big business and be precise about where corporate power comes from in specific cases. The determinants of size, and the possible associations of power with size, are examined in the first section. The second section is devoted to the importance of giant European firms, their turnover, their diversification and their multinational character.

DETERMINANTS OF SIZE

A starting-point for the following discussion has been put forward by Arrow: 'When the price system is fully operative, the large organisation is equivalent to a large number of separate activities whose connections are the same as those of unrelated firms. Hence, the large organisation would have no differential advantage in economic competition, and we would not expect to find it so dominant.'[2] This means the origin of the large organisation is to be found in the non-optimal allocation of resources by the existing imperfect market system and in the development of non-market means of allocation.

Apart from the explanations of horizontal and vertical concentration already discussed, which are also valuable for explaining large size (particularly economies of scale), reasons for large size can be found at three levels: the product-market level, the factor-market level and the socio-political level.

As far as the product market is concerned, growth, market power and risk avoidance are important factors.

First of all, the firm can increase its size by diversification, to sustain *growth* or even to survive. Otherwise, all its products become obsolete and the profits it earns are determined by the economic conditions of the later stages of the product's life.

> Having attained a satisfactory and reasonably secure position in its areas of specialisation, a firm with resources available for expansion over and above those required to maintain its position in those areas may well find that opportunities for expansion into new areas look more promising than further expansion in its existing areas. . . . Diversification is then seen as a solution to some of the problems that may be created for the individual firm by unfavourable movements in demand conditions.[3]

Empirically it has indeed been established that many products show the same pattern of market development. Four stages are distinguished (Figure 3.1): introduction, expansion, maturity and decline.

It is tempting, therefore, to relate the growth process and the corresponding increase in firm size to product-cycle developments.

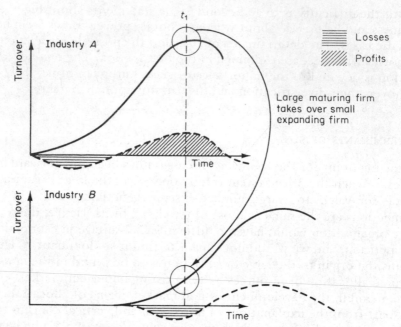

FIGURE 3.1   *The product cycle and diversification*

When introductory difficulties have been mastered, the growth of the
potential market, increasing actual market size and relatively large
cost reductions, based on technological improvements, induce firms
to enter the market. Attracted by profits and potential for growth,
the number of firms increases so that horizontal concentration
declines. But, with increasing competition, surplus capacity arises in
the maturing market (see Chapter 2, p. 35) and firms will be forced
to liquidate or merge, or cartel agreements will develop. Concentration increases again and the comparative stagnation of the market,
oligopolistic interdependence, combined with the uncertain outlook,
prompt the maturing firms to look around for alternative ways of
growth. Their accumulated profits and the urge to expand induce
internal and external diversification towards promising industries
(type B in Figure 3.1 at time t_1). Typically, diversified mergers take
place between large and slow-growing firms, and smaller rapidly
growing, actually or potentially profitable, firms, which are in the
first stages of the product cycle.[4]

Monopolistic leverage

Apart from growth or survival, a second reason for firms to expand
by diversification may be the existence of market power: a firm

exploits its dominant position in one market to expand its empire into another. This is known as *monopolistic leverage* and is closely connected with the classical analysis of industrial concentration as it depends on the existence of monopoly power in the original market. Very often a giant diversified firm which started by being dominant in one market progressively becomes the leader in a great number of product groups. As a result the largest enterprises which have a growing share in the whole manufacturing sector tend also to account for the high level of concentration in many product groups within manufacturing.[5]

Two traditional devices for carrying market power over to new products are *cross-subsidisation* and *tying arrangements*. Cross-subsidisation implies that a firm is able to use funds from one geographical or product market, from one stage of production, or even from its cash reserves ('deep pocket') to subsidise other areas of its operation. By means of cross-subsidisation, the firm may try to cover an actual loss resulting from a product sold below cost, to equalise profits in various markets, or, in the case of a vertically integrated firm, to 'squeeze' a non-integrated firm. But at the core of the concept is the idea that by subsidisation the firm may substantially weaken the competitive structure of the industry. Subsidisation is a profitable strategy for a firm only if it leads to a dominant position in a new area of activity and if this position can be maintained. The appendix to this chapter presents an analytical illustration of such a strategy (pp. 115–17).

By use of a tying arrangement, the sale of one commodity is made conditional on the sale of another (tied) product. Again, the tie enables a seller to use his market power in the tying product to acquire market power over the tied product; he may thus reduce the number of competitors in the tied-product or raise barriers to entry into that market.

As an illustration,[6] suppose that the minimum efficient scale in manufacturing of the tied product (B) is such that a seller must account for at least 20 per cent of total sales, which means that a maximum number of five efficient firms can produce B. In addition, suppose that a firm which has a monopoly in the market for the tying good (A) is able to foreclose 80 per cent of the market for B by tying sales of B to sales of A: this implies that some of the existing sellers of B will have to leave the industry, the exact number depending upon the steepness of the downward slope of their long-run average cost curves over the relevant output range (zero to the minimum efficient scale) and the magnitude of the difference between the 'minimum-efficient-output' price for B and the price adopted by the firm which has a monopoly of A. If initially there are five firms in the market for B, all but one may be forced to leave the industry if the slope of their cost curves is very steep and the monopolist does not charge far above the 'minimum-efficient-output' price for B.

There are other purposes for which a seller may find it advantageous to impose tying arrangements on its customers;[7] for example, where the arrangement enables price maxima or minima to be avoided or where the arrangement allows more effective price discrimination. But the most important potential danger of tying arrangements is that firms might use them to gain additional monopoly power by barring markets to their competitors. It is therefore not surprising that Article 86 of the Rome Treaty, which forbids the abuse of dominant positions, gives tying practices as a specific example of abusive behaviour.

To conclude with an example, the case of the British Oxygen Company (B.O.C.) is instructive because it exhibits both subsidisation and tying arrangements. The company controlled four of the five British manufacturers of oxygen-producing equipment. It provided this apparatus free of charge to the oxygen-consuming client companies, on condition that they bought the gas from B.O.C.*

Risk

A supplementary and important motive for increasing size through diversification is the reduction of risk. In a world characterised by change, the firm diversifies its production, not only to grow faster or to extend its dominant position to new markets, but also to guard against adverse changes in the demand for existing products and to stabilise its profit which is a random variable.† The attainment of

---

*For other examples (Kodak, Courtaulds, the British Match Corporation, and so on), see the Reports of the British Monopolies Commission.

†Let us recall that a *random variable* is a variable whose exact value is now known in advance but the range of its possible values is known, as well as the probabilities of occurrence for all the possible values in the range.

Expected value $E\{\Pi\}$ of such a random variable, in our case profit Π, is written:

$$E\{\Pi\} = \sum_{i=1}^{n} P(\Pi_i) \times \Pi_i = \overline{\Pi},$$

where each value of i represents one of n possible values of Π, and $P(\Pi_i)$ is the probability that the ith value of Π is observed. As all possible outcomes are accounted for by the probability function, all the probabilities must add to one:

$$\sum_{i=1}^{n} P(\Pi_i) = 1.$$

The degree of dispersion that affects outcomes of the variable Π can be represented by the *variance*, that is a weighted average of squared differences between all the actual values and larger size through diversification helps to increase the security of the firm, and such a motive is important in Europe where security is obviously sought after.

As a first step, it is easy to show that by producing a sufficient number of different goods, a firm is able to reduce the variability of its profits, and even to completely stabilise them. Such a demonstration is given in the appendix to this chapter and confirms that by not putting all their eggs into one basket, firms are able to protect themselves against the danger that one of their projects will turn out very badly.

However, the objective of firms is certainly not simply to minimise this instability; it also takes into account the level of the expected profit. A very simplified way of presenting the argument is to assume that the choice of variables for firms' decisions are the statistical parameters of the distribution of expected profits, so that particular assets or products are valued only in so far as they contribute to these statistical measures. The most obvious parameters are the mean $\bar{\Pi}$, a measure of the central tendency of profit, and the variance σ_{Π}^2 which serves as a measure of the riskiness of the profit. This assumption simplifies the analysis of choice under risk as it reduces all actions to those two dimensions and adds only one statistic to the static theory of choice under certainty which focuses on the mean and assumes a zero variance. The corresponding utility function of

---

the expected value. The weights are again the probabilities with which the value can occur:

$$\sigma_{\Pi}^2 = \sum_{i=1}^{n} P(\Pi_i) \times (\Pi_i - \bar{\Pi})^2 .$$

Usually, high risk is expressed by a high variance of returns, a zero variance corresponding to a certain outcome. The square root of the variance is called the *standard deviation*.

The *covariance* is a measure of the association between the movements of two or more different random variables, for example profit x from one product and profit y from another product:

$$\sigma_{xy} = \sum_{i=1}^{n} \sum_{j=1}^{n} P(x_i, y_j) (x_i - \bar{x}) (y_i - \bar{y}).$$

If both variables are always above and below their means at the same time, the covariance will be positive. If x is above its mean when y is below its means, and vice versa, the covariance will be negative.

Finally, the *correlation coefficient* is a standardised measure of the extent to which two variables move linearly together; contrary to the covariance that may have any value, depending on the size of x and y, this coefficient will always be between -1 (for two variables perfectly negatively related to each other) and $+1$ (for two variables perfectly positively related to each other). It is written as $r = \sigma_{xy}/\sigma_x \sigma_y$, that is the covariance of x and y divided by the product of the standard deviations of x and y.

the firm is written as follows:

$$u = u\left(\overline{\Pi}, \sigma_{\Pi}^2\right), \text{ with } \frac{\partial u}{\partial \overline{\Pi}} > 0, \frac{\partial u}{\partial \sigma_{\Pi}^2} < 0.$$

Hence it is assumed that, other things being equal, a greater expected return is preferred to a smaller one and a smaller risk (measured by the variance) is preferred to a larger one. The preferred combination of products is the one which maximises this function. Some utility trade-off between mean and variance could also be specified but many general results can be derived by simply assuming risk aversion, that is to say, that if the firm has a choice among outcomes that offer the same expected return, it will prefer the outcome with the smallest variance.

Figure 3.2(a) illustrates one set of indifference curves between mean and variance. A steeper slope corresponds to lower risk aversion* and curves further to the right represent higher utility. Points on the horizontal axis (such as B) show the mean profit, which combined with zero risk gives the same utility as the other mean—variance combinations on the indifference curve through B; such points are known as *certainty equivalents*.

It must be underlined that the use of a utility function which includes only the mean and variance of the probability distribution of profits requires that one (or both) of two conditions is fulfilled: either the probability distribution of returns can be fully described by its mean and some measure of dispersion, like the standard deviation (or the variance), so that the mean and standard deviation summarise all relevant information (this is the case of the normal distribution); or the utility function is quadratic so that moments about the mean higher than the second are zero.

As has been shown elsewhere, these conditions are not always plausible,† but as a first approximation this is a useful way of representing concisely and operationally a firm's attitude toward risk.

A second step in the presentation is to build up a frontier of efficient portfolios of products. We must determine the portfolio of different assets or products which has the smallest variance of all those which have an expected return equal to a given return $\overline{E}$. By solving this problem for a number of different values of $\overline{E}$, we will obtain a set of efficient portfolios which we can represent in implicit

---

*Indeed, the higher the degree of risk aversion, the greater the increase in expected profits a firm will require to accept greater profit variability.
†See the footnote on p. 186.[8]

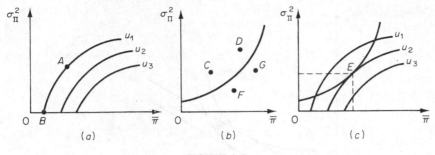

FIGURE 3.2

form by a relation: $f(\overline{\Pi}, \sigma_{\Pi}^2) = 0$. Thus, for every variance, the efficient portfolio offers the highest possible rate of return, and for every rate of return the efficient portfolio offers the lowest variance.

In Figure 3.2(b), each of these portfolios is represented by a point lying on the boundary curve. Points below the curve, such as F and G, are unattainable portfolios, and points above the curve, such as C and D, are attainable but inefficient portfolios. Having eliminated both unattainable and inefficient portfolios, a final selection of one portfolio from among the efficient ones is required.

The final step consists of maximising $u = u\ (\overline{\Pi}, \sigma_{\Pi}^2)$ subject to the efficiency condition $f\ (\overline{\Pi}, \sigma_{\Pi}^2) = 0$. In Figure 3.2 (c), the optimal portfolio is represented by the point E, where an indifference curve is tangential to the efficiency locus; the most preferred portfolio is also an efficient portfolio.

Such a straightforwad application of the theory of portfolio selection, mainly due to Markowitz,[9] to product diversification must, however, be considered with prudence.

First, the acquisition of activities differs from that of securities in certain ways: the conglomerate, unlike the investor, cannot vary the extent of the operation; cannot quickly change his mind; and the products of a conglomerate company are heterogeneous compared to the stocks of securities held by an investor. Second, a firm with some degree of market power and diversified production cannot be reduced to a 'market arbitrator' which considers its efficient opportunity set. If this was the case, there would be no need for a firm to diversify, as long as stockholders could have at their disposal a perfect security market, obtaining the same result by diversifying their own portfolios. But the large diversified firm not only has a wider range of investment opportunities than the specialised firm, and can allocate capital between diversified markets more efficiently, but may be able to shift its efficiency boundary to the right; this could enable the firm to obtain a lower profit variance

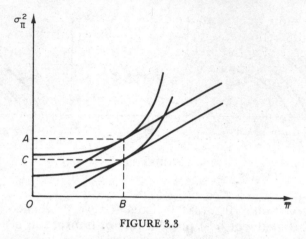

FIGURE 3.3

(OC instead of OA in Figure 3.3) for every level of expected profit, or a higher profit for every level of profit variance. This is an argument put forward by Hicks, Galbraith, Caves and others, for whom part of the reward of being in a position of market power is being able to reduce risk.

One aspect of this question is *financial*: if there exists for each firm some positive probability of suffering losses large enough to induce financial failure, the joint probability of such an event is reduced by a conglomerate merger if the income streams of the two firms are not perfectly correlated; the combination of the financial resources of the firms reduces lenders' risk. This will induce lenders to establish a new aggregate lending limit which exceeds the sum of the original limits established for the merger partners individually.[10]

Increased borrowing could reduce the tax paid by the firm as debt interest is deductible from taxable income.

Imperfect factor markets and synergy

The development of large firms may also be examined in the light of *imperfect factor markets*.

A first aspect is the market for managers itself. Let us assume there are 100 different industries in an economy A. In each industry there are 50 firms of the same size and making the same one product, so that the total number of firms in A is 5000. On the other hand, an economy B has 50 firms, which are of equal size, but each is diversified and makes 100 different products. Traditional analysis suggests that the two economies are similar because, in both cases, each firm has no more than 2 per cent of a market. In fact, it is to be expected that each of the 50 conglomerates will dominate their

economy more than each one of the 5000 specialised firms. One
reason is the reduced number of autonomous entrepreneurs in B, so
that the core of entrepreneurs will have more bargaining power. The
large corporate combination allows optimal allocation of scarce
managerial skills.

Second, increasing over-all concentration eases the task of
co-ordinating decisions. Whether or not firms recognise their mutual
interdependence 'depends on inter and intra-market fewness of
sellers, as well as on the character of their interrelations in each
market they share'. In addition, 'the extent to which barriers to new
competition exist depends on any previous relationships between
entrant and the established firms, and on the integration patterns and
total scale of both'.[11]

More generally, imperfections in factor markets, and even the non-
existence of markets for some factors, could explain the fact that the
cheapest way of acquiring some scarce factors is to buy the firm
which owns them. The limitations of capital markets are especially
important in the European context.

Capital markets work inefficiently because of uncertainty and lack
of information, but large firms could overcome this by taking over a
company with a surfeit of funds or a financial corporation, such as a
bank.

We have already noticed that a firm may have different optimal
sizes in its different functions and so *excess capacity* will arise in one
or more functions which the firm has an incentive to utilise by
internal or external diversification. Logue and Naert argue that
synergy exists when firms with complementary sets of under-utilised
resources merge.[12] The following example is suggested. Let V_x be
the market value of company x, V_y the value of company y and
V_{x+y} the value of the merged firm. The value of each firm is a
function of four interrelated factors: M = managerial resources, P =
productive resources, MP = market potential, and F = financial
resources. Each firm maximises its value, but is constrained by
different factors:

$$\max V_x = L_x \ (M_x^e, P_x^e, MP_x, F_x)$$
and
$$\max V_y = L_y \ (M_y, P_y, MP_y, F_y^e),$$

where the exponent e indicates that the corresponding resources are
limited.

If x and y merge, x can supply financial resources to y and y can
supply managerial and productive resources to x, so that

$$\max V_{x+y} > \max V_x + \max V_y.$$

This is one version of the transfer theory, which says that by combining the excess resources of one firm with the deficient resources of the other, a merger may lead to a synergy effect. The surpluses or shortages of resources could be explained by imbalances in functional optima or in growth, along the lines of the British School (Babbage, Robinson, Penrose). Synergy would then be the result of full employment of previously under-utilised capacity and a net benefit would be effected by means of a transfer of resources so that the new combination could work with the lowest average costs. Though the logic is impeccable, the result is nevertheless improbable.

First, the under-utilised resources must meet certain conditions. They should be complementary so that an unused factory will be able to make the products required by the sales organisation of the other firm. The more generally useful is a production factor, the better, so that liquid means obviously have the highest transferability.

Second, the quantities and proportions must match, otherwise new imbalances will be created.

Third, the surplus resources should be the cheapest available to the firm with shortages, otherwise it could better acquire them on the open market.

Fourth, an increase in the size disparities between merger partners will decrease the synergy effect, a conclusion which is in agreement with Kitching's findings that, in 84 per cent of the cases in which a U.S. merger failed, the merger partners differed widely in size.[13]

The transfer theory, therefore, though logically tenable, is not very realistic.

The socio-political dimension

A last word must be said about the *socio-political aspect*. Power in the market-place is but one facet of the firm's economic power and, in addition, the large firm possesses what might be called 'extra-market power', which consists of the numerous ways, social and political, in which it can transform the economic rules of the game in its favour.

> The branch manager of the company whose plant is the largest employer in a town or the vice-president of the firm proposing to build a plant which will become the largest employer in a small state treats with local government not as a citizen but as a quasi-sovereign power. Taxes, zoning laws, roads, and the like become matters of negotiation as much as matters of legislation.[14]

At the limit it could be argued that giant size and the intensity of political favours are positively correlated. Here lies an important explanation of the tendency of many large firms to become larger, even if such an expansion is obtained at the expense of economic efficiency. A giant firm, socially important because of the number of people it influences directly as employees, suppliers and customers, may be economically weak.

Today in Europe, extra-market power is probably more important than market power. This situation arises from the increasing institutionalisation of the market economy. Our system is no longer a delicate self-regulating mechanism but a set of institutions open to manipulation by the participants. In this view, the large corporation becomes more and more a 'body politic' for the accumulation and use of power. Reciprocally, there is a tendency for European governments to develop policies which use large enterprises to solve specific problems, as if they were agencies of the state.

GIANT EUROPEAN FIRMS

Size, structure, number and stability

It is well known that the largest European firms are quite small compared to the largest American firms, but it is not clear whether this is a good or a bad thing. On the basis of the 1973 *Fortune* list, twenty-four of the world's fifty largest industrial companies, that is 48 per cent, are based in the United States, representing 60 per cent of the total sales and 71 per cent of aggregate net income, while nineteen (38 per cent) are European (based in the nine E.E.C. countries), representing only 27 per cent of total sales and 22 per cent of net income.* The average rate of return on assets is 8 per cent for U.S. companies and 5 per cent for European ones. On the other hand, even allowing for inflation and devaluation, the sales of the largest European companies grew much faster than those of the U.S. ones: on the basis of the 1975 list, the twenty-nine U.S. companies' sales accounted for only 45 per cent of the total and their share of net income is reduced to 38 per cent, while the nineteen European companies now represent 33 per cent of total sales.

The number of very large European firms varies from one country to another. The distribution among the nine is given by Table 3.1:

West Germany, the United Kingdom and France have the greatest number of large firms and there is a systematic relationship between nation size and the number of very large firms. For the Six + the United Kingdom, we obtain a significant positive rank-correlation coefficient of $r = 0.956$ (significant at 1 per cent)

*It is useful to recall all the limits affecting the quality of the published data on large firms. However, these lists represent all that is available.

TABLE 3.1

Country	Number of companies with sales (in 1974)		
	more than 15 milliards of French francs	more than 10 milliards of French francs	more than 5 milliards of French francs
West Germany	19	34	66
France	13	19	38
Italy	5	8	11
United Kingdom	11	25	53
Netherlands	2	3	5
Belgium	1	2	5
Luxembourg	–	–	1
Netherlands/United Kingdom	1	–	–
West Germany/Netherlands	1	–	–
Europe	1	–	–

*1 French franc (1974) = $ 0.225 = £ 0.095.
SOURCE: *Le nouvel economiste* (December 1975).

between the classification by size of gross domestic product and that of the number of firms in the country with sales above 5.10^9 French francs. Furthermore, a sectoral classification shows that these big enterprises are in the same few industries: steel, chemicals, electronic equipment, vehicles, food and petroleum. The fact that the largest firms tend to arise in a small number of sectors seems to be a characteristic of industrial countries. The domination exercised by some large European corporations is illustrated in Table 3.2, which gives the five companies with the highest sales in 1974 for a number of industries. It appears that while U.K. firms control the food, drink and tobacco sectors and rubber products, German firms are ahead in chemicals and steel. Other sectors, such as automobiles and electrical equipment have large firms of various nationalities. It also appears that many leading European branches still exhibit a more or less symmetrical oligopolistic structure in which there is not a dominant firm, in contrast with the U.S. industry which knows in many of its sectors an asymmetrically concentrated structure where the role of the dominant firm is preponderant.

We may next ask whether the *relative size of U.K. and continental* firms has changed since the formation of the Common Market.

We notice that the size supremacy of U.K. firms is limited to a tiny leading group in 1962, as in 1971, while the opposite is true for smaller classes. Furthermore, the relative size of continental firms increased between 1962 and 1971 (see Table 3.3). This finding is

TABLE 3.2

1973	1974		Nationality	Sales (in French francs)
		Automobiles		
1	1	Volkswagenwerk	D	31,259,155
2	2	Daimler Benz	D	29,927,727
3	3	Régie Nationale des Usines Renault	F	25,674,103
4	4	Fiat	I	22,263,715
5	5	British Leyland Motor Corporation	GB	16,901,210
		Electric equipment		
1	1	Philips	NL	45,050,215
2	2	Siemens	D	31,738,905
3	3	I.T.T. Europe (I.T.T., U.S.A.)	EUR	25,929,600
4	4	A.E.G. Telefunken	D	22,087,890
5	5	Cie Générale d'électricité	F	15,366,000
		Petroleum		
1	1	Royal Dutch Shell Group	GB/NL	146,009,271
2	2	The British Petroleum Company	GB	82,767,534
3	3	E.N.I.	I	45,168,840
4	4	Cie Française des Pétroles	F	42,817,227
—	5	Elf Erap	F	28,359,000
		Non-ferric metals		
1	1	Pechiney Ugine Kuhlmaan	F	22,221,600
2	2	The Rio Tinto Zinc Corporation	GB	12,342,908
3	3	Metallgesellschaft	D	9,431,587
—	4	Metallurgic Hoboken Overpelt	B	5,955,488
—	5	Viag Vereinigte Industrietanlagen Gesellschaft	D	5,419,022
		Chemical		
1	1	B.A.S.F.	D	40,437,347
2	2	Farbwerke Hoechst	D	37,220,342
3	3	Bayer	D	34,784,001
5	4	Veba	D	33,283,282
4	5	Imperial Chemical Industries	GB	31,313,493

continued overleaf

TABLE 3.2 – continued

1973	1974		Nationality	Sales (in French francs)
		Food		
1	1	Unilever	NL/GB	61,410,086
4	2	Cavenham Ltd.	GB	14,691,314
2	3	Associated British Food	GB	11,305,201
–	4	Deutsche Unilever	D	11,239,250
3	5	B.S.N.–Gervais–Danone	F	9,781,022
		Steel		
1	1	August Thyssen Huette	D	38,942,527
3	2	Mannesmann	D	24,280,465
2	3	British Steel	GB	23,905,840
5	4	Estel N.V. Hoesch Hoogovens	NL/D	18,167,416
–	5	Denain Nord–Est Longuy	F	17,258,387
		Rubber–pneumatic		
1	1	Dunlop Pirelli Union	GB/I	16,903,012
2	2	Michelin	F	12,000,000
3	3	Dunlop Holdings	GB	9,410,380
–	–	Manufactureus des Pneus Michelin	F	5,747,349
4	4	Continental Gummi Werke	D	2,725,917

SOURCE: *Le nouvel economiste* (December 1975).

TABLE 3.3

Size ratio of the largest U.K. and E.E.C. firms

Size class	U.K./E.E.C. (1962)	U.K./E.E.C. (1971)
1—5	2.35	1.55
6—10	0.84	0.78
11—20	0.64	0.54
21—30	0.68	0.46
31—40	0.65	0.50
41—50	0.75	0.57

confirmed by examining the dispersion of firm size within the top 100 companies.

Table 3.4 reveals a tendency for dispersion (measured by relative entropy)* to decrease on the Continent since the creation of the Common Market, and to remain stable in the United Kingdom. At the same time the dispersion between the U.K. group considered as a whole and the continental group has increased, suggesting a faster growth of the continental firms.

Additional information may be gathered from examining the stability of the size distribution of firms. Turnover among the ranks of large firms as well as growth in their numbers may inform us

TABLE 3.4

Relative entropy of the top 100 firms in the United Kingdom and the E.E.C.

Year	Total entropy	Between groups	Inside E.E.C.	Inside U.K.
1962	0.8916	0.9658	0.8541	0.9083
1963	0.8935	0.9495	0.8631	0.9070
1964	0.8964	0.9363	0.8693	0.9097
1965	0.8978	0.9420	0.8695	0.9132
1966	0.8991	0.9132	0.8767	0.9097
1967	0.9037	0.9282	0.8826	0.9119
1968	0.9025	0.9378	0.8829	0.9015
1969	0.9077	0.9275	0.8936	0.9042
1970	0.9091	0.9190	0.8927	0.9097
1971	0.9117	0.8765	0.9044	0.9013

SOURCE: A. Jacquemin and M. Cardon, 'Size Structure, Stability and Performance of the Largest British and E.E.C. Firms', *European Economic Review*, no. 4 (1973).

*Let us recall that relative entropy is actual entropy as a percentage of maximum entropy equal to the logarithm of the number of firms. The use of this measure counteracts the sensitivity of the measure to the number of firms.

TABLE 3.5

Survival of the largest firms in similar rankings

Rank in 1962	Number of firms in 1962		Total surviving in similar rankings in 1971	Number of firms in 1971		Proportion surviving in 1971	Compared surviving proportion in 1971	
	U.K.	E.E.C.		U.K.	E.E.C.		U.K.	E.E.C.
1–12	5	7	8	4	4	0.66	0.80	0.57
1–25	8	17	17	6	11	0.68	0.75	0.65
1–50	16	34	40	13	27	0.80	0.81	0.79
1–75	31	44	62	24	38	0.83	0.77	0.86
1–100	43	57	74	29	45	0.74	0.67	0.79

about the ability of large corporations to become more or less insulated from broad shifts in the pattern of demand and to view themselves as quasi-private institutions controlling a substantial part of aggregate economic activity.

Table 3.5 shows how many of the 100 largest U.K. and E.E.C. firms maintained their size ranking between 1962 and 1971. Two conclusions can be drawn from Table 3.5. First, life is very secure for the 50 or 100 largest, which have a survival rate of four-fifths or higher. This is confirmed by Table 3.6,* which shows that of the largest 50 firms in 1962, 94 per cent were still among the top 100 in 1971.

Kaplan's result for the 100 largest U.S. firms over a twelve-year period (1948–1960) showed a 'death rate' of two companies per annum.[15] The European annual death rate would be around 2.8, so that European stability seems to be already well established.

Second, a comparison between U.K. and continental giants suggests that while their positions are very similar for the top 50 firms, this is not so for the top 100 where more E.E.C. than U.K. firms remain in the top 100 group (see Table 3.6).

A closer look at the firms moving into the top 100 class between 1962 and 1971 reinforces the idea of stability among the largest firms: 26 per cent of these 'new firms' were located between the 101st and the 133rd rank in the 1962 list. The other promotions are essentially due to mergers between firms not listed in the 1962 top 100.

Similar evidence is offered by Engwall.[16] Estimating *transition probabilities* of jumping from one size class to another (classes

TABLE 3.6

Survival of the largest firms in the top 100 class

Rank in 1962	Total surviving in the top 100 in 1971		Proportion surviving in the top 100 in 1971	
	U.K.	E.E.C.	U.K.	E.E.C.
1—12	5	7	1	1
1—25	8	17	1	1
1—50	15	32	0.94	0.94
1—100	29	45	0.67	0.79

Comparing homogeneous classes of the forty largest U.K. firms and the forty largest E.E.C. ones, we obtain a survival rate of 0.67 for the United Kingdom and 0.82 for the E.E.C.

TABLE 3.7

The estimated transition matrix

	0	1	2	3	4	5	Σ
0	0.924	0.076					1.000
1	0.024	0.893	0.083				1.000
2		0.038	0.892	0.070			1.000
3				0.948	0.041	0.014	1.000
4					0.947	0.053	1.000

numbered from 0 to 5), he shows (Table 3.7) that for a sample of the largest European firms between 1956 and 1965, the higher probability is of remaining in the same class and that jumps greater than one class are very rare.*

Last, we may consider to what extent the largest European firms have increased their degree of dominance in the economy over the post-war period. With respect to the E.E.C. before U.K. entry, Table 3.8 shows a remarkable increase in *overall* (or aggregate) *concentration* for each size class; giant enterprises account for an increasing share of economic activity.

As shown in Table 3.9, British evolution has been similar, although we cannot compare the percentages themselves because of the different sizes of the economies.

Thus, the growing weight of giant firms in the manufacturing sector as a whole confirms their growing importance in particular industries.

TABLE 3.8

*Shares of the largest E.E.C. firms in the gross output of
extractive and manufacturing industries (per cent)**

Size class	1960	1965	1970
1–4	5.8	6.8	8.1
1–8	10.4	11.8	14.6
1–20	20.9	22.6	29
1–50	35.1	35.1	45.7

*Gross domestic product equals added value, while sales are the numerator; this biases the obtained results upwards, but what is important is the trend.[17]

*The classes have been chosen so as to make the upper class limits twice as large as the lower ones. The class ranges are expressed in absolute terms and the firm sizes have been deflated to money value in the different years.

TABLE 3.9

Shares of the 100 largest quoted firms in total net manufacturing assets (per cent)*

Size class	1948	1957	1968
1–4	10.2	11.4	14.7
1–12	17.8	20.6	26.2
1–50	35	39.9	50.8
1–100	46.5	50.7	63.7

SOURCE: G. Whittington, 'Changes in the Top 100 Quoted Manufacturing Companies in the United States, 1948–1968', *Journal of Industrial Economics* (November 1972).

Product diversification

It is well known that the large companies are usually diversified. There exist several measures of *product diversification,* based on the number of different products produced by a firm or the different industries in which it operates or on the percentage of a firm's activities outside its main industry.

Such an index has been recently proposed by Berry:[18]

$$D_H = 1 - \sum_{i=1}^{n} p_i$$

where p_i is the ratio of the firm's sales in the ith industry to the firm's total sales in its n industries. This application of the Herfindhal index of industrial concentration has all the usual properties of this index itself; for example, when a firm is equally active in each of several industries,

$$D_H = 1 - \frac{1}{n}$$

where n is the number of industries in which the firm is active.

The rare empirical European studies of the importance of diversification use similar measures. For example, the U.K. 1963 and 1968 Census of Production uses a measure based upon the net output of the firm; a firm selling all its output in the industry to which it is classified has a specialisation index of 100, and a decrease of the index means an increase of diversification. Table 3.10 has been obtained. It appears that diversification is quite important, even at this level of aggregation, and that, with some exceptions, there is a trend towards greater diversification.

TABLE 3.10

Index of specilisation for U.K. industries (per cent)

S.I.C. order		1963	1968
III	Food, drink, tobacco	92	92
IV	Coal and petroleum products	75	68
V	Chemical and allied industries	82	79
VI	Metal engineering	81	68
VII	Mechanical engineering	83	84
VIII	Instrumental engineering	85	81
IX	Electrical engineering	85	79
X	Shipbuilding, marine engineering	71	83
XI	Vehicles	88	86
XII	Metal goods	75	72
XIII	Textiles	88	82
XIV	Leather goods, fur	90	89
XV	Clothing and footwear	94	94
XVI	Bricks, pottery, glass, cement, etc.	86	79
XVII	Timber, furniture, etc.	93	85
XVIII	Paper, printing, publishing	94	93
XIX	Other manufacturing industries	87	84
All Manufacturing industries		86	83

SOURCE: J.D. Gribbin, 'The Conglomerate Merger', *Applied Economics,* No. 8 (1975). Because of changes in the S.I.C., the two sets of data are not strictly comparable.

Such a trend is particularly impressive for the large firms. Gribbin obtains the following regression:[19]

$$S = 96.2 - 0.17 X$$

$$R^2 = 0.30, t = 2.49,$$

where S = specialisation index 1963, X = share of industry net output produced by firms with 1000 or more employees. It confirms that the more important are the larger firms in the industry, the greater is the degree of diversification.

The amount of diversification may be due to external as well as to internal growth of the firm. Using a sample of the 159 largest U.K. manufacturing firms, Kumps examines the evolution of the number and type of mergers over a six-year period (Table 3.11).[20] The increase in the percentage of conglomerate acquisitions over the period confirms the previous findings. Similar results are obtained for West Germany, where, according to Schwarz, the percentage has increased from 8 per cent in 1966 to 42 per cent in 1972.[21]

Hence the available information suggests that in Europe, as well as in the United States, there is a pronounced swing to diversification,

TABLE 3.11

Evolution of mergers among the 159 largest U.K. firms

Year	Conglomerate mergers* Number	Per cent	Other mergers Number	Per cent
1964	6	16.2	31	83.8
1965	14	46.7	16	53.3
1966	9	40.9	13	59.1
1967	24	51.1	23	48.9
1968	29	52.7	26	47.3
1969	21	63.6	12	36.4
Total	103	46	121	54

*Mergers between firms mainly operating in different S.I.C. industries.

through both external and internal growth. However, we must be cautious about any effort to measure the extent of diversification, as the results depend heavily upon the grouping of commodities defined as a single product or as an industry.

In *United States v. Continental Can* [1964], the Supreme Court held a merger between the second largest manufacturer of metal containers (Continental Can) and the third largest manufacturer of glass containers (Hazel–Atlas) to be illegal. Continental Can argued that the purpose of its merger was to 'diversify' into the glass-container field, but the Supreme Court held that the inter-industry competition between the manufacturers of these two types of containers brought both metal and glass containers under 'one combined product market'. On the other hand, at the European Court of Justice, Continental Can, accused of an abuse of its dominant position (because it acquired control of two big firms), argued that its market share was lower than that suggested by the European Commission because it was necessary to define the relevant market as the market for light containers which includes glass containers!

One possible test to distinguish between these situations is the use of cross-elasticity of demand. Table 3.12 suggests that when the cross-elasticity of demand is close to zero, the products may be considered as not being interchangeable.

A fundamental hypothesis behind the use of such a criterion is that 'other things remain equal'. Otherwise the observed change in the demand for product i may come not only from a price change in the related product but from increased advertising for product i or a more general market acceptance for this product (see also Chapter 4).

In any case it is useless to try to establish any 'absolute' meaning

TABLE 3.12

Substitute (horizontal concentration)	Complement (vertical concentration)	Diversification (conglomerate concentration)
$\in_{ij} = \dfrac{dq_i}{dp_j} \times \dfrac{p_j}{q_i} > 0$	$\in_{ij} = \dfrac{dq_i}{dp_j} \times \dfrac{p_j}{q_i} < 0$	$\in_{ij} \approx \dfrac{dq_i}{dp_j} \times \dfrac{p_j}{q_i}$

for terms such as 'a highly diversified' or an 'undiversified' firm, given that there is a continuum of products, going from very close substitutes to totally different products.

'If we are told that firm A produces 20 products and firm B produces 4 products, can we sensibly conclude that firm A is the most diversified? And would our judgement be changed if we knew that the 20 products of firm A were kinds of shoes while the four of firm B were tractors, radios, airplane engines, and automobiles?'[22] In fact, the computed degree of diversification will greatly differ according to the level of aggregation of the industrial classification used, i.e. two-, three-, four- or five-digit, and thus it becomes necessary to compute the index at different levels of aggregation but without the possibility of making weighted comparisons of the respective role of these different levels in the firm's diversification process.

This suggests the usefulness of a disaggregated approach which could distinguish between the diversification corresponding to activities in unrelated areas of production and diversification among closely related products. It would be desirable to determine the *intensity* of diversification, so that the relative specialisation of firms within a group of industries could be contrasted with diversification where the diversifying firm enters an industry far away from its original one.

In this context it has been proposed to use an entropy measure of diversification:[23]

$$D_E = \sum_{i=1}^{n} p_i \log \frac{1}{p_i},$$

where p_i is the ratio of the firm's sales (or another size indicator) in the ith industry to the firm's total in its n industries. This index takes the value 0 when a firm is active in a single industry and becomes $D_E = \log n$ when it is equally active in each of the n

relevant industries. But the main interest of the measure is that it can be decomposed into an intra-group component and an inter-group component.

Consider a given firm which is active in n four-digit industries, these industries being aggregated in S two-digit sectors. In agreement with the formula for disaggregated entropy previously presented, total diversification of a firm can be written as follows:

$$ D_E = \sum_{s=1}^{S} p_s \times \log \frac{1}{p_s} + \sum_{s=1}^{S} p_s \times D_s, $$

where the first term is inter-sectoral diversification, that is diversification among sectors, the second term is intra-sectoral diversification, that is a weighted average of diversification within sectors, the weight p_s being the share of each sector in total sales.

The use of such an index could contribute to a more realistic approach to the analysis of the diversification process considered as a whole spectrum.

Geographical diversification and multinationals

The large firm not only overcomes industry limits by its product diversification but also national boundaries through its geographical dispersion. Hence the multinational dimension can be viewed as an important step in the growth process of the large diversified firm.

The distinctive characteristic of the *multinational corporation,* which owns and controls production units in more than one country, as compared with its indigenous competitors is the transnational mobility and control of its resources.[24] It has the capacity to secure full and reliable information on investment opportunities beyond national borders; and it has the power to exploit differences between countries, in terms of availability and cost of labour, raw materials, capital and credit, as well as in terms of regulations, legal institutions, consumer behaviour and way of life. At the limit the multinational firm produces where the labour cost is lowest, borrows where the cost of capital is least, sells where the prices are highest and is taxed where the fiscal burden is lightest. Such a policy is favoured by intra-multinational enterprise *transfer-pricing.* This phenomenon has been studied from several points of view, including the following:

(i) an approach based on a revision of the theory of international trade which eliminates the inability of the classical model of static comparative advantages to explain international direct investment;

(ii) a related approach derived from location theory which tackles the question from the viewpoint of the individual firm;

(iii) approaches based on an extension of capital theory, explaining the origin of international and real capital flows.

A specially stimulating approach which overcomes the problems of the classical theory of international trade is based on the product-cycle theory. Such models have been mainly elaborated by Vernon and Wells.[25] Figure 3.4 is a schematic presentation of the course of the exports, imports and multinational production of a

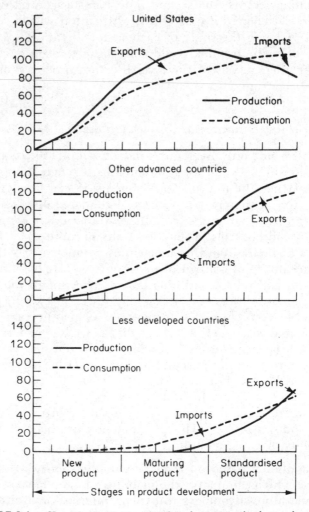

FIGURE 3.4   *Hypothetical international trade patterns in the product cycle*

new product.[26] Assuming that the product was invented in the
United States, production will accelerate fast there and exports
will be made to Europe and other advanced countries. As the
market expands in those countries (dotted consumption line),
European firms will start producing and American firms will
increasingly produce from their European plants in order to:
(1) compete on an equal basis with European companies; and
(2) to export from the lower-cost European plants to the expanding markets of less-developed countries. After some time the
process will be repeated, with the European market maturing, and
so on.

Many industrial economists have tried to determine the market
structure, conduct and performance which favour the activities of
subsidiaries of foreign firms competing with indigenous firms or
imports. Specifically, two aspects may be mentioned: the economic
characteristics and advantages of foreign firms over indigeneous
firms; and the characteristics of the industrial structure to which the
multinational firms are attracted. Most empirical studies made in
Europe and in the United States reach similar conclusions. The multinational corporation is mainly engaged:

(i)   in fast-growing and export-orientated industries;
(ii) in high-technology sectors;
(iii) in capital and advertising intensive sectors.

The corporations themselves, as compared with domestic firms, are:

(i)   larger than their domestic counterparts;
(ii) better export performers;
(iii) more capital intensive and more research and development
intensive.

All these are characteristic of broad trends in industrial structure,
mainly in terms of increasing aggregate and industrial concentration.
But the implications for competition are not so clear.

On the one hand, the entrance of foreign firms may have a
beneficial effect on productivity and prices by breaking up a local
monopoly or increasing competition in an oligopolistic structure, and
by introducing new techniques, processes, designs, products and
services. On the other hand, several authors have stressed the fact
that foreign direct investors can reduce competition by expanding
abroad the dominant position they occupy at home, and monopolis-
ing previously competitive markets. According to R. Caves, 'direct
investment tends to involve market conduct that extends the
recognition of mutual market dependence — the essence of
oligopoly — beyond national boundaries'.[27]

It must be stressed that almost all these studies have been made on the basis of U.S. multinational firms. Even from a European point of view, direct foreign investment means usually U.S. investment; from 1959 to 1972 the book value of direct investment in the E.E.C. by U.S. firms grew from 2.1 billion dollars to 16.8 billion dollars. A breakdown of international operations (holdings, joint or non-joint subsidiaries) in the E.E.C. into operations between firms from member countries and operations in which firms from non-member countries participate (Table 3.13) shows that U.S. firms were the outsiders most frequently involved, followed by U.K. firms.[28]

However, an obsession with the 'American challenge' may obscure the fact that large continental European enterprises based in the member countries of the E.E.C. are establishing and acquiring foreign subsidiary links elsewhere in the Community at a rate very similar to that of their large American counterparts. Multinational operations by European firms today are not confined to a select list of U.K., Swiss, Swedish and Dutch firms.

> On the contrary, the majority of today's large European companies have come first to sell and then to produce outside their home countries during the 157 years that have elapsed since Cockerill of Belgium put up its first foreign plant in Prussia in 1815. Today, fewer than five of the Continental European companies on Fortune [magazine's] '200' list have no foreign manufacturing activity.[29]

Table 3.14 indicates the distribution, by country of origin, of the foreign subsidiaries of non-American multinationals. Such subsidiaries account for almost half of the total number of foreign subsidiaries. The dominant position of the United Kingdom may be explained by the size of its firms, its tradition of overseas expansion and the role of the Commonwealth. The Dutch position is higher in terms of sales than in the number of subsidiaries because Dutch multinationals are located in highly concentrated industries (petroleum, chemicals, food). Both German and French foreign investment expanded very fast between 1968 and 1970.

Such a rise in multinational activities seems to be associated with structural changes inside large European firms. There is a tendency to replace the traditional holding company, comprising a loose collection of daughter companies, by multidivisional structures characterised by a separation of the general office (concerned with strategic decisions) from operating divisions. This more efficient internal organisation must be taken into account in the cost—benefit analysis of the multinational corporation.

TABLE 3.13

Shares of E.E.C. and non-member countries in international operations in the E.E.C. in 1966, 1970 and 1971 (percentages)

Year	E.E.C.	United States	United Kingdom	Switzerland	Scandinavia	Japan	Other Countries	Total
1966	58	21	9	5	3	–	4	100
1970	56	19	10	7	3	1	5	100
1971	55	17	10	7	4	2	5	100

TABLE 3.14

Country	Percentage of the total turnover of subsidiaries of non-American multinationals in 1970	Number of subsidiaries	Percentage of the total number of subsidiaries created in 1968–70	Share of the new subsidiaries in the total number of subsidiaries of each country
United Kingdom	35	2269	35	29
Holland	21	429	5.5	26
West Germany	10	792	19	39
Switzerland	8	397	4.3	20
France	7	429	10	49
Canada	5	201	2.4	18
Italy	5	133	1.3	23
Belgium–Luxembourg	3	276	6.5	44
Sweden	3	171	2.5	26
Japan	3	483	11	40

SOURCE: J. Vaupel and J. Curhan, *The World's Multinational Enterprises* (Harvard Business School, 1974).

CONCLUSION

In this chapter we have been examining the modern large corporation, the determination of its size and its importance in the
European context. Three kinds of explanation of the search for size
have been proposed. At the product-market level, the necessity to
master the product cycle, the strengthening of position in new
markets through monopolistic leverage and the reduction of risk by
a systematic strategy of diversification have been considered to be
relevant factors.

At the factor-market level, the imperfection or even non-existence
of such markets could mean that the cheapest way of acquiring some
scarce factors is to take control of the firms which own them.

Finally, at a socio-political level, it could be argued that giant size
and the intensity of political favours are positively correlated.

It is too often claimed that, in contrast with the United States, big
business is not a danger for Europe, and that on the contrary the
problem is to encourage it. In fact empirical analysis reveals rapid
growth by the largest European firms, the number in each nation
being closely related to over-all market size. Within Europe, the
largest continental firms have grown faster than the U.K. equivalents.
Furthermore, the largest European firms seem already to be securely
at the top of the industrial pyramid and to hold a growing share of
the European gross domestic product.

These firms follow a pattern of growth suggested by the previous
discussion of the determination of size. The larger the firm, the
greater its degree of product diversification and the wider its
geographical dispersion; today fewer than five of the continental
European companies on the *Fortune* magazine's '200' list have no
foreign manufacturing activity. Therefore, it seems justified to conclude that the role of large corporate aggregates and their impact on
the public welfare concerns not only some specific countries but the
whole industrialised world.

APPENDIX

The minimisation of the firm's profit variance

In this chapter we have asserted that by product diversification the
firm could fully stabilise its returns.

The proof is given by the following model. Let us assume a firm
which diversifies its activites between two independent products, A
and B. The total variance of profit is written as follows:

$$\sigma_\Pi^2 = X_A^2 \, \sigma_A^2 + X_B^2 \, \sigma_B^2 + 2X_A X_B \, r_{AB} \, \sigma_A \, \sigma_B, \qquad (3.1)$$

where σ^2 = the profit variance, X_i = the percentage of total
activities represented by product i, r_{AB} = the correlation coefficient
or the ratio of the covariance between A and B, to the product of
the standard deviations of A and B, namely $\sigma_{AB}/\sigma_A\sigma_B$.

Assuming that $X_A \neq X_B$ and $\sigma_A \neq \sigma_B$, and with $X_B = 1 - X_A$,
the problem is to minimise (3.1) by setting its partial derivatives
with respect to X_A equal to zero:

$$\frac{d\sigma^2_{\Pi}}{dX_A} = 2X_A\sigma^2_A + 2X_A\sigma^2_B - 2\sigma^2_B + 2r_{AB}\sigma_A\sigma_B - 4r_{AB}X_A\sigma_A\sigma_B = 0,$$

which implies

$$X_A = \frac{\sigma^2_B - r_{AB}\sigma_A\sigma_B}{\sigma^2_A + \sigma^2_B - 2r_{AB}\sigma_A\sigma_B}$$

or

$$\frac{X_A}{X_B} = \frac{\sigma^2_B - r_{AB}\sigma_A\sigma_B}{\sigma^2_A - r_{AB}\sigma_A\sigma_B}. \tag{3.2}$$

Let us now assume that profits are perfectly and negatively correlated ($r_{AB} = -1$): the minimisation of the variance implies that the
ratio between the percentages of activities in products A and B be
equal to the inverse ratio of their standard deviations.

Furthermore, expression (3.1) becomes

$$\sigma^2_{\Pi} = \{X_A\sigma_A - (1 - X_A)\,\sigma_B\}^2. \tag{3.3}$$

Substituting the optimal value defined by (3.2) for X_A in (3.3) we
have

$$\sigma^2_{\Pi} = \frac{\sigma^2_B\sigma_A + \sigma^2_A\sigma_B}{\sigma^2_A + \sigma^2_B + 2\sigma_A\sigma_B} - \frac{\sigma^2_A\sigma_B + \sigma_A\sigma^2_B}{\sigma^2_A + \sigma^2_B + 2\sigma_A\sigma_B} = 0. \tag{3.4}$$

Hence, the total profit is completely stabilised. Usually the value
of r will be between 0 and -1. It then follows from expression
(3.2) that the higher is the negative correlation between the two
streams of profit, the lower is the profit variance.

An illustration of monopolistic leverage through subsidisation

Let us assume that a firm holds a dominant position in industry A
and earns an annual profit of 5.5. In industry B, the firm is
confronted with a competitor and would like to eliminate it.

Let the demand function in sector B be

$$p = 10 - 2\,q,$$

where p = price, $q = q_1 + q_2$ = one-period production. The unitary cost function is assumed to be identical for the firms:

$$c_i = 5 - q_i + q_i^2 \qquad i = 1, 2.$$

Firm 1 has decided to stop the production of firm 2, $q_2 = 0$, and to suppress its revenue, $R_2 = 0$. More exactly, with fixed costs equal to unity, R_2 has to be equal to -1. To determine the expenditure required by such a policy, let us write the profit equation for firm 1:

$$\Pi_1 = (p - c)\,q_1.$$

Substituting for p and c their values as function of q_1 and q_2, and eliminating the terms including q_2, we have:

$$\Pi_1 = (10 - 2q_1)\,q_1 - (5 - q_1 + q_1^2)\,q_1 = 5\,q_1 - q_1^2 - q_1^3.$$

$$(3.5)$$

On the other hand

$$\Pi_2 = (10 - 2q_1 - 2q_2)\,q_2 - (5 - q_2 + q_2^2)\,q_2. \qquad (3.6)$$

We set the partial derivatives of (3.6) with respect to q_2 equal to zero:

$$\frac{\partial \Pi_2}{\partial q_2} = 5 - 2q_2 - 2q_1 - 3q_2^2 = 0.$$

Substituting zero for q_2 we obtain $q_1 = 2.5$, and substituting this value in (3.5), we have:

$$\Pi_1 = -9.375.$$

By taking into account the unitary fixed cost, it appears that the loss to be accepted by firm 1 in order to eliminate its competitor in market B is

$$\Pi_1 = -10.375.$$

This could be covered from two years' profits earned in market A.
    Once firm 1 obtains a monopoly position in market B, it can make

good the loss from the subsidisation in less than five years. Indeed, maximising (3.5) with respect to q_1 gives

$$5 - 2q_1 - 3q_1^2 = 0,$$

which implies $q_1 = 1$ and $\Pi_1 = 3$ or, taking into account the unitary fixed cost, $\Pi_1 = 2$.

Barriers to Entry, Product Differentiation and Price Elasticity of Market Demand

Although concentration has been accorded an important (and probably excessive) role in industrial-organisation studies, there are other aspects of market structure which must be given adequate attention as explanatory variables for industry conduct and performance. We shall now examine barriers to entry, product differentiation and the price elasticity of market demand.

One of the essential conditions of perfect competition is the freedom of entry and exit of firms in the market; such movements will eliminate super-normal profits in the long run. A monopoly position with freedom of entry for potential competitors cannot be exploited so that the monopolist, like a constitutional monarch, can reign as long as he does not govern.

Reality teaches us that established firms often have advantages over new entrants so that there is a risk in entering an industry. Such a risk may be expressed by the probability of earning less than competitive returns (or of suffering losses) and by the size of such possible losses. As recently noted,[1] the barriers to entry can then be considered as factors increasing the amount of risk faced by potential competitors.

Four types of barriers to entry must be distinguished: the existence of important economies of scale, an absolutely lower level of production costs, marked product differentiation and institutional and legal arrangements which favour established firms.

TYPES OF BARRIERS TO ENTRY

Economies of scale

Economies of scale, which were discussed when dealing with concentration and large size, affect entry when the potential entrant would have to produce a large output, say Oq_1 in Figure 4.1, to achieve minimum efficient scale.

If minimum optimal output represents an important share of total industry demand and if the cost curve slopes downwards steeply,

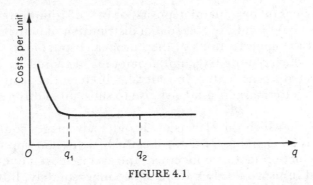

FIGURE 4.1

so that unit production costs rise appreciably as output falls below the minimum efficient level, the potential competitor faces an important barrier. The probability of capturing a substantial market share quickly is low. A related explanation is based on technological discontinuities: only a large firm with a significant market share could achieve the necessary technical and organisational levels; there would be a discontinuous variation of the production-function co-efficients, so that a new firm, with a low level of output, would be at a disadvantage as long as the established firms maintain their output.*

Absolute cost advantage

A second type of barrier to entry derives from an absolutely lower level of production costs of established firms (AC_2); such a level is absolutely lower because it is lower for every comparable output (Figure 4.2). The sources of such advantages are various: the control of a better production technique, exclusive ownership of sources of

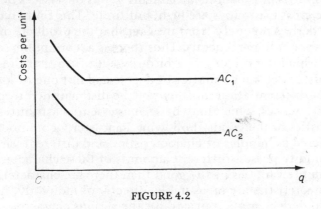

FIGURE 4.2

*This assumption may not be valid in all circumstances.

supply, such as oil or mineral deposits, or of a distribution network, significant liquid funds, better spatial distribution of activities. Because of the imperfections of the European capital market, industries which require large initial amounts of capital are especially well protected against entry. In general, a preferential position in imperfect factor markets may give rise to substantial differences in costs.

One way in which the effects of absolute advantages could be mitigated is by charging rents for specific benefits and imputing them to the production factors concerned; the average-cost curve of established firms would then be raised commensurately. But the absence of efficient markets for such types of factors of production prevents such a process actually occurring.

Production differentiation

The third type of entry barrier is provided by strong consumer preferences for established differentiated products. Product different-iation transforms goods with similar technological characteristics into imperfect substitutes so that their prices can differ significantly and the market can be segmented. This type of barrier is connected with the notion of an industry which may be defined, as we have seen (see Chapter 3), by means of the cross-elasticity of demand, $(\partial q_i/\partial p_j)(p_j/q_i)$, where q_i is the quantity demanded of product i and p_j is the price of product j. An industry strictly defined would comprise products, between which the cross-elasticity of demand would be positive and infinite, while the cross-elasticity *vis-à-vis* products of other industries would be zero. Less strictly, an industry is made up of firms or divisions of firms, producing goods or services between which the cross-elasticities are high, but finite. This finite nature of elasticity derives precisely from the fact that the products of such an industry are not homogeneous. Thus there is a 'continuum' of products which is more or less arbitrarily cut off so that the definition of an industry becomes a matter of degree and not one of kind.

Product differentiation must *a priori* be distinguished from real quality differences, which may be seen as essential attributes or characteristics of the goods. Following Lancaster,[2] commodities can be considered as bundles of characteristics, and different varieties of the commodity possess different amounts of these characteristics. If there are more varieties of the good than there are characteristics, and if the characteristics are measurable, directly or indirectly, it becomes possible to derive 'implicit prices' for the various characteristics. Several empirical studies have been made from this angle,[3] measuring the importance of quality, its impact upon price, profitability or market share.

The respective influences of price and quality policies on the sales or market share of a firm may also be studied.[4] So, theoretically, in the case of 'objective' product qualities or characteristics, all consumers are expected to rank close substitutes in the same way, while in the case of product differentiation, consumers differ in their ranking of close substitutes. However, the distinction is not as clear as this because according to the desired characteristics and their weighting, two goods may be considered to be close substitutes by one category of consumers and not so close by another. It does not seem possible to determine an 'objectively' social optimal degree of product differentiation either for the economy as a whole or in a particular industry.* The problem is made still worse once we admit that we are in a world in which every consumer does not know exactly what he prefers and does not know exactly how to achieve personal optimality in the face of the constraints upon his action.

In fact, a main source of differentiation is the lack of information that leads consumers to differ in their rankings of technically close substitutes. In the case of consumer goods, such as pharmaceutical products where the doctor chooses but does not pay for the product, and in the case of durable consumer goods where the consumer has insufficient technological knowledge and where information costs are high, the price—quality relationship is the source of grave distortions.

This phenomenon may also be seen when identical products are sold at different prices in neighbouring areas over a long period; inertia, the force of habit and the consumer education play a destructive role here. Correspondingly established firms acquire information about their customers which gives an advantage over potential entrants.

To a certain extent advertisements are meant to show the quality of products, to reduce information costs for the consumer and to create brand loyalty based on genuine superiority. On the other hand, the principal object of advertising is not a disinterested service of consumer information: it is selling. Therefore, apparent differences may be promoted in order to exploit irrational elements in consumer behaviour, with the aim of destroying information through dubious claims and unfounded or even treacherous appeals. Advertising expenditure can simply waste resources in so far as the effects of competitive advertising cancel out. Such advertising battles do not

*In a recent paper, Lancaster reaches the same conclusion. But he defines product differentiation (measured by comparing the proportions in which the various characteristics are possessed by different goods within the same product class) so broadly that the restrictive value of the selected characteristics and the origin of their selection are not discussed.[5]

usually benefit the consumer. To see this, the effect of advertising expenditures on actual competition may be divided into the expansion of the whole market by the joint efforts of all competitors and the effect on relative market shares, which depends on the effectiveness of the advertising efforts of each separate competitor. In expanding markets the second effect will usually be outweighed by the first; even the firm with small outlays on publicity will benefit from the joint efforts made to differentiate the product from others — the demand generated by market expansion will be distributed between firms, in accordance with price differences, speed of reaction in increasing or changing production, and so on (see Figure 4.3(a)).

In stagnating markets the second effect becomes dominant and the wastes of advertising are more visible, in that high expenditures are made to highlight trivial differences. Whether or not consumers appreciate these differences is a secondary matter. They will have to pay heavy costs, because oligopolistic producers feel compelled to act in a parallel fashion (see Figure 4.3(b). In the appendix to this chapter, a simple model illustrates this phenomenon, but at an empirical level we may take as an example the pharmaceutical market, where demand for drugs is highly inelastic with respect to price. For this kind of product, the doctor prescribes, the National Health Service or an insurance company pays the bill, and the consumer cannot judge what he gets. A high level of concentration exists in mature pharmaceutical markets (for example antibiotics, tranquillisers) and firms have a habit of heavily promoting a new variety of essentially an old drug at higher prices, thereby lifting the demand curve as in Figure 4.3(b) from D_1 to D_2. With the same marginal and

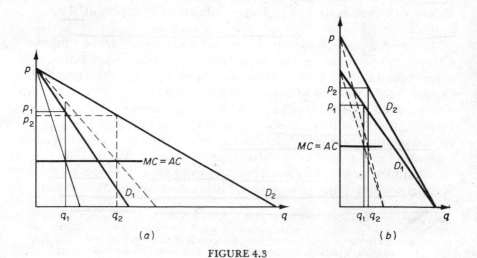

FIGURE 4.3

average production costs at any level of output (assumed constant for simplicity), the amount of profits is raised from $p_1 q_1 - q_1 \times AC$, to $p_2 q_2 - q_2 \times AC$. On the contrary, in rapidly expanding markets (for example sterilizers or contraceptive pills), innovating firms will benefit from keeping their prices stable (or reducing them slightly), as exhibited in Figure 4.3(*a*).

Advertising investments for existing products build up goodwill, which, reinforced by consumer inertia, constitutes an important barrier to entry. The expected profitability of investment by entrants varies inversely with the total level of expenditure on advertising by established firms. The problem will be especially obnoxious if the maximum of expenditure which the entrant can afford lies just below the required threshold, due to the imperfection of capital markets.

Institutional barriers

The last type of barrier to entry is of an *institutional* nature: patent and tax laws, financial conditions, insurance systems, tariff regulations, health and safety legislation, systems of subscription for public works, are all factors for barriers to entry which play an important role in the European situation.

BARRIERS TO ENTRY IN THE EUROPEAN CONTEXT

The formation of the Common Market has given a specific meaning to the term 'freedom of establishment and the provision of services' in two senses: on the one hand, a producer enlarges his geographical market or changes his location while continuing to produce the same type of output; on the other hand, he will benefit from the new market if he enlarges his product range or enters new sectors. This double opportunity for entry into new markets is facilitated both by reduction of institutional barriers and also by the transformation of economic barriers.

Within the E.E.C., institutional barriers due to customs duties and tariffs have been suppressed. The opportunities for entry are improved, moreover, by fiscal and financial harmonisation and by the granting of legal status to European companies which will open up the market to international operations.

As a consequence, economic barriers to entry are being lowered. Economies of scale or technological discontinuities are the less important the more the geographical market is extended and the absolute cost advantages are endangered through technological progress, which is easily diffused in a large common market. This is true, not only for E.E.C. producers but also for producers outside the

TABLE 4.1

Importance of advertising investments by country in 1970

	Percentage of G.N.P.	Percentage of private consumption	In $ by inhabitant
West Germany	1.50	2.54	44.6
Denmark	1.27	1.93	37.7
United Kingdom	(1.30)*	(1.79)	(22.2)
Netherlands	1.38	2.43	30.0
Sweden	0.91	1.50	33.3
Switzerland	1.42	2.38	44.2
Belgium	0.64	1.06	17.0
France	0.56	0.88	15.1
Italy	(0.56)	(0.76)	(9.1)
United States	1.70	2.56	76.9

SOURCE: *Informations CREDOP* (Brussels).

Community: although they are confronted with a Common External Tariff* that does not change the tariff disadvantage to exporting; they are induced to increase their direct investments inside the E.E.C. as the unified market allows the exploitation of scale economies which were unattainable within the limits of the previously segmented national markets. Established markets and preferential positions are also undermined by the free circulation of goods, the extension of choice and the internationalisation of preferences. This is encouraged by the fact that, in comparison with the United States, expenditure for product differentiation is still relatively low in most European countries (see Table 4.1).

At the same time national authorities have sometimes found subtle ways of protecting their national enterprises and of erecting new barriers against the entry of foreign firms. In particular, they have developed systems of discriminatory aid for regional or sectoral purposes. For instance, the European Commission has instituted procedures against the Belgian government, which passed a law on 30 December 1970 concerning economic expansion that required foreign companies to declare important shareholdings they intended to acquire in Belgian enterprises. In the shipbuilding, textile, aircraft, and cinema industries, the Commission has intervened to counter national activities which discriminate against foreign firms. Many

*The rates of the common external tariffs result from averaging the rates for individual products previously existing in the tariff schedules of the member states.

technologically advanced industries (for example telecommunications, information-processing, nuclear energy, transport, and so on) depend essentially on public expenditure, which frequently respects national boundaries. The Commission has reacted against the agreement signed in 1971 between the French government and the Compagnie Internationale pour l'Informatique (C.I.I.) which grants C.I.I. preferential access to public contracts as long as C.I.I. equipment remains techno logically and economically competitive. Another way in which the national differences between goods, especially consumer goods, can be preserved is through different national legislative standards relative to composition, penetration, weight of products, and so on, which form an important technical barrier. This is the case for motor vehicles, agricultural materials, electrical machinery, textiles, food products and pharmaceutical products. The Council of Ministers has adopted a series of directives to harmonise these national rules but the process is very slow (compare the situation in which new national standards appear almost every day, under the influence of scientific and technical progress). Finally, various legal, fiscal and political obstacles may still hamper the free movement of firms and products.

Also, the private sector has sometimes, in agreement with governments, contributed to the creation or maintenance of national barriers. Large, concentrated industries, such as food, drinks and household cleaning products, are probably not much affected by the suppression of tariff barriers. If products are differentiated, heavily advertised and price inelastic, the withdrawal of tariff barriers does not have much affect on the industry as a whole. When products are differentiated the limited effects of tariff removal can be judged by the amount of resource reallocation that takes place between industries. In perfectly competitive markets with homogeneous products, the suppression of tariff protection would lead protected inefficient national industries (or some portion of them) to go out of business and the corresponding resources would be reallocated to other industries in which the country enjoys a comparative advantage. Instead it seems that each E.E.C. country's exports to its partners rose in most product groups, rather than rising in some and falling in others. The suggested explanation is that when products are different-iated or when the output of an industry is diversified into sub-products, 'the common removal of trade barriers may lead some firms in the x industry of both countries A and B to contract or expire, others to expand; neither industry undergoes a general shut down, and each expands its exports to the other.' Hence, in such a case, substitute goods produced in different countries could appeal to each other's consumers so that large amounts of differentiated goods are exported in both directions, and increased intra-industry

TABLE 4.2

The determinants of advertising intensity
(stepwise regression results, n = 103)

Determinants of advertising intensity by order of entry	Partial regression coefficient	Multiple correlation coefficient
Concentration ratio	0.487	0.397
Level of retail prices	0.219	0.537
Position on life-cycle curve	0.283	0.561
Market share	0.200	0.590

rather than inter-industry specialisation in production occurs.[6] However, it would be dangerous to generalise too much as it seems that important redistribution of activities has also occurred between industries, especially in small countries (for example food and drink and woollen textiles in the Netherlands).

A recent study by Lambin,[7] concerning 104 individual markets, sixteen product groups and eight European countries, provides information on the importance of product differentiation in Europe (among the products studied were food, petroleum products, chemicals, durable goods and services). He found, first, that the degree of concentration is one of the most important determinants of the intensity of advertising (see Table 4.2).

Second, the study suggests that in European countries consumer inertia and brand loyalty, showing an attachment to brand names and established habits, is high; moreover, advertising for a brand creates a considerable stock of goodwill, as shown by the lagged effects of advertising.

Finally, let us recall that there exist many cartels striving for the segmentation of national markets and the exclusion of outsiders. However, the efficacy of such a policy is limited by the dynamic and unstable nature of the European economy, as well as by the competition policy of the Commission.

LIMIT-PRICE POLICIES

The theory of limit-pricing shows how the firm, by a policy of reducing its price, exploits and sustains existing barriers to entry. This theory obviously concerns only those cases where entry is not already blocked by existing barriers. If entry were completely impeded, the protected firm would have no reason whatsoever to reduce its prices and profits; it could simply exploit its position.

Various authors have shown how this limit-price, that is the maximum price that can be fixed without attracting any entry, could be determined according to different hypotheses.[8]

Let us suppose that:

(i) established firms and potential entrants maximise their long-term profits;

(ii) established firms are able to concert their behaviour so as to agree on a fixed limit price;

(iii) potential entrants assume that established firms will maintain their level of output and therefore expect only to sell the balance of total industry demand not satisfied by the established firms; and

(iv) the product is homogeneous.

In the case of an absolute inferiority of costs, the determination of the limit price, p_L, is illustrated by Figure 4.4; if AC_1 is the average cost of established firms and AC_2 that of potential entrants, the limit price $p_L = AC_2$ will impede entry. At that price non-satisfied potential market demand is represented by the segment AC of the demand schedule. The distance AB shows how far price can be raised above average cost without attracting entry. If we suppose that the barrier to entry is formed by the existence of important scale economies, Figure 4.5 permits comparison between the entry-impeding limit price p_L and the monopoly price p_M, which assures short-term profit maximisation.

More generally, the excess of price over the competitive price varies directly with minimum efficient scale and with the number of firms in the industry, and inversely with market size and the price-elasticity of industry demand.

Despite its apparent simplicity, this theory is not very convincing as an explanation of real problems. The supposition that the entrant will restrict himself to supplying the non-satisfied portion of demand is not realistic. If a market is homogeneous, as Sylos-Labini and

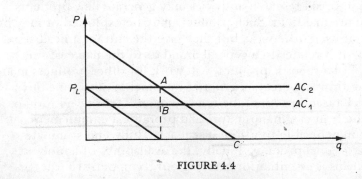

FIGURE 4.4

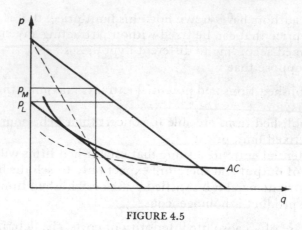

FIGURE 4.5

Modigliani explicitly assume, why should an entrant not expect to share the market with the established firms? Entry is not usually undertaken by a new firm but by a firm diversifying from another industry, and in this case the decision on whether to enter depends not so much on the prices and profits of established firms but on the confrontation of respective competitive advantages.

Two effects are discernable. On the one hand, there may be an expansionary effect, that is an enlargement of the total market. The entering firms base their strategy, not on a static demand, but on demand which is growing due to finding new customers, new geographical areas, new distribution chains, and so on. On the other hand, a substitution effect can transform a symmetrical oligopoly in which everybody has a similar position into an asymmetrical one in which the newcomer assumes leadership. In this case there will be two sets of factors operating, one favouring the established firms and the other the newcomer, who is more likely to be successful in establishing a dominant position under certain circumstances; for example, a large budget devoted to research may facilitate entry, because widespread research activities may generate new products outside the original field. Such products may be exploited or may be exchanged or used otherwise, but they give the entrant a head start. Advertising, if it relates to a general brand or to the name of the firm instead of a specific product, will work for other products made by the same firm and create a generic consumer loyalty: one buys a 'Yves Saint Laurent' product, be it a gown, an after-shave lotion or a watch. If the firm can manufacture and promote a complementary product, it may be able to utilise its capacity fully and stimulate sales of the original product. Finally, the availability of abundant financial means is essential for carrying out a competitive war (or

threat of one) with established firms. In general, the firm with a lot
of diverse resources in manpower, technology and finance will be
able to shift its activities within broadly defined fields, such as
chemicals, electrical equipment and transport, and thereby enhance
its staying power against outside attacks.

The best protection of dominant positions against entry does not
reside in static barriers to entry, but in firm's ability to anticipate and
meet demand for new products, new patents, new selling techniques,
new distribution methods. Nearly all products mature and die after a
shorter or longer period, and the real assets which a firm has are therefore not so much the existing facilities for producing an established
product, but rather the capacity to adapt itself to new trends, with
perhaps the ingenuity to create them.

A second criticism relates to the choice between an entry-blocking
price and a monopoly price which allows entry but maximises short-
run profits. In the preceding theories nothing has been said about
such an alternative. Indeed the problem has been examined in a
static and certain context while the real perspective should be
dynamic and uncertain.

(1) Pashigian has suggested a dynamic model in which industry
demand and average long-term costs are given, and the rate of entry is
simply a function of the time period during which price p is above the
limit price p_L.[9] Because market share does not depend on price, the
dominant firm will fix its price at the monopoly level as long as $p \geqslant p_L$.
Figure 4.6 illustrates the outcome. The (non-discounted) monopoly
revenue is indicated on the ordinate axis. The monopolist will maintain his price during the period Ot_1, but as from t_1 he will have to
choose between the two policies. If he reduces his price to the limit
price (solid line), his monopoly profit A will fall to the level B. If, on
the other hand, he maintains the monopoly price in period $t_1 t_2$
(dashed line), his net revenue will decrease towards C as a result of

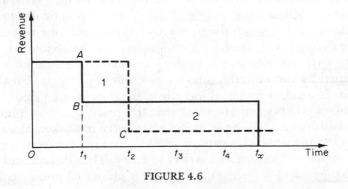

FIGURE 4.6

entries at t_2. In period $t_1 t_2$ his profits (the rectangle 1) will be higher than in the former case, but from t_2 entries will reduce his market share so that his new revenue C will be reduced below the level B in periods t_2 onwards.

Thus in order to determine the usefulness of reducing the monopoly price to the limit price, the monopolist should compare areas 1 and 2. If $2 > 1$, it would be better to adopt the limit price. Obviously such a decision can only be made if the moment t_x, at which the market will stop consuming the product in question, can be ascertained or estimated with reasonable accuracy (for example on expiry of a patent).

This model still ignores gradual changes in price policy or switching backwards and forwards between the limit price and monopoly price according to circumstances. It also ignores barriers to entry which determine the limit price. In Chapter 6 we will see that models based on optimal control theory go much further.

(2) In an effort to abandon certainty, various authors have developed models with a probability distribution for the entering firms in a given period. The probability P that x_n firms enter in period n is assumed to be a function of the price p_n adopted by established firms, which in its turn is an indicator of the profitability to be expected by the entrant. It is also a function of the number of firms in the industry X_n with a reduction in the degree of concentration diminishing the chance that entry will be rewarding:

$$P(x_n \mid p_n, X_n).$$

One may also expect that entry barriers affect the probability of entry, that is the higher the barriers, the smaller the probability of entry, for a given price and a given number of firms. As we shall see in Chapter 6, the most complete approach combines the dynamic nature and the uncertainty of entry, but these studies soon become very complex without adding much in the sense of new general propositions. Finally, one may well question the practical value of limit-price theories, given the many assumptions relating to collusion among existing firms, product homogeneity, the behaviour of potential entrants, and so on. In the European context, such a doubt is amplified by the imperfect degree of economic integration already achieved. Instead of undertaking subtle analyses of the price charged by established firms and assuming that this price is a good indicator of profitability and will be in effect after entry has taken place, we suspect that the potential entrant will be more concerned with the nature, forms and extent of barriers to entry. Thus differences in fiscal charges, land acquisition, regional or industrial public assistance, credit terms, employment policy, vertical integration, diversification and structural market traits will play a preponderant role in entry (or exit) movements.

PRICE-ELASTICITY OF MARKET DEMAND

Apart from the types of market structure already analysed, other characteristics, less easily measurable and less often examined, nevertheless influence both the behaviour and the performance of firms. This is notably true with the elasticity of demand to the industry. If two otherwise identical industries, but with different demand elasticities, are compared, it is *a priori* evident that the industry facing higher elasticity will lower its price more quickly than the other in order to benefit from expanding amounts sold. As reasons abound for supposing that demand elasticities differ between industries, it is useful to examine this aspect.

Johnson and Helmberger have shown that a low industry price-elasticity of demand reduces the gain from price competition and increases incentives for concentration to facilitate collusion.[10]

The potential effect of the elasticity of demand for the product of an industry on the firm's profitability is also important. Suppose profits are given by $\Pi = pq_i - C(q)$, in which C is total cost (assumed to be equal for all firms) and Π is profit. The inverse market demand function is given by

$$p = f(Q) = f(q_1 + q_2 + \ldots q_n).$$

The first-order condition for a maximum can be written as

$$\frac{d\Pi_i}{dq_i} = p + \left(q_i \frac{dp}{dQ} \right) \frac{dQ}{dq_i} - \frac{dC}{dq_i} = 0, \qquad i = 1, \ldots, n.$$

We know that $Q = q_i + \sum\limits_{j \neq i}^{n} q_j$, so that

$$\frac{dQ}{dq_i} = 1 + \frac{d \sum\limits_{j \neq i} q_j}{dq_i} = 1 + \lambda,$$

where λ captures the expectations about the behaviour of potential entrants as well as actual rivals.

The Cournot model would imply that $\lambda = 0$.[11] On the other hand, if positive responses are expected, we obtain, by calculating the sum of n firms in the market:

$$np + Q \frac{dp}{dQ} (1 + \lambda) - n \frac{dC}{dq_i} = 0.$$

Dividing by p, gives

$$n + \frac{1 + \lambda}{\epsilon} - n \frac{dC}{dq_i} \Big/ p = 0,$$

in which ϵ is again the price-elasticity of industry demand. This expression can be written:

$$\frac{p - \dfrac{dC}{dq_i}}{p} = \frac{1 + \lambda}{n \times \epsilon},$$

which shows that the profit margin (price minus marginal cost) will be inversely related to the number of firms in the industry and to the elasticity of industry demand. On the contrary, recognition of interdependence allows firms to achieve higher price—cost margins.

It is thus clear that elasticity of demand for the industry's products is an important structural characteristic. If rough distinctions between industries are made (high versus low elasticity), one can make cross-sectional studies. Also, comparisons over time can be made for a given industry, furnishing clues for policy decisions.

CONCLUSION

To conclude, market structure — that is the characteristics of the industrial environment of the firm, stable in the short run — is a multidimensional concept. It embraces not only the number, size and distribution of sellers and buyers but also such features as the presence or absence of barriers to the entry of new firms, the degree of differentiation among competing products, the amount of diversification and the price-elasticity and rate of growth of market demand. A correct appraisal of the competitiveness of an industrial sector or of the relative position of a firm must take into account all these characteristics and not only the degree of concentration or some other specific feature. A 'structural balance-sheet' has to be drawn up, however difficult this may be.

Furthermore, the elements of market structure are a priori interdependent. For example, the relation between concentration and barriers to entry is obvious: very high barriers to entry mean that equilibrium is likely to be reached with a small number of firms in the industry, given the positive exit rate of firms from any industry. In the same way, a high rate of industry growth provides opportunities for entry and expansion of smaller firms, leading to decreasing concentration.

A theoretical implication of the interdependence of all aspects of market structure is the possibility of an equilibrium or steady-state condition in which all these elements would have reached mutually consistent values.

But in the European context, where economic integration is far from complete, it is likely that we observe a transitory market structure so that the existing interactions between its elements are likely to give birth to a future type of industrial organisation which could be very different from the present one.

APPENDIX

The cancelling effect of competitive expenditures

A simple model can illustrate the possibility that in an oligopolistic structure, the competitive handling of advertising expenditures will lead to an equilibrium position in which a great many messages merely cancel one another out.

Let $q = q(a, A)$ be the demand function for a monopolistic firm, where q = quantity demanded to the firm, a = advertising expenditures by the firm, A = advertising expenditures by all the other firms in the industry, and with $\partial q/\partial a \geqslant 0$, $\partial q/\partial A \leqslant 0$. This function could also be expressed in terms of market share:

$$q = m(a, A) \times Q(a, A),$$

where m = market share of the firm, and Q = quantity demanded to the industry.

Furthermore, suppose that A depends upon a, in the framework of oligopolistic interdependence. Hence we incorporate a reaction function, $A = A(a)$, with $dA/da > 0$, that is an increase of advertising by the monopolistic firm will induce an increase in advertising by the competitors. In the case of Cournot behaviour, $dA/da = 0$.

Let Π be the firm's profit function:

$$\Pi = (p - c)\{m(a, A) \times Q(a, A)\} - a,$$

where c = constant unit production cost. The first-order condition for maximising Π can be written:

$$(p - c)\frac{\partial q}{\partial a} = (p - c)\left\{m\frac{\partial Q}{\partial a} + Q\frac{\partial m}{\partial a}\right\} - 1 = 0.$$

As $A = A(a)$, the expression in brackets can also be written:

$$m\frac{\partial Q}{\partial a} + m\frac{\partial Q}{\partial A}\frac{dA}{da} + Q\frac{\partial m}{\partial a} + Q\frac{\partial m}{\partial A}\frac{dA}{da}.$$

The effect of an increase in advertising expenditure on the quantity demanded from the monopolistic firm is made up of an industry sales effect ($m \, \partial Q/\partial a + m \, \partial Q/\partial A \times dA/da$), itself resulting from the advertising of the firm and the induced advertising of its competitors, and a *net effect on the firm's market share* $(Q \ \partial m/\partial a + Q \ \partial m/\partial A \times dA/da)$. If the market is a stagnating one $(\partial Q/\partial a = \partial Q/\partial A = 0)$, we have to consider only the second expression. Its first term is positive but the second is negative, as $\partial m/\partial A < 0$. Therefore the induced negative effect of the firm's increased advertising expenses through its competitors' reactions could more or less cancel out the direct positive effect. By contrast with price competition, the consumer will not benefit from such a competitive battle.

Effects of Market Structure and Size on Performance

Within the field of industrial economics, a growing role is played by quantitative studies relying on regression analysis, which tests the impact of market structure upon various aspects of performance. But while in the United States there exists an impressive body of econometric work,[1] similar European research is scarcer and less well known, at least on the Continent. One explanation is the often insuperable difficulty of obtaining the relevant data: on the one hand, the European business world keeps its secrets very efficiently, so that even data like firm's sales are sometimes hard to obtain; on the other hand, there is little co-ordination between or within national administrations, so that there is a lack of standardised information. Furthermore, the few European economists concerned with industrial economics often show scepticism towards quantitative studies which assume a direct link between market structure and performance; they prefer to undertake case studies, analysis of business policies and institutions. Despite these reservations, the purpose of this chapter is to present, after a discussion of the concept of 'performance', recent European econometric studies from which the foundations of statistical knowledge of European industrial economics could be built.

MICRO AND MACRO PERFORMANCE: THEORETICAL ASPECTS

The concept of performance is usually analysed at the level of the industry or the firm. A well-known basic result expected from a competitive economy is marginal-cost pricing. By contrast, an imperfectly competitive market structure will lead to an inefficient allocation of resources; a high degree of concentration increases ability to collude and to maximise joint profits, significant barriers to entry and product differentiation allow excess profits, with a price above marginal cost, to persist.

Social-welfare losses

The social-welfare loss from monopolisation of a competitive industry is shown in Figure 5.1. With a competitive industry, price equals

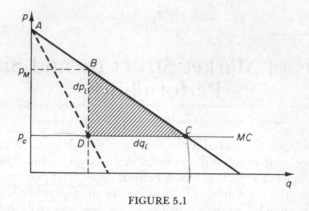

FIGURE 5.1

marginal cost or the supply curve of the competitive industry: $p_c = MC$. Consumers' surplus, that is the greatest sum that consumers are ready to pay for consuming quantity $p_c C$, is given by the triangular area $Ap_c C$. Monopolisation of the industry has two effects. First, the monopolist takes the part of consumers' surplus shown by the profit rectangle $p_M BDp_c$: it is a simple transfer with no consequences for efficiency (unless we specify different marginal utilities of money for different income recipients). Second, another part of consumers' surplus is lost, to the producer as well as to the consumer; this is the 'deadweight loss triangle' DBC, due to the misallocation of resources because of the existence of market power.

This welfare loss can be measured by the following formula:

$$w = \frac{1}{2} \sum_{i=1}^{n} dp_i \, dq_i,$$

where dp_i = the amount by which the monopoly price is in excess of the competitive price, dq_i = the amount by which the monopoly output is less than the competitive output, and n = the number of monopolistic sectors in the economy. Defining $\eta_i = (dq_i/q_i)(p_i/dp_i)$, we have also:

$$w = \frac{1}{2} \sum_{i=1}^{n} \left(\frac{dp_i}{p_i}\right)^2 p_i q_i \eta_i.$$

The dead-weight loss increases as a quadratic function of the relative price distortion and as a linear function of the demand elasticity. Finally, defining $\Pi_i = dp_i q_i$ as the excess profit, we obtain:

$$w = \frac{1}{2} \sum_{i=1}^{n} \left(\frac{\Pi_i}{p_i q_i}\right)^2 p_i q_i \eta_i.$$

The welfare loss increases as a quadratic function of the monopolistic rate of profit. When this formula has been numerically estimated, several criticisms have been made of this way of measuring resource misallocation due to monopoly. Beyond the usual reservations made about the data, the following have been argued:

(i) excessive aggregation biases dead-weight loss estimates downwards by submerging the high monopoly returns earned on individual products within broad industry averages;

(ii) the transmission of monopoly distortions through vertical price flows is overlooked;

(iii) this model does not take into account the possible effects of monopoly power on variables other than price or output, such as the rate of innovation, the absorption of the firms' resources into corporate consumption, misallocation in factor markets (shrinking the production curve), which could increase the dead-weight loss.

The concept of 'X-inefficiency' is also important here. While economists have usually been content to analyse the efficient allocation of resources between firms and markets, the specialist in business administration has always been concerned with the question of efficiency within the firm, that is non-market allocation. Once external competitive pressures are reduced so that cost minimisation and profit maximisation are not required for survival, technical inefficiency and organisational slack could emerge in the firm.

> Firms and economies do not operate on an outer-bound production possibility surface consistent with their resources. Rather they actually work on a production surface that is well within that outer bound. This means that for a variety of reasons people and organizations normally work neither as hard nor as effectively as they could.[2]

To incorporate this supplementary welfare loss, Figure 5.1 should be amended, as in Figure 5.2.

The monopoly marginal cost becomes MC_2, higher than the competitive marginal cost MC_1. Let us define $X = x/a$ as the ratio of the difference between MC_2 and MC_1, to the margin between p_M and MC_2. The loss due to monopoly price is $w = aq_1/2$. The total loss due to monopoly pricing and monopoly costing is, therefore,

$$w_T = \frac{(a + x)(q_1 + q_2)}{2} = \frac{(a + aX)(q_1 + q_2)}{2}.$$

It is clear that

$$\frac{w_T}{w} = \frac{aq_1 + aq_2 + Xaq_1 + Xaq_2}{aq_1} > 1.$$

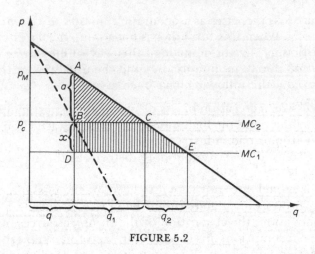

FIGURE 5.2

There is another way of presenting this argument: it is to insist, as we have done previously, that the firm's objectives and behaviour can deeply affect the link between structure and performance. While the textbook model of perfect competition implies that the role of the firm's conduct is unimportant, because conduct is structurally determined, the existence of imperfect market structure and the corresponding decline of competitive pressures leave room for discretionary attitudes and X-inefficiency. There are therefore two possible causes of internal inefficiency. First, it could be due to unintentional loss of control, or failure to adopt new technologies, inability to reduce chronic excess capacity, errors in exploiting the production function, bounded rationality or irrational behaviour. Second, the firm may deliberately choose a level of price, cost or output different from the perfectly competitive level, and in this case the firm can only be described as 'inefficient' in a conditional sense. Indeed, according to the general definition, a decision is efficient if it is not 'dominated' by any other possible decision. A decision x dominates a decision x' if, in the light of any selected criterion, x is at least as satisfying as x' and is better than x' on the basis of at least one criterion. It is therefore clear that the efficiency concept depends upon the selected criteria. Once the objective function and/or the constraints of the firm differ from those of the profit-maximisation model, its output will automatically be different, as we shall see later on.

For example, one set of outputs of the production processes are the non-pecuniary benefits received by the workers. Workers may get a higher level of satisfaction or morale from more participation in the work process even though market outputs may be lower as a result.[3]

As an example, an observer, comparing the efficiency of an American firm established in Europe and the corresponding European firm, could ignore such non-market outputs which are related to the quality of life. He gives them a zero price and is then tempted to judge in terms of efficiency, while in fact he makes a value judgement. Therefore, any observed performance could be considered to be inefficient according to one organisational model and efficient according to another. More specifically, the performance of a high-concentration, high-entry barrier industry can reflect something other than profit-maximising behaviour. It is then difficult to interpret the meaning of an indicator of performance such as reported profits if we ignore the behavioural pattern which lies in the background. When a dominant corporation shows, for example, an average or below-average rate of return, this could demonstrate long-run profit maximisation, internal inefficiency, sensitivity to the public interest, managerial discretion allowing income transfers in favour of management, or a decision to trade excess profits for an increased amount of the 'quiet life'.

Second-best considerations

The preceding analysis, which focuses attention upon the performance of individual firms or industries, is susceptible to criticism on the grounds that inter-industrial relations are ignored. This is a defect common to all *partial-equilibrium* constructions. For example, by isolating one monopolistic sector from the rest of the economy, this view assumes that substitutes from other sectors are not themselves monopolised or that there is no interaction between sectors. But, in fact, conduct which apparently yields an economic loss (benefit) in a partial-equilibrium context could result in a benefit (loss) in a general-equilibrium framework. To illustrate the point, let us assume that the production cost of metal containers is 10 and its monopoly price is 14. Suppose that the nearest substitute is a glass container which is sold at a price of 12. The monopolisation of the metal-container sector will induce people to buy more glass containers. But if the glass-container sector is competitive, its price equals its marginal cost so that the substitution is inefficient: resources are diverted from a lower (10) to a higher (12) cost means of meeting consumer demand.

On the other hand, if the glass-container sector is also monopolised with a selling price of 12 and a marginal cost of 9, there will again be an increase in demand for glass containers because their monopoly price is still less than the monopoly price of metal containers (14). This would lead to a desirable reallocation of resources since glass containers cost less to produce. A partial 'welfare economics

policy' suppressing the metal container monopoly* and provoking
a competitive price of 10 in this sector would induce a substitution
of metal containers for glass containers and, for a general-
equilibrium point of view, would bring about a welfare loss. In this
situation the first-best solution would be no monopolies, and the
second-best solution, if it is impossible to suppress both
monopolies for technological or institutional reasons, is to
maintain a monopoly in the metal-container sector.[4]

More generally, the *second-best theorem* tells us that if an
unavoidable constraint is introduced into a general-equilibrium
model, so that it is impossible to satisfy one or more of the optimum
conditions, the remaining conditions, although still attainable, are
not necessarily desirable. Unfortunately, there are no *a priori* simple
general rules to evaluate different situations in which the first-best
optimum conditions are not all satisfied. In our example where a
specific imperfection is assumed, it was possible to find another
imperfection which leads to a second-best solution, but finding such
a countervailing imperfection is not usually easy and requires detailed
and complicated analysis.

Apart from building *ad hoc* complex general-equilibrium models
where the value of the welfare function is maximised subject to the
constraints which prevent attainment of the first-best solution, two
approaches are suggested for overcoming the problem.

First, the industrial economy could be considered as being made
up of industries or sectors sufficiently distinct for the interactions
between them to be negligible. By partitioning the set of commodities
into sub-sets, including products that are closer substitutes or
complements to each other than to members of any other sub-set,
it could be possible to take into account only the welfare effects at
the level of each separable group and to ignore the eventual cross-
effects between groups. While this could be defensible for some
sectors, we must admit that there is a growing interdependence
between sectors; the increasing diversification of large firms across
product lines is one form of this interdependence.

Macroeconomic objectives

An alternative method is to determine a direct link between market
structure and the over-all performance of the economy.

A starting-point is to be found in Tinbergen, who distinguishes
between 'targets' and 'instruments'.[5] The set of targets comprises
national non-economic and economic goals: full employment, price

*See the Continental Can case (pp. 229–30) and Chapter 7.

stability, maintenance of international peace, and so on. Hence:

> the vagaries of social welfare maximization with its attendant
> theoretical defects, are rejected in favour of the simpler processes
> of macroeconomic target attainment. This does not mean that the
> analysis of public policy is divorced from welfare economics.
> Indeed, the target approach can best be interpreted as a change in
> the form of the social welfare function. The conventional social
> welfare function, somehow predicated upon individual utilities, is
> replaced by a list of dominant social objectives.[6]

The instruments are variables that are susceptible of control by
government agencies and affect targets. When the full set of relationships among instruments and targets are discovered, government
policy can be determined.

Applying this methodology to the concept of workable competition, Ferguson suggests investigating the relationships between
industrial structure on the one hand and the set of macroeconomic
objectives on the other; industrial structures are regarded as
instruments that may be partially controlled for the purpose of
achieving the targets. As a first step, one must find out in which
direction structure is likely to change the target objectives. Having
obtained more or less reliable evidence about the kind of relationships to be expected, a programme of business regulations can be
put forward, and if the objectives are realised, it can be concluded
that, in the short run, the selected set of policies is optimal. Hence an
economic system is workably competitive if there is no feasible
change in industrial and union structure that would make attainment
of the targets more likely, given the probability limits imposed upon
our knowledge by its origin in empirical research.

This macroeconomic theory of workable competition, which refers
to the operations of the entire economy and which tends to avoid
piecemeal welfare economics, finds an expression in European anti-
trust policy. Indeed, the Commission has explicitly expressed its
concern with the relationship between industrial structure and
macroeconomic performance. According to the First Report on
Competition Policy:

> the Commission would also like to underline the importance it
> attaches to competition policy as a means of fighting inflation,
> especially now, since inflation presents in many respects a
> structural obstacle to adaptation. Competition policy also
> contributes considerably to the better use of labour, since ill
> adjusted structures which are encouraged by inflation give rise to
> under-utilisation of the labour potential within the Community
> and to under-payment of skilled workers.[7]

Whatever the merits of this approach, two reservations must be
expressed. First, the theoretical basis for this pragmatic view is not as
solid as that of the concept of Pareto optimality. Second, statistical
evidence on systematic relationships between industrial structure on
the one hand, and price stability, employment, the growth and
distribution of income on the other, is limited and inconclusive. Even
the hypothesis of administered prices is, as we shall see in the
following section, still controversial. More work is needed at both the
theoretical and empirical levels.

EUROPEAN MARKET STRUCTURE – PERFORMANCE RELATIONSHIPS

It is now time to look at some recent studies which illustrate the use
of econometric analysis in European industrial economics. We shall
look at the impact of market structure upon four aspects of
performance: profitability, wages, prices, R and D activities. Second,
we shall look at the effect of large size on performance. Our purpose
is not to completely survey the empirical studies in a field where new
results appear almost every day, but to briefly describe the main
hypotheses tested and to select some recent illustrations of the
findings. A brief discussion of the main econometric concepts and
difficulties encountered in these studies is presented in the appendix
to this chapter.

Profitability

The relationship between market structure and *profitability* is that
most often studied and also the most problematic. One basic
difficulty is the measurement of profitability. Accounting measures
of profits give a very rough approximation to true entrepreneurial
profits. For example, it is known that accounting profits include
some rent and some interest on invested capital and, conversely,
some returns which conceptually are part of corporate profits are
not reported; the executive incentive bonus on top of salary, is a
classic example. In computing the rate of profit, the choice of the
denominator is also difficult. Some authors consider that the rate of
return on sales, or the 'price–cost margin', is the most appropriate
measure of allocative efficiency, but then it is necessary to take into
account possible variations in capital output ratios; indeed variations
in the capital intensity of production could lead to different
profitability. Others argue that equity is the appropriate denominator,
on the theory that firms maximise equity-ownership returns and that
such rates of return should be equalised in competitive industries in

the long run. An alternative is the rate of return on assets; but as assets are usually recorded in balance-sheets at historic cost, inflation will bias the computed profit rates upwards. Furthermore, such an approach depends upon the rate of depreciation adopted. It also includes debt, and therefore could be affected by the capital structure of the firm. In fact, however, there is a high correlation between the rate of return on equity and the rate of return on assets; for the 100 largest European firms, we find a rank correlation of 0.85 between the two rates.

Besides these difficulties, we must also mention the choice of a time period long enough to be able to detect 'equilibrium values' and to avoid short-run influences, the selection of a big enough sample of industries to be representative, excluding badly defined industries. All these problems are multiplied in the European case by the poor quality of the data, differences in accounting practices, the well-established practice of under-evaluation of reported profit for fiscal reasons, the role of foreign markets and international trade, all of which affect the effective degree of concentration and reported profits.

Despite all this, several studies have tried to check the value of the American models using European data.

For a sample of forty-four French three-digit manufacturing industries, Jenny and Weber[8] study the relationship between profit on asset (A) and the following explanatory variables:[7] concentration (C), expressed by the share of the largest four firms; economies of scale (E), measured by the average size of the largest establishments employing 50 per cent of the total employment of the industry divided by total employment of the industry; barriers to entry (B), defined on the basis of the capital cost; average level of exports (X), as a percentage of total sales; product differentiation (D) a dummy variable; and growth of industry sales (g).

The following effects are expected. First, industrial concentration, as a proxy for monopoly power and an indicator of the probability to collude, should be linked with higher profitability. The same effect is expected from the barriers to entry, which reduce potential competition, and from product differentiation.

Second, an important level of export means that the sector is open to foreign competition (if it is impossible to discriminate between the domestic and the international market) and that the national monopolies or oligopolies are constrained to behave more competitively; in this case one should expect a negative impact on the profitability.

Third, the relationship between growth of demand and profit rate must be positive. Indeed, in the absence of excess capacity, a fast increase in demand would result in increased profits unless it is fully anticipated. Nevertheless, a negative sign is possible because of the accounting bias; slowly growing industries tend to use a larger proportion of old plants, and hence to exhibit understated assets and, therefore, overstated profit rates.

An example of the obtained equations is the following:*

$$\frac{\pi}{A} = 0.10 + 0.08\ C - 0.34\ E - 0.52 \times 10^{-7}\ B - 0.2\ X$$
$$\qquad\quad (0.03)\quad (0.17)\quad\ (0.5 \times 10^{-7})\quad (0.05)$$

$$- 0.012\ g + 0.018\ D$$
$$(0.07)\qquad (0.002)$$

$$R^2 = 0.47 \quad n = 44.$$

Clearly, concentration has the expected positive and significant effect (as well as product differentiation). On the other hand, the export variable, expressing a measure of international competition, has a significant and negative impact. The other variables are not significant but there is a high degree of collinearity between the variables 'economies of scale', 'barriers to entry' and 'concentration'.† The same difficulty is met with in a study of sixty three-digit U.K. industries made by Khalilzadeh-Shirazi.[9] In the context of a simple regression, the association between price—cost margins and five-firm seller concentration is large and highly significant, confirming a previous study by Shepherd.[10]

When proxy variables for economies of scale and product differentiation are introduced, their coefficients are found to be significant, while seller concentration ceases to have a significant impact. Multicollinearity obscures the separate effects of this variable and of the measure of minimum efficient plant scale. We are left with the impression that, although research seems to confirm most of the American findings on the positive association between profitability and imperfect market structure, the part played by the different aspects of market structure has not yet been precisely specified. Furthermore, as expected, concentration is an *ad hoc* measure of only one of the dimensions of industrial structure which influences profitability; even a whole set of market-structure variables explains only a small proportion of the variation in profitability and leaves room for other influences, which vary in nature and in strength between industries.

*Figures in parentheses are the standard errors of the regression coefficients. R^2 is the coefficient of determination, telling the percentage of the variance of the dependent variable that can be explained by the independent variables, and n is the number of observations.
†This appears from an examination of the matrix of the partial correlation coefficients.

Wage rate

Another dimension of performance which could be related to imperfect market structure, especially concentration, is the *wage rate*. A positive association would reflect a higher qualification of the labour force hired in the more concentrated industries, so that their incomes contain few monopoly rents, as well as a sharing of monopoly profits in order to limit union power, to obtain a protection against potential competitors or to avoid frequent adjustments of wage rates reflecting changes in market conditions.

Horowitz uses entropy as an inverse measure of (employment) concentration and estimated a four-equation model for each of the original six E.E.C. countries.[11] The first equation is

$$W = \alpha_0 F^{\alpha_1} S^{\alpha_2} P^{\alpha_3}, \tag{5.1}$$

where the exponents are elasticities measuring the responsiveness of wages (W) to changes in concentration (F = antilog of entropy), firm size (S) and labour productivity (P). The second equation is written:

$$T = \beta_0 F^{\beta_1} N^{\beta_2} P^{\beta_3}, \tag{5.2}$$

where total industry turnover (T) is a function of concentration, the number of firms (N) measuring market size, and labour productivity is P.

The average level of investment per firm is determined by the third equation:

$$I = \gamma_0 F^{\gamma_1} S^{\gamma_2} P^{\gamma_3}, \tag{5.3}$$

and the fourth equation tests the determinants of concentration:

$$F = \theta_0 N^{\theta_1} S^{\theta_2}. \tag{5.4}$$

One of the conclusions is that labour does not generally find the less concentrated industries to be as lucrative as the more highly concentrated one; but this result could be imputed to differences in unionisation as well as in the state of technology. For Belgium, France and Italy, Phlips confirms that concentrated industries do pay higher wages.[12] A more recent study for the French manufacturing sector introduces differences between the 'quality' of the labour force in concentrated and unconcentrated industries.[13] Systematic differences are found but the specific positive association between concentration and wages is preserved even when the 'quality effect' is taken into account. Unionisation is clearly positively related to wage incomes in weakly concentrated industries but not significantly related when concentration is high.

Price stability

The positive wage-concentration relationship is compatible with the assumption of an indirect contribution to inflation. This leads to the well-known controversy over administered prices. At a theoretical level the basic assertion is that in non-competitive industries, usually characterised by a high degree of concentration, barriers to entry and product differentiation, prices will be un-responsive to short-run changes in demand or cost conditions, and will be administratively set by corporate management.

But in the framework of the static models of competitive and monopolistic price-setting, it is hard to explain why a monopolist's profit-maximising price will fluctuate less than a price set under conditions of pure competition; both of them will move up down with marginal cost and there is no *general* argument to justify differences in fluctuations. Of course, it is possible to argue that price-makers are able to depart from profit maximisation and, furthermore, that there is a large class of oligopoly theories in which price is more or less insensitive to short-run changes in market conditions, for example a kinked demand curve theory or the full-cost pricing model. But the main point is that this phenomenon is essentially in search of a dynamic theory. This is even more true of the new argument developed by Means and Blair, who accuse concentrated industries of raising prices by more than is justified by market conditions and thus causing inflation.[14]

This view has been considered to contradict the previous one:

> Since the price inflexibility argument adopted earlier by Means alleged that prices were unresponsive to market conditions, it implied that prices in concentrated markets would fall less during deflation and rise less during inflations than would prices in unconcentrated markets. This pattern of price changes would exhibit no secular tendency for prices to increase faster in con-centrated industries.[15]

But, according to Kahn,[16] the phenomenon that Means purported to explain in the 1950s, and the explanation itself, were the same as those of the 1930s: 'it was the resistance of prices and wages to deflation in the presence of market power'.

In a recent paper, Ross and Wachter try to build up a dynamic theory compatible with these arguments.[17] They suggest that since price changes are costly to make, and, if mistaken, carry the risk of substantial loss, it is necessary for the firms to agree on a price structure which is stable, that is on a mark-up on certain costs that are both important and nearly identical for all firms in the industry. Prices based on a mark-up on wages meet these requirements. In order to insulate the firm from short-run changes in the economy-wide demand for labour and frequent adjustments, it is necessary for the long-term contracts to include a wage premium; whereas competitive firms may be viewed as setting wages and prices continuously, the non-competitive firm acts discontinuously. This does not mean that concentrated industries originate inflationary movements; they simply pass on inflationary impulses after a lag.

But others have argued that the 'lag thesis' is inadequate because market power affects not only the long-run equilibrium level of price, when it is reached, but also its trend.[18] A valid dynamic theory would then have to explain how profit margins in industries with monopoly power can continue in the long run to widen relative to profit margins in competitive industries. A starting-point is that 'it is somewhere in the inter-relationship between product market power and the wage determination process that monopoly profits get transmitted into increasing unit costs, first in the concentrated sector, then by spillover into economy at large.'[19]

Empirical studies of these theories are numerous. In the United States, one of the recent studies by Stigler and Kindahl shows that administered prices are not stable if actual buying prices, and not wholesale price indices (that is seller list prices), are used, but this does not tell us whether those prices are as unstable as competitive prices.[20] In Europe, an analysis of Belgian, Dutch and French wholesale prices concluded that concentrated industries, as far as upward flexibility is concerned, appear to behave in the same way as unconcentrated industries.[21] But, according to the previous arguments, the administrative inflation hypothesis could be, more subtly, assuming that oligopolistic industries could indirectly contribute to inflation by granting wage increases more easily because they can pass on increases in unit labour costs to prices. The following equations would then have to be estimated separately:

$$\frac{p_t}{p_{t-\theta}} = a_0 + a_1 \frac{W_t}{W_{t-\theta}} \tag{5.5}$$

and

$$\frac{p_t}{p_{t-\theta}} = b_0 + b_1 \frac{W_t}{W_{t-\theta}}, \tag{5.6}$$

where (5.5) relates to the group of concentrated industries and (5.6) to the unconcentrated ones. According to this theory a unit increase in wage costs would lead to a higher price increase in the concentrated group than in the unconcentrated group. Preliminary tests for the European countries provide some empirical support for such a hypothesis.

To conclude, we have the feeling that, at least in Europe, the preceding approach to the inflation problem is quite partial and that a more comprehensive explanation is required. A starting-point is to admit that the origin of inflation is probably to be found in the confrontation of social groups to keep or expand their share of national income. All the economic mechanisms by which inflation spreads could then be viewed as the varied reflections of the tactics adopted by the different groups; the social body, divided, disputes about the benefits of growth and requires more than what is available. A systematic analysis along this line has still to be built but would require to largely overcome the conventional framework of industrial organisation.

Research activities

According to the Schumpeterian theory, imperfect competition and monopoly power favour *research activities* because the accumulation of monopoly profits provides the firm with the necessary financial resources for research and for facing the uncertainty of the results. Furthermore, monopoly power and the ability to impede entry allow imitation to be prevented and high profit ability to be maintained. Therefore, a positive relationship could be expected between concentration and R and D activities. On the other hand, it has been argued that technological advance related to the progress of basic science applied in specific industries is a much more important stimulus than market structure and the search for profit. The importance of basic science should show up in strong inter-industry differences in research input as well as in inventive output. An example of a European study testing both possibilities is given by Finet,[23] who has partitioned a sample of 300 Belgian firms into a chemical sector (I_1), an electronic sector (I_2), a moderately progressive sector (I_3) and the rest (I_4), using four dummy variables. One of his results is the following:

$$RP = 0.026C + 138.4I_1 + 195.2I_2 + 53.8I_3 + 47.1I_4$$

$$(0.04) \quad (46.1) \quad (30.1) \quad (26.6) \quad (14.3)$$

$$R^2 = 0.42 \qquad n = 300,$$

where RP is the ratio of research personnel to total employment in the industry and C is the four-firm concentration ratio and standard errors are given in brackets. The explanatory power of the degree of concentration appears to be rather weak, while the coefficients for different sectors are significantly different. Similar results have been obtained by Adams in his study of French industries.[24]

As the Schumpeterian and Galbraithian views emphasise the role of firm size as well as concentration as determinants of progressiveness, these results will be completed by discussing in the next section the relationship between R and D activity and firm size, before making an over-all appraisal.

A (provisional) conclusion from this sample of European econometric studies is that the structure—conduct—performance paradigm has some relevance in the European context and that this will be strengthened as the process of integration advances. But it also appears that the explanatory power of the structural variables, especially concentration, is limited. In our opinion this confirms that the progress of quantitative analysis of industrial organisation must be accompanied by a better understanding of the objectives and strategies of the firm as well as of the organisational and institutional factors. It would be very naive to believe that an increasing degree of sophistication in econometric methods could bring about much improvement without a better specification of variables and assumptions, based on a better knowledge of the actual firms which make actual decisions in the actual industrial economy. This could be a justification of the attitude of many European economists, who, instead of spending much time running regressions of concentration ratios of doubtful theoretical meaning against profit figures of questionable accuracy, have analysed the structure of internal organisations, the decision-making processes within firms, the quality of information flows, the firm's perception of its environment, and the role of financial and business institutions, which replace costly market mechanisms in the co-ordination and control of several financial, industrial or commercial activities.

THE EFFECTS OF LARGE EUROPEAN SIZE

Even before Servan-Schreiber's famous book *The American Challenge*,[25] Europeans were obsessed with the small size of the largest European firms compared to their U.S. rivals (see Chapter 3) and with the differences in performance which were thought to be associated with the size difference. The 'bigger the better' is a belief which has obtained widespread adherence. It has been argued that large corporations can do anything smaller firms do, but can also act in fields that require such a scale which excludes smaller firms.

However, it is only recently that empirical studies have been undertaken in Europe to test such *a priori* assertions about the relationship between size and performance. Three dimensions of performance will be examined in this section: profitability, growth and research.

Profitability

According to Baumol,[26] a positive profitability—size relationship is to be expected independent of scale economies because large firms can benefit from reaching a higher echelon in imperfect capital markets. This argument could be generalised to include all imperfect factor markets. To some extent this idea has been confirmed by empirical evidence for the United States, although with many qualifications. European studies, on the contrary, suggest a different picture. Usually the authors find either no relationship or a negative one between size and profitability. For a sample of the largest European and Japanese corporations in 1972, Jacquemin and Saëz obtained the following equation (corrected for heteroskedasticity):[27]

$$\frac{\pi}{A} = 11.41 - 0.61 \log S + \sum_{i=1}^{8} u_i I_i + 1.23N$$
$$\qquad\qquad (1.9) \qquad\qquad\qquad (3.6)$$
$$R^2 = 0.38 \qquad n = 223$$

where π/A = profits on assets, S = size, measured by sales, I_i = industrial sector, expressed by a dummy variable, and N = nationality, expressed by a dummy variable equal to one if the firm is European and to zero if it is Japanese. Firm size has a negative impact upon profitability, while the European group is, *ceteris paribus*, more profitable than the Japanese.

A similar negative effect of size on profitability is obtained by Jenny and Weber for a sample of large French firms,[28] confirming the previous finding of Morvan.[29] In the United Kingdom, Samuels and Smyth have found a significant negative relationship,[30] but, according to Weiss,[31] this could be due to the fact that the sample was drawn from Moody's, which covers almost all large firms but only those small firms which are publicly listed, that is the more profitable ones. As a result of the heteroskedasticity of profit rates, the most profitable small firms earn more than the average large firm. Finally, Singh and Whittington found that differences in the average profitability of U.K. firms between size classes were not statistically significant for most of the samples of firms considered.[32]

Among the possible explanations, it may be suggested that for European firms lack of control or some other form of internal inefficiency may more or less cancel out the possible scale-economies effect. It could also be argued that the large dominant firm frequently takes the option of trading high profits for an increased amount of the quiet life. (Models taking into account such risk-aversion behaviour have been presented in Chapter 3.) For the present let us underline that empirical studies confirm that the *profit variation* declines substantially with increasing size for European corporations. The result is obtained by cross-sectional studies of profit variability among size classes as well as analyses of the variability of profit rates over time for firms of various sizes. As we have seen (Chapter 3), the corresponding strategy is a greater diversification in the large firm which produces and sells more products, more varieties of any given product and operates in a greater number of geographically segmented markets. 'The large firm, then, may be viewed as an aggregate of small firms, each of them $1/n$ of its size. The variance of the profit rates for the large firms should then be approximately $1/\sqrt{n}$ of the variance of the profit rates of firms $1/n$ as large.'[33]

For a sample of 716 French firms, Morvan obtains the figures presented in Table 5.1.[34] One clear result is the high rank correlation ($R = 0.73$) between the variance of profit rates and average firm size. For U.K. firms, Singh and Whittington, Samuels and Smyth confirm these results. For the largest European and Japanese firms, we see that the average rate of profit (1962–72) has a significant positive effect on the firm's profit variance and that the logarithm of initial size has a significant negative effect on the logarithm of the coefficient of variation of profit $\sigma_\pi^2/\bar{\pi}$. The reward of being a large firm appears to be not higher profitability but greater security, as expressed by profit stability.

TABLE 5.1

Size class (10 million French francs)	Rates of return			Percentage of losing firms	Variance of profit rates	Variance of average profit rates (1953–64)
	All firms	Profitable firms	Unprofitable firms			
0–499	7.7	20.4	−18.4	21.4	144.5	358.5
500–1499	13.1	22.4	−7.6	14.2	100.1	93.2
1500–3999	17.6	21.2	−8.4	10.8	69.1	80.1
4000–7499	18.8	29.3	−8.3	9.7	57.7	69.3
7500–19999	16.5	18.4	−7.0	6.1	53.2	46.5
20000–49999	15.2	17.7	−7.4	5.4	43.4	37.2
50000–74999	13.0	14.7	−6.8	6.1	31.5	26.1
75000 and more	14.4	10.8	−5.2	2.1	17.2	21.4

Growth rates

Generally, the rate of growth of sales seems to be independent of size. Attempts have therefore been made to consider the growth–size relationship as a stochastic phenomenon, the nature of the stochastic processes being defined by the mathematical characteristics of theoretical statistical distributions, such as Pareto, Yule or log normal distributions. In the latter case, size distribution is assumed to result from a number of small random factors affecting all sizes of firms in a similar, multiplicative manner.

The change in size between two periods may be written as follows:

$$(S_t - S_{t-1})/S_{t-1} = \epsilon,$$

where S_t = the size of a firm at time t, and ϵ = a random variable.

This implies that a large firm has the same chance of a given proportionate growth as the small firm, so that concentration in any industry will increase over time. One way of testing such a hypothesis is to estimate the following equation:

$$\log S_t = \alpha + \beta \log S_{t-1} + u.$$

If $\beta = 1$, growth is independent of size; if $\beta < 1$, the smaller firms are growing at a faster, proportional rate; and if $\beta > 1$, larger firms grow faster, accelerating the concentration process. Empirical results for France,[35] the United Kingdom,[36] and for the largest European firms[37] suggest that the estimates of β are not very different from unity and that luck plays a significant role in the growth process of firms.

However, it also appears that the dispersion of growth rates is usually negatively correlated with size; large firms seem to enjoy more stable growth.

Research activities

Finally, we turn to another standby in the field: *research and development*. The Schumpeterian hypothesis suggests that absolute size as well as monopoly power and concentration will have a positive effect on research activity. Indeed, large size may bring about scale economies in R and D from lower risk, as the large firm is usually more diversified, and from greater opportunities to exploit the results of research. It is necessary here to distinguish between the relationship between size and R and D input, and size and R and D output.

To the question whether large firms *spend more on R and D*, relative to their size, empirical studies of European firms suggest a negative answer. Adams, using a sample of the largest 300 French firms, shows that R and D is less concentrated than production.[38] Table 5.2 shows that industries in which average firm size is small are able to undertake R and D activity.

To avoid the effect of arbitrary size classes (which may impede discernment of critical thresholds), as well as that of the presence of small research subsidiaries of large firms or co-operative R and D organisations, Adams has also tested regressions for a sample of selected firms which show a significant negative impact of size on R and D intensity. In Belgium, studies using 157 Belgian firms, which between them account for about 70 per cent of all research expenditure, conclude that for small and medium-size firms it is difficult to undertake research, but once this is overcome the results are at least proportional to the firms' size. Using a cubic function that involves high collinearity of the exogenous variables but allows detection of inflection points, Biname and Jacquemin find that only

TABLE 5.2

Intensity of research expenditure by industry and size of firm, France, 1966

Industry	R and D expenditure sales (percentage)					
	For firms employing:					
	0–499* people	500–900 people	1000–1999 people	2000–4999 people	5000+ people	For all firms
Aerospace	12.5	15.5	17.0	17.0	3.4	27.4
Electrical and electronic measuring and computational equipment	6.2	4.5	6.0	2.0	4.5	4.9
Other electrical and electronic equipment	5.7	19.0	7.0	7.0	7.0	7.4
Chemicals and pharmaceuticals	5.8	4.1	3.9	4.4	3.9	4.2
Automobiles	17.0	2.3	5.7†		0.5	2.3
Machinery	2.2	4.6	2.3	2.2	4.7	3.2
Non-ferrous metals		3.6‡	—	1.1	1.8	1.7
Ferrous metals	14.0		0.5§	0.6	0.4	0.5
Wood, paper	0.4	0.7	0.7	0.4	0.0	0.5
Textiles	1.0	4.1	1.4	0.3	3.6	2.4
All firms	3.2	5.0	3.3	2.6	3.3	3.4

*This size class includes most of the co-operative research organisations.
†Pertains to firms employing 1000–1999 people.
‡Pertains to firms employing 0–999 people.
§ Pertains to firms employing 500–1999 people.

the linear term of sales has a significant impact upon R and D expenditures.[39] Defay obtains the following equation:[40]

$$RE = 0.146TE^{0.737}, \qquad R^2 = 0.42 \quad t = 10.71$$

where RE = research employees, TE = total employment and where the exponent is significantly less than unity.

Finally, testing various forms of equations (log linear, quadratic, cubic, and so on) for a sample of 300 Belgian firms, Finet confirms the previous results.[41]

Two remarks must be made. First, the samples are biased in that they usually include only those firms which do research, that is almost all large firms but only a small proportion of other firms. Second, as we already know, the selected measure of size selected could affect the results; in this respect, sales seem a better measure than employment, which depends upon the proportion in which factors are utilised and underestimates the size of large capital-intensive firms.

Although tests show that size has no more than a proportional effect on R and D input, it is still possible that the R and D input of large firms leads to proportionally greater *inventive output*. The alternative links between size and inventive output, through the R and D input—output relationship, are presented in Figure 5.3, where S = firm size, Y = inventive output, RD = R and D expenditures, $\eta = (dRD/dS) \times (S/RD)$ = elasticity of R and D input with respect to size, and $\epsilon = (dY/RD) \times (RD/Y)$ = elasticity of inventive output with respect to R and D input. It is clear that if $\eta \leq 1$, the final impact of size upon inventive output will depend upon the value of ϵ.

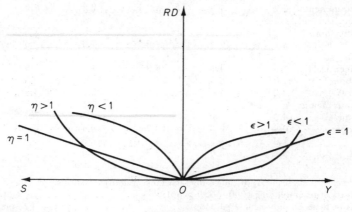

FIGURE 5.3

In the United States, the existence of a linear and homogeneous relationship between input and output of R and D cannot be rejected.[42]

In Europe, the meagre stock of knowledge is gradually growing and confirms the American findings. Dividing French firms in the aggregate and by industry into three size groups, each containing an equal volume of employment, Morand has found that, in eight out of ten industries, and in all of them combined, the mean ratio of patents/sales to R and D expenditures/sales, that is of R and D output to unit input, is lower in large than in small firms.[43] Using a sample of 181 Swedish firms, divided into twelve industrial sectors, Johanisson and Lindstrom showed that large firms' share of total patent applications were consistently less than their share of employees (except in chemicals).[44] The number of patented inventions is of course an imperfect proxy for R and D output. One reason is that the desire of patenting may decrease with firm size, not because of less R and D output, but because largest firms are as well (or even better) protected by their 'know-how' as by a legal monopoly.* Instead of using patents, Freeman has directly analysed 1200 innovations in the United Kingdom since 1945.[46] On the whole, there is quite a good rank correlation between the share of small firms in output and their share in industry innovations. Small firms contribute more than proportionally to innovations in low capital-intensive industries and less in industries of high capital intensity. Smyth, Samuels and Tzoanos have found for eighty-six U.K. firms that the number of patents obtained increases faster than firm size in the chemical industry and in the electrical engineering and electronics industry, but not in the machine-tool industry.[47]

We can conclude with Kennedy and Thirwall that 'the evidence appears to be heavily weighted against the hypothesis that a necessary condition for technological change and progressiveness is that firms should be large scale and dominate the market in which they operate'.[48] From the very origins of technical change, in the work that is put into research, to the commercial application of new knowledge, it does not appear that large firms or monopolistic industries are necessarily more dynamic or progressive, or produce more fundamental technical change. In fact, we suspect that the firm's planning objectives, its policy in terms of products and marketing, its internal organisations, are more important

---

*Furthermore, Weiss suggests that high R and D intensity, being positively related to the propensity to patent, patents could reflect new R and D inputs better than R and D output.[45]

factors for exploiting technological opportunities than firm size
and market structure.

CONCLUSION

A first conclusion of this chapter is that the concept of performance is ambiguous: it could be defined at the firm, the industry of
the macroeconomic level; it could include non-market allocation as
well as allocation between markets and industries; it could be
linked with the traditional concept of 'optimality' or with a set of
'targets' politically determined. Despite its theoretical weakness,
this last approach seems to have been adopted by the European
authorities.

Second, our examination of the effects of market structure and
size on the various dimensions of performance suggested that
although there is a growing amount of evidence that industrial
structure and size are relevant to determination of performance in
the European context, the explanatory power of the structural
variables, especially concentration, is strongly limited. We suspect
that the usual American industrial-organisation theory is unable to
capture several important features of the industrial pattern char-
acterising the European Community.

The role of conduct in determining market structure, communi-
cations aimed at establishing collusive agreements among firms, the
co-ordination of control between several industrial, commercial and
financial institutions, their imperfect structure of financial markets,
the co-operation between public and private bureaucracies, all are
so important in Europe that it is essential to extend the structure—
conduct—performance paradigm to encompass these phenomena.
An effort along these lines will be attempted in Chapter 6.

A third interim conclusion is that European concentration leads
to higher profit and higher wages, but not to greater research
efforts. The administrative inflation hypothesis requires not so
much more empirical testing as a better dynamic formulation.

Fourth, as far as the effects of large size in Europe is concerned,
no evidence of increasing profit, faster growth or more intensive
research activities can be found to support the 'size mystique' that
has prevailed in Europe. The main consequence of very large size is
to reduce the variability of the firm's results, and hence the firm's
exposure to risk. The social-welfare effects of this result are not
clear; it could be argued that it increases welfare through the
pooling of risks of the individual parts of the firm's total activity
so that the large business organisation engages in some risky
activities which would not otherwise be undertaken. This would be

a partial answer to the absence or the incompleteness of insurance markets or other institutions for risk-bearing. On the other hand, it could also be argued that the large corporation transfers risk from itself to other markets or economic agents, be they small firms, customers, local or national public authorities; it would stabilise its own position by destabilising its environment. Much more research is needed on these aspects of oligopoly behaviour.

APPENDIX

Some econometric difficulties in industrial economics

The econometric tool most commonly used in quantitative industrial economics is multiple regression analysis. The usual dependent variable is a specific indicator of performance such as profitability or growth, and the independent (explanatory) variables are drawn from the set of market-structure variables, lagged as well as current. Usually the model reduces to a single linear equation, eventually after having eliminated *non-linearities* by redefining the variables or transforming the form of the equation. For example, if non-linearity applies only to the variables, but not to the parameters,

$$P = a_0 + a_1 S^2 ,$$

where P = a performance variable and S = a market structure variable, it is easy to define a new variable $X = S^2$, which is substituted into the model so that least-squares regression of P on this new X variable gives the solution. When non-linearity involves the parameters, it may still be possible to linearise the equation. For example, the model may suggest a multiplicative interaction between the market-structure variables so that a logarithmic transformation will make this model linear:

$$P = A S_1^\alpha S_2^\beta$$

becomes, by taking natural logarithms of both sides,

$$\ln P = \ln A + \alpha \ln S_1 + \beta \ln S_2 ;$$

where the slope coefficients, α and β, are elasticities. Let us also notice that it is possible to replace the value of a given function, $f(S)$, by an approximate linear expression, $S, f(S) = \alpha + \beta S$, for a small range of values of S.

Even with a linear multiple regression, several econometric problems arise. One of these is the linear relation between two or

more explanatory variables, that is *multicollinearity*. When collinearity exists, the standard errors of the estimated population
parameters are very large and the relation of P to either S_1 or S_2
cannot be sensibly investigated. Given the interdependence which
frequently exists between different aspects of market structure, it
is not surprising that such a problem often occurs in econometric
studies of industrial organisation. Little can be done about this
problem, except to try and choose meaningful explanatory
variables which are not related to one another.

Another difficulty is when the variance of the error term is not
constant: the errors are said to be heteroskedastic. As an example
of *heteroskedasticity*, when studying the relationship between
profitability and firm's size, it is well known that the variance of
the error decreases as the firm's size increases. Thus observations
on small firms give a less precise indication of where the true regression line lies, but it is possible to allow for this by attaching
more weight to the observations with small error variance.[49]

It is apparent that in industrial economics the observer is often
confronted with *simultaneous-equation* models and all the related
econometric problems. For example, it could be argued that the
relationship between concentration and profitability could reflect
greater efficiency which may increase the size of the more profitable firms, and hence lead to concentration. Instead of a single
equation, it is then necessary to build up models such as the
following one:

$$\pi = k \times C^{\alpha} \times X^{\beta}$$
$$C = g \times \pi^{\gamma} \times Z^{\delta},$$

where π is profitability, C is the concentration ratio, X and Z are
two distinct variables which are assumed to affect π and C
respectively.

The simultaneous-equation approach allows us to consider that
a specific variable could be an explanatory variable in one equation
of the system and an endogenous variable in another, and also to
test two-way relationships among variables and to determine the
direction of causal links.

Although it is true that important contributions can be made in
our field with fairly simple techniques because of the character of
our assumptions and data, it is undeniable that the complex interrelationships which characterise the structure—conduct—performance paradigm offer a promising future for simultaneous-equation
systems.

6

Objectives and Strategies of the Firm: Static and Dynamic Aspects

In contrast with the traditional profit-maximising economic theory of the firm where managerial discretion is unimportant, there is an impressive and growing body of literature which suggests that the firm is a complex organisation made up of a coalition of agents pursuing various goals, and co-ordinating and controlling economic activities by non-market as well as market allocative mechanisms.

We have already mentioned that once the assumption of perfect competition is abandoned and the existence of imperfect market structure, including capital-market imperfection, is admitted, the use of the profit-maximisation assumption as a general survival condition is no longer acceptable. Those in control of the corporation will have a margin of discretion to select various objectives which could differ, in nature and in weight, according to the identity of the controllers: stockholders, managers, employees and workers, regulatory agencies, and so on.

These differences in objectives will of course affect the firm's policies, in terms of price and output, advertising and research, and will also affect the impact of public policies on the behaviour and efficiency of the firm. Furthermore, in a rapidly changing economy such as the European one, the theory should not be limited to static situations in which change is treated as essentially exogeneous to the system and where market structure and behaviour are taken as structurally determined; we must consider the changing contours of business structure and behaviour and examine to what extent the firm is actively attempting to mould its industrial environment over time.

According to the 'structuralist' school in industrial-organisation theory, the structure—conduct—performance paradigm could be reduced to aspects of market structure and firm or industry performance, ignoring questions of firm behaviour; the structure of the industry determines conduct, which in turn determines performance, so that differences in structure are the only explanation of differences in performance (see the solid lines in Figure 6.1). By contrast, a 'behavioural' approach would emphasise that in a similar structural situation, various firms could adopt different policies,

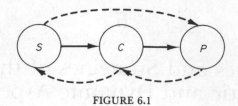

FIGURE 6.1

according to their objectives, their attitude towards risk or their time horizon, and that this will lead to different performance and results. More generally, the direction of influence in the S—C—P paradigm cannot be asserted *a priori* and it is useful to analyse the possible reversed links as well as two-way relationships, where different forms of market conduct have the ability to produce gradual changes in the structure of industries or where conduct tends to change over time, in response to performance (see dashed lines in Figure 6.1).

It is only when such a broad view is taken, that a central concern of industrial economics, namely the consequences of alternative forms of industrial organisation for resource allocation, can be adequately dealt with.

In the following sections, we shall focus attention on three main topics: first, comparing how firms are run in the United States and in Europe; second, examining the firm's private planning process intended to help it control its economic and socio-political environment; and third, analysing the policy implications of a new distribution of power within the firm which allows workers to participate in decision-making. After a general discussion of each of these problems some recent models dealing with each are presented.

OWNERSHIP AND CONTROL

A U.S. managerial revolution?

In 1960 Mason stated that in the United States, 'almost everyone now agrees that in the large corporation the owner is, in general, a passive recipient; that typically control is in the hands of management; and that management normally selects its own replacements.'[1] Such a separation of ownership and control and the emergence of an increasingly important class of professional managers seem to be confirmed by various statistical studies. For example, according to Larner,[2] in 1963 84.5 per cent of the 200 largest U.S. corporations had no group of stockholders owning as much as 10 per cent of stock.[3]

Such a 'managerial revolution' could have important implications, the basic idea being that the interests of those in control may differ from the interests of ownership: corporate mangement could expand those classes of expenditure for which it has a positive preference (large salaries, expense accounts, bonuses, retirement pensions, stock options at the shareholders' expense) beyond the level required by a strict profit maximisation; it could also retain a high proportion of earnings for the pursuit of selective expansionary objectives of the firm even if the shareholders consider that the same capital could be better invested elsewhere or spent upon consumption.

Several criticisms of this view have nevertheless been made.

(a) First, the criteria used to determine the lack of control by owners are arbitrary. The percentage of stock necessary to give a position of control could be quite low and varies from one case to another.

(b) For various reasons listed below, it may still be true that, in spite of the dispersion of shares among a large number of holders, managers are constrained to satisfy the owner's expectations, so that the separation of ownership and control would be no more than a division of labour within a capitalist society. These reasons include the following.

(i) Competition in the capital market could be so strong that a mismanaged enterprise runs the risk of being driven out of business, which is reinforced by the potential danger of takeover raids if the market value of the firm's common stock is depressed relative to the net book value.

(ii) Where capital markets are imperfect the divisional organisation of the firm, contrasting with a unitary or holding-company structure, could play the role of a mini capital market where divisions compete for capital, retained earnings and cash flow. Williamson argues that 'a more self-conscious examination of internal organization and an assessment of the efficiency properties and system consequences of the multidivision form lead, from the standpoint of neoclassical analysis to a somewhat reassuring result'.[4] However, such a divisionalised structure for the firm may be a necessary but insufficient condition for the efficient allocation of resources. 'Some compromises with the operating divisions may, as a matter of political reality have to be made.'[5]

(iii) Independent of the use of internal audits that monitor performance and responsibilities, one way of reinforcing internal control is to transfer large shareholdings to the management group, which then has to combine the double role of manager and stock-holder; this should induce a shift in the manager's objectives towards profit. Similarly, it is possible to link managers' salaries and non-pecuniary benefits to the levels of profit earned so that managers

will wish to pursue the shareholders' objectives. This is not the case
if executive compensation or directors' pay are more closely related
to some measure of firm size, sales revenue or growth than to profitability, and only empirical work can find out whether this is the case.

(c) It is too simplistic to draw a clear-cut distinction between
control by owner and managerial controls; there are several degrees
of separation and several domains of control varying with the types
of decision concerned. The shift in power from owners to managers
could be limited to the level of the divisional and departmental
committees or be extended to reach the board of directors; the
spheres of decision could be limited to operating decisions or include
strategic and structural decision-making. Therefore, to determine who
controls what, it is necessary to undertake a detailed analysis of the
internal organisation of the firm.

(d) Finally, it could be argued that even if, according to the
classical theory, shareholders often exercise only limited control over
the operations of the firm, it does not follow that the only possible
substitute is management. Financial intermediaries, such as institutional investors (mutual funds and insurance companies), banks and
holding companies could play an important role. In the United States,
the *Patman Report* concludes that 'the major banking institutions in
this country are emerging as the single most important force in the
economy, both through the huge overall financial resources at their
command and through the concentrations of the resources and other
interrelationships with a large part of the nonbanking business
community in the country'.[6] This conclusion is not widely accepted,
mainly because the managers of these funds are assumed to avoid
interfering actively in the affairs of the companies whose stock they
own; however, the situation is viewed quite differently in Europe.

Control of European firms

Although empirical research is still very scarce, corporate control in
European firms appears to be mainly in the hands of wealthy families
and holding companies.

In the United Kingdom, a rigorous classification of companies
according to control type was undertaken by Florence.[7] His information related to 1951 and covered 268 industrial and commercial
companies.

Companies are called owner-controlled, when:

(a) one person owns more than 50 per cent of the vote-carrying
shares;

(b) the largest shareholder owns 20—50 per cent of the vote-carrying shares, or the largest twenty shareholders own colectively at least 20 per cent of the vote-carrying shares.

Companies classified under (b) are called owner-controlled when:

(i) the main vote-holders are persons; or
(ii) the board of directors collectively owns more than 10 per cent of the shares; or
(iii) two or more members of the board are among the largest twenty shareholders.

The U.K. control system differs from the German system, because German company directors do not usually hold shares in the company. In this way shareholders' influence company control more directly and U.K. companies can be classified as owner-controlled at a relatively low percentage of share-ownership. Bank control is not classified as a separate category in the Florence investigation. Can we use the 1951 data as representative of an actual picture of ownership and control patterns? An investigation undertaken by Radice shows that few changes in control type occurred in the period 1957–68.[8] This is confirmed by a study undertaken by the Department of Applied Economics in Cambridge which has classified companies into size categories according to data for the period 1948–60. The Cambridge Data Bank contains data for about 4000 U.K. companies quoted on the stock exchange. Size was measured by net assets. Subsidiaries are consolidated by the Cambridge Data Bank while the Florence study uses data related to parent companies only. But the two sets of information are comparable because subsidiaries are controlled by the parent and consolidation does not change control type. Holl has combined the Cambridge and Florence data relating to the same companies.[9] In this way classification of companies by control type on one hand and by size on the other has been made possible.

Table 6.1 leads to the conclusion that about 30 per cent of U.K. companies are owner-controlled. However, it is dangerous to consider that the other firms are automatically managerially controlled: the role of government or quasi-government agencies, as well as the growing intervention of financial institutions, as large corporations have increasingly relied on external funds to finance expansion, are also evident in the United Kingdom.

In West Germany, the Aktiengesellschaft (A.G.) is the most widely used legal form for large companies. The A.G.s are controlled by two boards: the supervisory board (Aufsichtsrat) and the executive board of directors (Vorstand). The supervisory board is elected by the Annual General Meeting of shareholders.

TABLE 6.1

Classification of firms by industry, size (net assets) and control type

	Very large MC	Very large OC	Medium large MC	Medium large OC	Smaller large MC	Smaller large OC	All sizes
1 Bricks, pottery, etc.	4		1				5
2 Chemicals	2		1				3
3 Metal manufacture				1			1
4 Non-electrical engineering	1	1	4	2	3		11
5 Electrical engineering	7	3	3	1	3	1	18
6 Vehicles	8	2	2		1	2	15
7 Metal goods n.e.s.	3		2		3	1	9
8 Cotton and man-made fibres							
9 Woollen and worsted	1		1	1	2		5
10 Hosiery, etc.							
11 Clothing and footwear		2		1	1		4
12 Food	4	5	2		2	2	15
13 Drink	9	6	15	2	3		35
14 Tobacco	1	1					2
15 Paper, printing, etc.	7	1		1		2	11
16 Leather, etc.	2		2	1		1	6
17 Construction					1		1
18 Wholesale distribution	2		2	1	6	2	13
19 Retail distribution	6	4	2	2	5	4	23
20 Entertainment and sport		2					2
21 Miscellaneous services	1	1	1		1		4
All industries	58	28	38	13	31	15	183

Total MC*: 127

Total OC†: 56

*MC = managerially controlled
†OC = owner-controlled

SOURCE: P. Holl, 'Effect of Control Type on the Performance of the Firm in the U.K.',
           Journal of Industrial Economics (June 1975).

These three organs control the company according to the powers
and reponsibilities vested in them by law. The Vorstand is the official
representative of the company and takes the day-to-day decisions.
The Aufsichtsrat appoints the Vorstand and the Vorstand needs their
approval for important long-term decisions such as the taking up of
long-term loans, diversification and takeover. Another task of the
Aufsichtsrat is to approve the company's annual accounts. Vorstand
members are usually appointed for a five-year period, but they can
be dismissed by the Aufsichtsrat, if their managerial performance is
judged to be below standard.

   As usual, the real power of shareholders depends on whether the
ownership of shares is concentrated in a few hands, or is widely
dispersed. When families, foundations, financial institutions or the

state own a considerable part of shares, they are represented in the Aufsichtsrat. Vorstand members are not usually large shareholders, but they often have a seat on the supervisory board of one or more subsidiaries.

By their membership of the Aufsichtsrat, large shareholders can exert significant control over the company. It is not necessary for them to own a majority of shares, because German company law prescribes that important company decisions have to be taken by 75 per cent of the votes of the company's shareholders. Every major company decision can thus be blocked by a person or group which owns 25 per cent of the shares.

The managerial freedom of the Vorstand is more restricted when the supervisory board consists of large shareholders than when shares are owned by many small shareholders. The risk of being dismissed by the Aufsichtsrat is much more real in block-owned companies than in companies where share-ownership is widely dispersed.

Thus Volkswagen's chairman Kurt Lotz was forced to resign by the Aufsichtsrat in 1971 and Herr Beitz, the chairman of the Krupp Trust, which owns all Krupp shares, dismissed two Vorstand chairmen in the years 1971 and 1972.

What are the facts about ownership and control in the largest West German companies? A company is considered as managerially controlled when more than 75 per cent of the shares is dispersed over more than ten shareholders. Table 6.2 shows that eight of the twenty-two largest companies are wholly managerially controlled, and of the ten largest companies, six are managerially controlled.

From Table 6.2, one may also conclude that family control is more important than control by financial institutions (banks, insurance companies, and so on). However, bank control is probably underestimated because the banks are the only stockbrokers in West Germany and exert the voting rights of the shares they hold on deposit for their clients. The real shareholding power of the banks is difficult to detect because they do not publish all their holdings.

The large German banks (Deutsche Bank, Dresdner Bank, Hypo-Bank) have large interests in, for instance, the tyre industry, the retailing business and the breweries. Usually bank controlled companies are not owned by a single bank, but all the banks with an interest in a company will co-operate with each other.

In France a study of the 200 largest firms shows that half of them are family-owned corporations (see Table 6.3). The next most important control type is control by foreign corporations followed by technocratic control, where banks are dominant. Furthermore, the most frequent case (87 — see last column in Table 6.3) is where one owner or group of owners has absolute control. The weight of family

TABLE 6.2

Method of control in the twenty-two largest West German companies, 1972

No. Name	State	Family or foundations	Block	Financial institutions	Managerial	Remarks
1 Volkswagen	+				□	State owns 36 per cent
2 Siemens					○	
3 Thyssen—Hütte	+				□	Two family-owned found. own 36 per cent
4 Hoechst					○	
5 Bayer					○	
6 B.A.S.F.					○	
7 Daimler Benz		□		+		Flick & Quandt owns 45 per cent, Deutsche Bank 27 per cent
8 Veba	+					State owns 40 per cent
9 A.E.G.—Telefunken					○	General electric owns 10 per cent
10 Ruhr Kohle					○	Majority of shares owned by more than ten companies
11 Mannesmann					○	
12 Gutehoffnungshütte		+	+			Three families own a large part of shares
13 Krupp		○				Owned by the Krupp Trust
14 Flick		○				
15 Robert Bosch		○				
16 Rheinisch Westfälischer Elektrizitätswerk	+					
17 Hoesch					○	Merged with Hoogovens in 1972
18 Salzitter	○					100 per cent state-owned
19 Metallgesellschaft				□		
20 Gelsenberg			+			R.W. Elektrizitäts-werke owns 48.5 per cent; merger with Veba expected
21 Klöckner Humbold	+					
22 Klöckner			+			Dutch concerns own over 25 per cent

+ owns 25—50 per cent of shares.
□ owns 50—75 per cent of shares.
○ owns 75—100 per cent of shares.
SOURCE: F. Vogl, *German Business after the Economic Miracle* (Cologne, 1973).

TABLE 6.3

Types of control	Family	Technocrats		State	Foreign corporation	Co-operative	Total
		Bankers	Managers				
A group of stockholders with more than 50 per cent and without blocking minority (holding more than 33.3 per cent)	36	2	1	7	40	1	87
A group of stockholders with more than 50 per cent and with a blocking minority	2	3			1		6
A group of stockholders holding between 5 and 50 per cent	62	20	4	1	15		102
No group of stockholders with more than 5 per cent			5				5

SOURCE: F. Morin, *La structure financière du capitalisme français* (Paris: Calmann-Levy, 1974) p. 65.

control is of course strongest for small and medium-size firms, where, according to the Review *l'expansion* (October 1973), 77 per cent are family-controlled.

In Belgium, an analysis of large non-financial corporations has established that there is a dominant owner in each case (see Table 6.4). In the eight cases of family-owned corporations, the family has a monopoly of the executive posts, while in the eight corporations whose main owner is a Belgian holding company, namely the Société Générale de Banque, the holding company selects the top executives and controls the cash flow. Notice that in eighteen of the corporations under study, the Société Générale has powerful stockholders' interests.

Although it is dangerous to generalise at this stage, the impression is that the U.S. concept of managerial capitalism does not fit the European experience and it would be better to speak of *financial capitalism* and, in addition, especially for France and Belgium, *family* influence.

The evolution of the holding company in several West European countries is especially important. According to Daems, the banks and holding companies have been able to co-ordinate and control the

TABLE 6.4

Types of main owner	Number of corporations	Percentage of total assets of the corporations under study
Family	8	23.4
Belgian holding company	8	18.6
Foreign corporations	16	25.5
Joint ownership between Belgian holding companies and a foreign company	7	24.8
Joint ownership between Belgian family and a foreign company	2	7.7

SOURCE: M. de Vroey, *Propriété et pouvoir dans les grandes entreprises* (Brussels: C.R.I.S.P. 1973).

accumulation and allocation of wealth, and thus become the obvious suppliers of funds to industry. 'In exchange for funds, they obtained control over the industrial sector. The institutions for organizing corporate control in Europe were consequently financial institutions.'[10]

It is clear that such corporate control could have important adverse consequences for the firms concerned; for example, it could lead up to ill-defined corporate policy through the existence of loose structures, or the lack of uniform control systems, such as standardised accounting practices; it could also entail management systems relying more on trust than on efficient organisation, or weak co-ordination of subsidiaries and concentration, that (a) is mainly based on financial participation and interlocking directorates, and (b) avoids real technological integration which might lead to scale economies.* It is doubtful whether these probable defects have been made up for by the role of the holding companies in organising the accumulation and allocation of funds within the capital market.

THE BEHAVIOURAL IMPLICATIONS OF NEW BUSINESS GOALS

We have seen already that, whatever the form of corporate control, once profit is no longer the only objective to be maximised, business policies will be modified. This is easily seen with the help of a simple general model.

*In the case of Belgium, for a sample of 385 corporations, it appears that a tiny 0.6 per cent of directors held 5.3 per cent of all positions and were responsible for 34.6 per cent of all interlockings. In the United States, on the contrary, no directors has more than seven positions. The Gini coefficient of concentration is 0.25 for Belgium and 0.18 for the United States. Furthermore, the main source for the interlocking directorships are the large financial holding companies.[11]

A simple static model

Let u be the utility function of the firm, assumed to be continuous, twice differentiable and strictly quasi-concave in Π and W, where Π = profit and W = any other distinct objective such as size, welfare expenditures, leisure or financial autonomy.

We have

$$u = u(\Pi, W),$$

with

$$\frac{\partial u}{\partial \Pi} > 0, \quad \frac{\partial u}{\partial W} \geqslant 0.$$

Furthermore, there is a technical relationship between Π and W, expressed by a transformation function:

$$\phi(\Pi, W) = 0.$$

The controllers will select Π and W so as to maximise the utility function subject to the transformation constraint. There exists a multiplier, λ, such that the Lagrangian is:

$$L(\Pi, W, \lambda) = u(\Pi, W) - \lambda\phi(\Pi, W).$$

The first-order conditions require that:

$$\frac{\partial L}{\partial \Pi} = \frac{\partial u}{\partial \Pi} - \lambda \frac{\partial \phi}{\partial \Pi} = 0 \tag{6.1}$$

$$\frac{\partial L}{\partial W} = \frac{\partial u}{\partial W} - \lambda \frac{\partial \phi}{\partial W} = 0 \tag{6.2}$$

$$\phi = 0 \tag{6.3}$$

Dividing (6.1) by (6.2), we have

$$\frac{\partial u}{\partial \Pi} \bigg/ \frac{\partial u}{\partial W} = \frac{\partial \phi}{\partial \Pi} \bigg/ \frac{\partial \phi}{\partial W}. \tag{6.4}$$

For a given level of the transformation function, we also have

$$d\phi = \frac{\partial \phi}{\partial \Pi} \times d\Pi + \frac{\partial \phi}{\partial W} \times dW = 0,$$

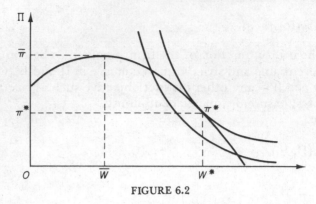

FIGURE 6.2

or

$$\frac{\partial \phi}{\partial \Pi} \Big/ \frac{\partial \phi}{\partial W} = -\frac{dW}{d\Pi}.$$

Substituting in (6.4), we obtain:

$$\frac{\partial u}{\partial \Pi} \Big/ \frac{\partial u}{\partial W} = -\frac{dW}{d\Pi}, \tag{6.5}$$

that is, the marginal rate of substitution is equal to the marginal rate of transformation, and the tangency solution occurs along the declining part of the transformation curve.

This result is displayed graphically in Figure 6.2, in which the co-ordinates corresponding to the equilibrium solution are given by Π^* and W^*. It is clear that in a profit-maximising firm, W would have been undertaken only to the extent that it increases profit; the equilibrium level of W would have been that which corresponds to a maximum of profit, $\bar{\Pi}(\bar{W})$. With a positive utility attached to W, whether it stands for size, growth, managerial welfare, or whatever, the controllers will sacrifice some profit, $\bar{\Pi} - \Pi^*$, in order to obtain an increment in W, $W^* - \bar{W}$.

Various behavioural models have been built on this basis, by specifying the new argument in the objective function: Marris uses the rate of growth of sales;[1,2] Williamson uses managerial expenses;[1,3] and Baumol uses sales and growth.[1,4]

One general implication of these models is that, in equilibrium, the level of profit will be lower than under traditional assumption of owners' control. Several American empirical studies have tested this proposition with mixed results.[1,5]

Empirical testing

After a critical survey of these studies, where the role of hetero-skedasticity in the test as well as the absence of any interaction between monopoly power and the control type were emphasised, Palmer presented a study which shows that among U.S. firms with a high degree of monopoly power (as shown by very high barriers to entry), management-controlled firms (where no single party owned 10 per cent or more of the outstanding common stock of the corporation) report significantly lower profit rates than owner-controlled firms.[16] A very valuable aspect of this analysis is the explicit recognition that a manager operates under two constraints — one from shareholders and one from competition in the market. It is only if both constraints are very weak that significant divergence from profit-maximising behaviour would be expected, and this was observed to be the case. Reservations are the qualitative nature of the variable used to measure monopoly power and the limited value of the percentage of shares held by the main owner to reflect the separation of ownership and control.

For a sample of large U.K. firms, Radice found that although owner-controlled firms do have higher rates of profit on average than management-controlled firms, they also have higher rates of growth.[17] More recently, however, Holl found, for a different sample of U.K. firms, that the difference between the mean values of profits and growth rates for owner- and managerially controlled firms were not statistically significant.[18] He then suggests that the existence of an active market for managers might constrain managers to act so as to meet the interest of owners. A recent analysis of the largest French manufacturing firms by Jacquemin and de Ghellinck leads to a still different conclusion: the profitability is not directly influenced by the type of control of the firm; however, the positive effect of the firm's size is significantly higher in the case of a familial control as compared with non-familial control.[19]

Related studies deal with the determinants of executive compensation; if executive salaries are closely correlated with criteria other than the firm's profitability, deviations from profit-maximising behaviour become more probable, and vice versa.* Again, various empirical studies have been made of U.S. firms, the majority of them concluding that compensation is more closely correlated with sales (or size) than profits. One of the recent studies, using quite a small sample of large firms, shows that size (assets or equity size) has a significant positive effect on compensation, while profit rates have an insignificant positive effect in cross-sectional studies where industrial differences are not taken into account.[20] But profits appear to have a significant effect in producer-goods industries, if industry dummies are included.

---

*Let us underline that the compensatory system cannot imply that profit is or is not really maximised; compensation is just another argument in the utility function.

Yarrow argues that the previous studies could have made a specification error arising from a failure to identify differences in the marginal productivity of the managers. By taking into account industry differences in pay, these differences in management productivity can be incorporated.

The first work using European data was done by Meeks and Whittington.[21] With a sample of 1008 major U.K. quoted companies operating primarily in manufacturing and distribution, and continuing in existence from 1967 to 1971, these authors test various hypotheses.

Two of the estimated relationships are the following, with t values in brackets:

$$D_{1971} = -24025 + 4002 \log S_{1970} + 46\Pi_{1971} \qquad (6.6)$$
$$\quad (15.6) \quad (25.6) \qquad\qquad (2.8)$$
$$R^2 = 0.395$$

$$\Delta D = -62.6 + 1601 \, \Delta \log S + 108\Delta\Pi \qquad (6.7)$$
$$\quad (3.6) \quad (3.1) \qquad\qquad (8.7)$$
$$R^2 = 0.09$$

where D = salary, including bonuses, of highest-paid director, S = sales, Π = rate of return (per cent), and Δ = differences between 1969 and 1971 flows.

The main conclusion is the overwhelming importance of size in the explanation of the level of directors' pay. On the other hand, growth and profitability have a lesser impact, their relative importance depending on the director's time horizon. No allowance is made here for possible differences in managerial productivity.

Quasi-dynamic models

The need for managerial models to be dynamic rather than static is as clear as in the traditional profit-maximisation model, and may be greater as it has been argued that dynamic managerial models might lead to profit-maximisation. Following the well-known Baumol's model, it can be assumed that the firm maximises the sum of discounted sales (under some constraints to be determined) over an infinite time period:

$$\sum_{t=0}^{\infty} \frac{R_t}{(1+r)^t} \qquad (6.8)$$

where R = total revenue, r = the rate of discount, t = time, or, for a constant rate of growth, g, we also have:

$$\sum_{t=0}^{\infty} \left(\frac{1+g}{1+r}\right)^t \times R_0,$$ (6.9)

knowing that $R_t = R_0(1+g)^t$, where R_0 = initial total revenue. Assuming $(1+g)/(1+r) < 1$, a sufficient condition for this being $r > g$, the expression

$$\sum_{t=0}^{\infty} \left(\frac{1+g}{1+r}\right)^t$$

is the sum of the terms of a geometric progression, the common ratio being less than one. The value of such an expression is therefore

$$1 \Big/ \left(1 - \frac{1+g}{1+r}\right).$$

Hence, expression (6.9), to be maximised, reduces to

$$R_0 \left(\frac{1+r}{r-g}\right).$$

An alternative objective is the discounted present value of future dividends:

$$V = \sum_{t=0}^{\infty} K_0 \frac{(1+g)^t}{(1+r)^t} \times \frac{(1-a)}{(1+r)} \times \Pi_t,$$ (6.10)

where Π = rate of profit, a = the proportion of profits retained, and K_0 = the initial capital stock.* Using this objective function, and following the approach proposed by Marris[22] and Williamson[23] Heal and Silberston[24] have developed a stimulating model which has been completed by Seton.[25]

They assume that the firm's growth is financed entirely by retained profits and that the higher the retention ratio, the higher the growth rate: $g = a\Pi$, so that $a = g/\Pi$. It is also assumed that the relationship between Π and g is such that $\Pi = f(g)$ $f'' < 0$ and $f' > 0$ for low g, $f' < 0$ for high g. With $g < r$,

$$\sum_{t=0}^{\infty} \left(\frac{1+g}{1+r}\right)^t = \frac{1}{1 - (1+g)/(1+r)},$$

---

*The profit, ΠK_0 is regarded as accruing at the end of the first year, and not synchronously with the capital stock, K_0.

so that expression (6.10) becomes:

$$V = K_0 \frac{f(g) - g}{(r - g)}.$$

(6.11)

The valuation ratio of the firm is then:

$$v = \frac{V}{K_0} = \frac{f(g) - g}{(r - g)}.$$

For shareholders to be willing to invest in the firm, v must be greater than unity, since unity would be the valuation ratio of capital invested risklessly at an interest rate identical with the rate of discount.

The necessary condition for maximising (6.11) is

$$\frac{dV}{dg} = \frac{K_0(r - g)\{f'(g) - 1\} + \{f(g) - g\}}{(r - g)^2} = 0.$$

This implies that

$$f'(g) = \frac{r - f'(g)}{r - g},$$

or

$$f'(g) = 1 - \frac{f(g) - g}{r - g} = -(v - 1).$$

The expression $v - 1$ is the margin over unity of the valuation ratio. In equilibrium, the selected growth rate will not maximise the rate of profit (implying $f'(g) = 0$) but the valuation margin corresponding to a higher growth rate. As the valuation ratio is usually taken as an indicator of the profitability of takeover, maximising the valuation margin is also equivalent to minimising the probability of takeover.

This is shown in Figure 6.3. We assume that the segments $AD = OD$ correspond to the level of the discount rate. The negative slope $AC = (r - f(g))/(r - g) = -(v - 1)$ must equal the slope of the transformation function between the rate of growth and the rate of profit, that is $CB/AB = f'(g)$.

The value of g that maximises the present value of dividends, and hence the valuation margin, is g_V, clearly above the growth rate g_Π that maximises the rate of profit. This confirms the general conclusion of Williamson that in all cases except those where profitability is at the minimum level necessary to prevent takeover, the policies the firm pursues will depend on the form of its objectives. Profit- growth- and sales-maximisers will act differently.

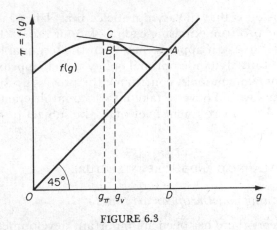

FIGURE 6.3

Such models, however interesting, are limited by *their very partial dynamic nature*. The basic assumption is that there is a constant growth rate or steady growth path, so that it is optimal for the firm to make a 'once-for-all' selection of the values of its policy variables for an infinite time horizon.

In a changing environment, a fully dynamic model would surely be more realistic. Leland proposes such a model, using optimal control theory.[26] He assumes that the firm chooses $L(t)$ to maximise discounted sales:

$$\int_0^T e^{-\rho t} F(K, L)\, dt, \tag{6.12}$$

subject to two constraints: all capital growth is internally financed, and profit must be equal to or greater than zero:

$$K = a\{F(K, L) - WL\} \tag{6.13}$$

$$\{F(K, L) - WL - i_0 K\} \geqslant 0, \tag{6.14}$$

where K = capital, L = labour, a = proportion of profit retained, i_0 = the minimum acceptable return on capital, W = unitary wage, and ρ = the discount rate. The current value Hamiltonian is written:*

$$H = F(K, L) + \lambda a\{F(K, L) - WL\} + \mu\{F(K, L) - WL - i_0 K\}.$$

*According to the method of Lagrange multipliers, it is possible to solve various problems of static optimisation under constraints by introducing new variables, Lagrange multipliers, one for each constraint, defining a Lagrangian expression and finding a saddle point of this expression. The maximum principle is an extension of the method of Lagrange multipliers to dynamic optimisation or control problems. The Hamiltonian function is defined as the sum of the objective function, here $F(K, L)$, plus the inner product of the adjoint or costate variables and the constraints. As for the Lagrange multipliers, the costate variables can be interpreted as 'shadow prices', that is the sensitivities of the optimal value of the objective function to changes in the initial state variables.[27]

One conclusion is that the asymptotic capital–labour ratio will be less than the profit-maximising capital–labour ratio.* Furthermore, if and only if $\rho > g$, it appears that when the terminal horizon is distant, the fully dynamic optimal policy is well approximated by the quasi-dynamic models, confirming the previous results. Further developments would have to take into account interactions between the firm and its environment over time, the subject of our subsequent section.

CORPORATE PLANNING AND MARKET STRUCTURE

Private planning and European attitudes

In recent years there has been an important development in business planning, especially in the United States. A growing number of firms try to make a general forecast of the trends in the economy as a whole, a prognosis of the future development of the markets in which they are currently operating, or could enter in the future, a selection of the goals to be attained and of the strategies to be elaborated. Various plans are drafted for the multiple functions of the firm: sales, purchases, production, personnel, capital investment, research, and so on. Budgets are the principal embodiment of these business plans and increasingly take on a dynamic dimension. They range from the short-run budget of operating expenses to long-run planning for capital expenditures and become a continuous process for replanning the firm's path into the future with short-run experience as a guide to the longer run. What must be underlined is that business budgeting and planning imply an interaction between the individual firm and its environment and an attempt to enlarge the area of business discretion as well as to capitalise on whatever discretion is already enjoyed. This means that budgeting implies more than forecasting. It involves the manipulation of the variables which determine the firm's performance in the future.

> The manipulation of variables in advance, on paper, if it is to be more than an intellectual exercise, implies a belief that at least certain of these variables can in fact be controlled as planned, or that certain of these variables can at least be partially controlled. If the plan is expected to provide an outcome superior to what would have been gained through simple response to external ('market') pressures, there is an underlying assumption that the company can in fact control, within some limits, the variables of markets, men, and money on which the planned performance rests. An element

---

*Thus one would set the marginal productivity of labour equal to W.

of control is implied not only over and through the budget, but over the firm's environment as well.[28]

Beyond this corporate strategy determined by the working of the market as an institutional framework for the interplay of demand and supply, the firm manipulates its political and social environment in various ways: pressure to obtain favourable tax and subsidy laws, better credit conditions, important government contracts and good labour relations (see Chapter 3). Firms even set themselves up as trend-setters, style leaders and social models in our society. In this view, our system is no longer seen as a delicate self-regulating mechanism but as a set of institutions open to manipulation by the participants. The powerful corporation becomes a 'body politic', a 'rationalized system for the accumulation, control and administration of power'.[29]

One of the best advocates of this concept is Galbraith, who argues in *The New Industrial State* that the corporation has a secure source of capital from its own earnings, integrates backwards to control the supply of necessary raw materials, replaces blue-collar workers by mechanisation or by more easily integrated highly qualified employees.[30] Besides its control of factor markets, the large corporation is able to regulate aggregate as well as specific demand, leading to a higher propensity to consume and a lower propensity to save. Prices themselves are administered, facilitating control and minimising the risk of a price collapse that could jeopardise earnings and the autonomy of the technostructure. Finally, the industrial system has extended its influence over the state, emphasising those public policies that are vital for the industrial system: regulation of aggregate demand, maintenance of the large public sector on which this regulation depends, underwriting of advanced technology and provision of an increasing volume of trained and educated manpower.

It is clear that although the large firm does control its environment to some extent and is able to adopt various strategies for avoiding uncertainty (see Chapter 3), the degree of control varies from one firm to another, one sector to another and one period to another. Corporate planning meets severe economic and institutional constraints, so that there is an incessant dialectical relationship between the firm and its uncertain environment. As Cyert and March have stated, 'within rather large limits, the organization substitutes the plan for the world — partly by making the world conform to the plan, partly by pretending that it does!'[31]

At this level, it is useful to emphasise a specific point relating to Europe. Business planning practices have been slower to take hold in European business and it is American experience that has given it an important impulse, whether directly through contact with American subsidiaries in Europe, which are involved in the planning exercise of their parent companies, or indirectly by employing the services of management-consultancy firms, many of which either are American or have adopted American methods.

But it must also be recalled that, in almost every European country, there exists a long tradition of co-operation between state and private business. With their sustained scepticism towards competition, European governments have usually encouraged the major interest groups to co-ordinate their policies so that economic evolution could follow the desired path. Businessmen are called for meetings with the government and trade-union officials in one of the many forms of *économie concertée*.

Thus, instead of relying on market mechanisms to solve industrial problems, the tendency has often been to promote some form of planning agreement between industry and the state. The European industrialist, like his American colleague, is increasingly interested in ascertaining the future of his industry, rigorously expressed in a series of detailed forecasts over a period of years, against which he can check his own investment programme. The difference is that the European 'can do so directly by questioning one another in a smoke-filled room under official auspices, with the Government's plans thrown in too, while the Americans have to get it all second hand'.[32]

This is probably truer for the French, the Italian, the British or the Dutch businessman than for the German, but the tendency is still present, as we shall see again when looking at the conflict between European anti-trust and industrial policies.

Reciprocally, European governments are tempted to use large private corporations as instruments of national and regional planning; but this is much harder as the new generation of European multi-nationals may be less and less responsive to national or even E.E.C. authorities.

General static and dynamic models of the firm moulding its industrial environment

It is not easy to embody planning behaviour in a dynamic model. In the framework of industrial organisation and the structure—conduct—performance paradigm, a starting-point is to consider that market structure is no longer thought to be a state of nature, as a set of exogenous factors, but as a set of variables open to some manipulation by the firm.

For a firm which has some amount of market power, it is possible and profitable to try to increase or at least to maintain the degree of concentration, through mergers, absorptions, collusion or loss-leader selling; to try to maintain or to increase the degree of product differentiation through advertising and the various forms of selling costs; to try to sustain or develop barriers to entry through the acquisition of patents, retail outlets or scarce resources whose markets are imperfect, in order to impede or prevent the entry of new firms. *Different forms of market conduct can bring about, either directly or as side-effects, gradual changes in the structure of industries.* According to this approach, the more market power a firm has, the more it looks on market structure as a strategic variable and not as an exogenously determined parameter. In the 'market–structure–performance' pattern, the direction of causation can run from conduct to structure to performance.

By analogy with the *prix crié par hasard* of Walras, we may suppose that the powerful firm works on the initial industry structure until some kind of equilibrium is reached. Within a limited period of time, the firm will arrive at a position combining a certain level of concentration, product differentiation and barriers to entry such that the highest level of profit is attained. As Andrews writes: 'we can still retain ideas of a firm in balance, a sort of equilibrium; but this would be a balance with its environment, the industrial environment.'[33]

This conception implies the existence of what may be called a 'structural maximum' for the firm. Expenditure or investment aimed at altering the market structure is assumed to suffer from diseconomies beyond a certain level. Indeed it is inconceivable that, within a given time span, a firm will be able to increase its size without being handicapped by problems of budget control, decentralisation of operation, reorganisation; similarly, the expansion of advertising and the multiplication of barriers to entry will be halted by various forms of saturation and decreasing efficiency.*

Furthermore, such changes in market structure will be constrained by the anti-trust legislation. This legislation is concerned more with market conduct than directly with market structure or market performance. Among the practices generally condemned are restrictive agreements, price discrimination, exclusive dealing and full-line forcing, resale price maintenance, and so on. It is important to recall that, in so far as these practices do arise in conjunction with monopoly, they are more often a symptom of monopoly power than its source.

---

*However, if a 'static' analysis is the appropriate method of exploring the conditions of equilibrium because of a limit to the amount of change any firm can undertake in a given period, there is no reason to assume that there is a limit to its expansion over time.

A worse danger lies in the predatory practices whose aim or effect is to modify the market structure by making the industrial environment less favourable to actual or to potential competition. Horizontal and vertical mergers, pooling of patents and extensive advertising may be dangerous, not so much as ways of exploiting the given market power of the firm, but as ways of increasing this power over time through changes in the market structure. Such conduct, which feeds back into market structure, could then lead to socially inefficient market performance in the long run.

Those considerations may be illustrated by a model of a single-product, imperfectly competitive firm whose objective is profit maximisation. Profit is defined as

$$\Pi = p(q, \alpha)q - c(q, \beta) - (\alpha + \beta)$$

$$\frac{\partial p}{\partial \alpha} > 0, \quad \frac{\partial^2 p}{\partial \alpha^2} < 0; \quad \frac{\partial c}{\partial \beta} < 0, \quad \frac{\partial^2 c}{\partial \beta^2} > 0,$$

where p = price of one unit of input, q = output, $R = pq$ = total revenue, c = total variable cost, α = total expenditures for increasing the price of the product at a given output, and β = total expenditures for decreasing cost at a given output. α expenditures can be thought of as advertising and sales-promotion expenditures, or as other expenditures which increase product differentiation, collusion between firms, concentration, and so on. β expenditures represent costs such as purchases of patents and control of factor supplies which constitute barriers to potential entrants. Since both α and β have the effect of decreasing competition in product markets, anti-trust legislation aims to impose ceilings on α and β; these are denoted by $\bar{\alpha}$ and $\bar{\beta}$.

The entrepreneur's problem is then to maximise profit subject to the anti-trust constraint. There exist multipliers such that, for the Lagrangian:[34]

$$L = p(q, \alpha)q - c(q, \beta) - (\alpha + \beta) + \lambda_1(\bar{\alpha} - \alpha) + \lambda_2(\bar{\beta} - \beta),$$

the following Kuhn–Tucker conditions are obtained:

$$\frac{\partial R}{\partial q} - \frac{\partial c}{\partial q} \leqslant 0, \quad \left(\frac{\partial R}{\partial q} - \frac{\partial c}{\partial q}\right)q = 0, \quad q \geqslant 0 \qquad (6.15)$$

$$\frac{\partial R}{\partial \alpha} - 1 - \lambda_1 \leqslant 0, \quad \left(\frac{\partial R}{\partial \alpha} - 1 - \lambda_1\right)\alpha = 0, \quad \alpha \geqslant 0 \qquad (6.16)$$

$$-\frac{\partial c}{\partial \beta} - 1 - \lambda_2 \leqslant 0, \quad \left(-\frac{\partial c}{\partial \beta} - 1 - \lambda_2\right)\beta = 0, \quad \beta \geqslant 0 \qquad (6.17)$$

$$\bar{\alpha} - \alpha \geqslant 0, \quad \lambda_1 (\bar{\alpha} - \alpha) = 0, \quad \lambda_1 \geqslant 0$$
$$\bar{\beta} - \beta \geqslant 0, \quad \lambda_2 (\bar{\beta} - \beta) = 0, \quad \lambda_2 \geqslant 0. \tag{6.18}$$

In the equilibrium position, if legal constraints are not binding, there is equality between the marginal effects of expenditures on increasing total revenue and expenditure on reducing total cost:

$$\frac{\partial R}{\partial \alpha} = -\frac{\partial c}{\partial \beta} = 1.$$

In the case $\alpha = \bar{\alpha}$, $\beta = \bar{\beta}$, that is where firms are prevented by anti-trust legislation from spending optimal amounts on price increasing and cost reducing factors, we have

$$\frac{\partial R}{\partial \alpha} = 1 + \lambda_1$$

and

$$-\frac{\partial c}{\partial \beta} = 1 + \lambda_2.$$

The λs can then be interpreted as the marginal advantage to the firm of liberalising anti-trust legislation, or as the maximum price the firm will pay, through lobbying, for changing the legislation. When the expected value of the penalty for a violation of the anti-trust legislation is known, it can be determined whether or not the advantage to be gained from systematically violating the law outweighs the expected cost.

In contrast with the preceding presentation, it must be admitted that the interaction between corporate strategy and market structure is fundamentally *dynamic*. Time plays two crucial roles. First, it is through the temporal dimension that competitive forces work against the market power of the firm and the imperfections of market structure; a high growth of market demand tends to be associated with a low degree of concentration; the introduction of new products and new demands, the effect of the passage of time on consumers' memories, both tend to destroy brand loyalty; industries with rapidly changing technologies offer strong inducements to entry in the form of opportunities for gains to innovating firms. Second, the impact of expenditure, aimed at changing market structure, is not limited to a given time period, but affects the whole time path of the firm.

In order to reformulate our model to take account of these phenomena, let

$$\Pi = \{ p, s(t), x(t) \}$$

be the firm's profit function at time t, as a result of having an 'inherited' market structure, x, that is, a given market share, a given level of product differentiation and a given level of barriers to entry at that particular date, together with the set of current strategies, s, aimed at moulding market structure at time t. More precisely:

$$\Pi = p(q, s, x)q - cq - s,$$

with

$$\frac{\partial p}{\partial q} < 0, \quad \frac{\partial p}{\partial s} \geqslant 0, \quad \frac{\partial p}{\partial x} \geqslant 0, \quad \frac{\partial^2 p}{\partial s^2} < 0, \quad \frac{\partial^2 p}{\partial x^2} < 0.$$

The firm attempts to maximise the present value of the stream of profit:

$$V = \int_0^\infty e^{-\rho t} \Pi\{q, s, x\} \, dt,$$

where the discount factor ρ is taken to be positive and constant.

The state variables representing market structure are related by state equations to the control variables of market conduct:

$$\frac{dx}{dt} = \dot{x} = f(x, s),$$

with $f'(s) \geqslant 0, f'(x) \leqslant 0$. More specifically, we may assume a linear state equation:

$$\dot{x} = s - \beta x,$$

with $\beta \geqslant 0$. This implies two assumptions.

First, given the initial market structure, $x(0) = x_0$, these imperfect market structures depreciate over time. The constant proportional rate of depreciation β expresses technological conditions as well as the competitive forces which operate, through the temporal dimension, against market imperfections.

Second, market conduct produces not only a direct effect on the firm's current profit but also changes in the industrial structure. For example, advertising expenditures, besides their direct impact on the quantity demanded, have an indirect long-run effect by changing the stock of goodwill and the degree of product differentiation.

We construct the Hamiltonian function:[35]

$$H = e^{-\rho t}\{\Pi(q, s, x) + \lambda(t)(s - \beta x)\},$$

where the costate variable $\lambda(t)$ can be interpreted as the shadow price of a unitary increase of the state variable, in our case of the marginal unit of imperfect market structure, along the optimal control path. It is the implicit price attached by the firm to its industrial environment.

The first term of this equation is the instantaneous profit and the second term is the effect of the current change in x on future profits. If we assume the existence of an upper unit on s, we may apply the 'maximum principle' for an infinite horizon, as stated by Chetty.[36] The necessary maximum conditions are as follows:

$$\frac{\partial H(t)}{\partial q} = p + \frac{\partial p}{\partial q} q - c = 0 \tag{6.19}$$

$$\frac{\partial H(t)}{\partial s(t)} = \frac{\partial \Pi}{\partial s} + \lambda(t) = \frac{\partial p}{\partial s}(q - 1) + \lambda(t) = 0 \tag{6.20}$$

$$\frac{\partial H(t)}{\partial x(t)} = \rho\lambda(t) - \dot{\lambda}(t), \quad \text{with} \quad \lim_{t \to \infty} e^{-\rho t}\lambda(t) = 0 \tag{6.21}$$

or

$$\lambda(\rho + \beta) = \frac{\partial \Pi}{\partial x} + \dot{\lambda}$$

$$\frac{\partial H(t)}{\partial \lambda(t)} = \dot{x}(t), \quad \text{with} \quad x(0) = x_0. \tag{6.22}$$

From equation (6.20), it appears that along the optimal path of the decision variable, at any time, a positive shadow price $\lambda(t)$ associated with imperfect market structure implies that the marginal revenue generated by s is less than the marginal cost generated by s. Thus, unlike the static profit maximiser for whom $\partial \Pi / \partial s = 0$, the dynamic firm has to sacrifice some current profit in order to obtain larger profits in the future.

It can also be proved that the optimal level of s_H will always be above the short-run, profit-maximisation level at every point along the optimal path. In the case of maximising instantaneous profits, the myopic profit-maximising s_Π is the solution to the equation (see p. 181):

$$\frac{\partial p}{\partial s}(q - 1) = 0, \tag{6.23}$$

while maximising the Hamiltonian at every point along the optimal path implies that

$$\frac{\partial p}{\partial s}(q - 1) = -\lambda(t), \tag{6.24}$$

with $\lambda(t) > 0$. Given that $\partial^2 \Pi / \partial s^2 < 0$, equations (6.23) and (6.24) are both satisfied only if $s_H > s_{\Pi}$.

Finally, it could be proved that if the equilibrium state $(\hat{s}, \hat{x})$ (that is, the point at which $\dot{x} = 0$, $\dot{s} = 0$) is a saddle point, the optimal strategy of the firm, for $x_0 < \hat{x}$, is to use most of its strategy expenditures s in the initial period, creating favourable market structure, and to reduce the effort as x approaches its equilibrium value $\hat{x}$. In other words, it is in the beginning period that the firm diverges most from short-run profit maximisation, accepting reduced profits in order to mould its industrial environment.

At this stage, it is useful to present briefly some specific applications of control theory to industrial organisation which follow more or less the above pattern.

Specific dynamic models of firms controlling demand or supply

Through changing market structure the firm could on the one hand modify demand conditions and on the other hand the production and cost functions.[37] From the *demand side*, several models treat *advertising* as a capital good and use a state variable $K(t)$, called 'goodwill', which summarises the effects of the past advertising outlays, habit formation arising from past consumption and brand loyalty linked with product differentiation.

A demand equation for the product of a given firm could then be defined:

$$q(t) = q\{p(t), a(t), K(t)\},$$

where a = current advertising expenditures by the firm. This could also be expressed in terms of market share and by taking into account competitive reactions:

$$q = m(p, a, A, K) \times Q(p, a, A, K),$$

where m = firm market share, Q = industry sales, and A = advertising expenditure of competitors, with $\partial m / \partial A \leqslant 0$, $\partial Q / \partial A \geqslant 0$. According to this formulation, selling expenditure not only affects the firm's market share but also industry sales. Oligopolistic interdependence is expressed by a reaction function:

$$A = f(a), \qquad \frac{dA}{da} \geqslant 0.$$

Either there is no competitive reaction as in the Cournot-type oligopolist, $dA/da = 0$, each firm being assumed to believe that no matter what value of advertising it selects, the other firm(s) will not alter its (their) advertising; or either there is a positive Stacklberg-type reaction $(dA/da > 0)$ — the given firm behaves as a leader, considering that the other firm(s) will behave as follower(s), setting its (their) advertising strictly on the basis of the leader's advertising.

The evolution of goodwill is expressed by a differential equation identical to the one of our general model:

$$\dot{K} = a - \beta K.$$

The corresponding Hamiltonian is then:

$$H = e^{-\rho t}\{(p - c)[m(p, a, A, K) \times Q(p, a, A, K)] - a + \lambda(a - \beta K)\}.$$

From this framework it is possible to generate the well-known Dorfman–Steiner* and Nerlove–Arrow† results as special cases.

Uncertainty could also be introduced. For example, a demand function where uncertainty enters additively is given by

$$q(t) = q\{p(t), a(t), K(t)\} + e(t),$$

where $e(t)/t \geqslant 0$ is a sequence of identically and independently distributed random variables with zero mean. The expected utility of the firm's profit is then written:

$$E\{u(\Pi)\},$$

where u is the utility function assumed to be continuous and twice differentiable. It is known that a concave utility function means risk aversion, a convex utility function risk preference and a linear utility

---

*According to the simplified version of the Dorfman–Steiner model, the firm, to maximise profits, will equate its advertising-to-sales ratio to the advertising elasticity divided by the price elasticity:

$$\frac{a}{pq} = \frac{\epsilon_a}{\epsilon_p},$$

where p = price, q = quantity, a = advertising outlay, and ϵ = elasticity.[38]
†The Nerlove–Arrow dynamic model leads to the following result:

$$\frac{K}{pq} = \frac{\epsilon_k}{\epsilon_p(\rho + \beta)}.$$

where K = goodwill, ρ = a discount factor, and β = rate of depreciation.[39]

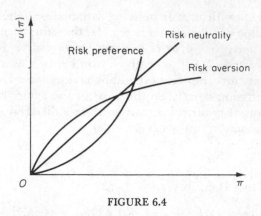

FIGURE 6.4

function risk neutrality (see Figure 6.4).* Usually risk aversion, that is diminishing marginal utility of profit, is assumed.

One general conclusion derived from these models is that whatever *the firm's attitude towards risk*, the optimal level of advertising expenditure is higher under dynamic than under static conditions.[40]

A second topic on the demand side is the *limit-pricing model*. We have already noted the criticisms of the static models (see Chapter 4), especially the hypothesis that the dominant firm faced by potential entry will either charge the short-run, profit-maximising price, allow entries and accept a declining market share, or set price at the limit price and preclude entry. A superior model would avoid this strategic dichotomy and suggest a strategy which trades off current profits against future market share.

Defining a state variable $x(t)$ to mean all the competitive firms on the fringe of the industry and $\dot{x}(t)$ as the rate of entry of rival producers, Gaskins assumes that the rate of entry is directly

---

*Indeed, let us assume a choice between (initial) profit Π_0 with probability 1 and a random profit taking on the values $\Pi_0 - v$ and $\Pi_0 + v$ with equal probabilities, i.e. 0.5 each, where v is a given amount. By definition a risk averter will prefer the certain profit

$$u(\Pi_0) > 0.5 \times u(\Pi_0 - v) + 0.5 \times u(\Pi_0 + v),$$

or

$$u(\Pi_0) - u(\Pi_0 - v) > u(\Pi_0 + v) - u(\Pi_0).$$

Thus the utility function of a risk averter is such that the utility differences corresponding to identical changes in profit are decreasing as the profit increases: this implies $u''(\Pi) < 0$. To introduce risk-aversion by using the mean—variance utility function, as in Chapter 3, it is necessary to give one specific form to the utility function, namely a quadratic form:

$$u = a + b\Pi - c\Pi^2,$$

where a, b and c are positive constants and $d^2u/d\Pi^2 = -2c$. But such a function also implies that for $\Pi > b/2c$, $du/d\Pi < 0$, which is not plausible. This seriously limits the relevant range of this specification.

proportional to the difference between the current price $p(t)$ and the limit price p_L:[41]

$$\dot{x} = k(p - p_L),$$

where k is a constant response coefficient; the difference between p_L and the dominant firm's average cost c measures the level of barriers to entry, that is the cost advantage enjoyed by the dominant firm. It is assumed that $p_L \geqslant c$.

The firm maximises

$$V = \int_0^\infty e^{-\rho t} \{p - c\} \{f(p) - x\} \, dt,$$

where $f(p)$ is the market demand curve. The corresponding Hamiltonian is then:

$$H = e^{-\rho t} \{p - c\} \{f(p) - x\} + \lambda(t) k(p - p_L).$$

The costate variable $\lambda(t)$ is the shadow price of an additional unit of rival entry at any point in time.

Among the results, it appears that for $x_0 < \hat{x}$, the dominant firm will sacrifice market share by initially pricing substantially above the limit price and gradually lowering product price towards the limit price, p being equal to p_L for $t \to \infty$.

Furthermore, with a fixed market demand curve, it is shown that the dominant (in terms of market share) firm with no cost advantage ($p_L - c = 0$) prices itself out of the market in the long run, so that the stationary state is similarly characterised by a competitive situation.

Ireland points out that for an increasing market demand curve, an analogous result is obtained, once it is assumed that the increase is shared out among the established firms according to current market shares.[42]

Jacquemin and Thisse suggest that, in the static case, once the net rate of entry does not depend exclusively upon price policy but also on the non-price policies of the dominant firm, then if this firm has no cost advantage it will not ultimately leave the market.[43] This argument could be extended to include the possibility that the dominant firm will adjust its policy to the product cycle and build up a portfolio of products.

Kamien and Schwartz, examining the consequences of free entry for a Cournot oligopoly, view the appearance of new firms as uncertain and dependent upon current industry price.[44] Their results confirm Gaskins's findings of decreasing industry price in the absence of scale economies. De Bondt, using a generalised Gaskins model to allow for scale effects and non-linear dependence of the rate of entry on the difference between current industry price and a constant limit price, finds again that entry retarding modifies free-entry conclusions only if the firm has a cost advantage over potential entrants.[45]

Models in which the firm is assumed to be able to control the supply side over time are scarce. Usually the production function and cost conditions are defined as entirely exogeneous. In fact, through various expenditures, especially on R and D, the firm is able, to a certain extent, to modify its technology by altering certain parameters of its production function.

Several authors have applied optimal control theory to this problem, trying to develop a theory of induced technical change. One of the most stimulating models has been proposed by Kamien and Schwartz, who assume that the firm can change the current state of technology x by devoting resources to research.[46] The corresponding state equations are as follows:

$$\dot{x}_1 = \frac{s_1^k x_1}{R_1}; \quad \dot{x}_2 = \frac{s_2^k(1-x_2)x_2}{R_2}; \quad \dot{x}_3 = \frac{s_2^k x_3}{R_3},$$

with $x_1 \geqslant 0, 0 \leqslant x_2 < 1, x_3 \geqslant 0$. The symbols are defined as follows:

x_i, the current state of technology, corresponds to the parameters of the production function $\phi\{x_1 f(z_1, z_2; x_2, x_3)\}$ — the shape of the isoquants will be determined by the values of the parameters x_2, x_3 (non-neutral technical change), while neutral technical advance is realised through increase in the positive parameter x_1;

s_i is the amount of expenditure for achieving technical change at the rate $\dot{x}_i$, when the technology is at a level x_i;

R_i is a positive constant reflecting the relative cost of the ith type of technical change; and

k is a parameter $(0 < k \leqslant 1)$ indicating whether research effort brings about decreasing returns in technical change $(0 < k < 1)$ or constant returns $(k = 1)$.

Note that the state equations are obtained from specific equations for the cost of achieving technical change at the rate $\dot{x}$ when the technology is at the level $x : s_i = \dot{s}_i(\dot{x}_i; x_i)$. Among the results obtained, it is shown that the relative effort devoted to each type of technical change varies inversely with the relative cost R_i, directly with the elasticity of production costs with respect to that type of change, and directly with firm size.

Other models have tried to examine the Schumpeterian hypothesis that large, monopolistic firms will undertake more research than smaller firms,[47] but these R and D analyses, by ignoring aspects such as diseconomies of scale in research, arrive at the doubtful conclusion that optimal levels of R and D will occur only in a pure monopoly with R and D subsidies.

Finally, let us mention the model of the Hochmans which deals simultaneously with demand-creation investments and investment in the production process.[48] The state of the firm is described by the two variables W and Z, whose rates of change over time are given by

$$\dot{W} = I - \gamma W$$

and

$$\dot{Z} = a - \gamma Z,$$

where W = the stock of productive capital, I = gross investment in productive capital, Z = amount of capital devoted to demand creation, a = current outlays on advertising, R and D and any other expenditure that directly influences the price of the product for a given output, and γ = the constant rate of depreciation of both stocks.

It is shown that in the early expansion phase of the firm's productive capacity, there is no demand-creating activity. This phase is followed by a second one in which all investments are channelled to demand creation. In the last phase the firm chooses to invest in both types of capital and the steady state is reached in regions of decreasing marginal returns to both types of capital. One notable aspect is *the occurrence of 'investment cycles' both in productive and demand-creation activities*.

To conclude, the increasing application of dynamic analysis to the strategies of the firm in relation to its industrial environment have overcome several limitations of the static models commonly used in industrial-organisation theory. More and more, the whole complex of interrelationships between the various aspects of the structure—conduct—performance paradigm over time are being explored on a theoretical basis.

In 1942, Schumpeter wrote:

> the fundamental impulse that sets and keeps the capitalist engine in motion comes from the new consumers' good, the new forms of production or transportation, the new markets, the new forms of industrial organization that capitalist enterprise creates . . . . Now a theoretical construction which neglects this essential element of the case neglects all that is most typically capitalist about it; even if correct in logic as well as in fact, it is like Hamlet without the Danish prince.[49]

There is now some hope that optimal control theory will help us to reintroduce the Danish prince on to our industrial stage! But it must be admitted that, even within the limits of the previous simple models, the analysis quickly leads to tedious mathematical complications and to results with no valuable economic meaning. This would be the situation if it were necessary to embody all the various aspects of the firm's expansion process in the model; that is why institutional and historical research or case studies remain essential in this field. Our hope is that the optimal trajectories of the various methodologies will converge.

WORKERS' PARTICIPATION AND CONTROL OF THE FIRM

Workers' participation in Europe

Workers' participation in decision-making is receiving growing attention among academics as well as among businessmen and labour representatives. Despite the various experience of the Israeli *kibbutz* the Latin American farm co-operatives and the Yugoslav worker-managed firm, it is only recently that this new form of industrial organisation has become a major political issue in European countries, especially in West Germany, the United Kingdom, France, Belgium and the Scandinavian countries.

As there is growing dissatisfaction with the capitalist market economy, efforts are being directed toward reshaping the system in order to provide better information, to improve working conditions, to develop 'job enrichment', to reduce the feelings of alienation of the worker and to bring into play new methods by which those most directly involved in activities participate in taking decisions which affect them.

Although the major European countries seem likely to follow a similar philosophy in this matter, several different forms of participatory organisation are possible. Three levels of participation may be distinguished:

(1) At the first stage, workers may demand to receive complete and detailed *economic information*, to enable them to exercise some control. As in France and Belgium, the *conseils d'entreprise* are able to see from company data what the present situation is and where a company's financial breakeven point is when they frame their demands. Because of the old-fashioned European idea of 'business secrecy', full disclosure of the relevant economic information would represent significant progress.

(2) At the second stage, workers could participate in decision-making and be ready to assume various responsibilities.* *Labour participation* in managerial decisions implies collaboration with

*This is distinct from a participation to the *results*, i.e. profits, of the firms activities.[50]

capitalist partners, mainly shareholders who could still bear the financial risks. There is then real power-sharing with workers. This is the 'cogestion' (codetermination) applied in West Germany in the coal and steel industry, where supervising boards have had fifty-fifty representation for more than twenty years. In most other industries, the supervising boards at present consist of one-third employee representatives with the rest being nominated by the shareholders.

The West German government has recently introduced a fifty-fifty arrangement similar to that which exists in the coal and steel industry for all companies employing more than 2000 people. Businessmen seem to agree with unions on the fact that codetermination has been a valuable experience and that union representatives have shown themselves willing to act according to the over-all needs of the enterprise. Yet a generalisation of such experience requires better education of union representatives and the acceptance of shared responsibilities. Similar beginnings can be seen in Sweden and the Netherlands, but some trade unionists are not happy about the idea of a worker director being transformed into a boss and collaborating with the capitalist system.

The European Commission itself is much in favour of worker councils having a say in the conduct of a company, including its major policy decisions. It has suggested that full worker representation on the supervisory board is desirable but has left the precise forms of worker participation to be decided at a national level. According to the Green Paper on *Employee Participation and Company Structure* 'Member States must be free to adopt the principles of participation with the maximum degree of flexibility possible'.

(3) At the third stage, *labour management* or self-management implies that workers exercise full control, hiring capital instead of capitalist entrepreneurs hiring workers. This is mainly the case of a co-operative in which workers get together, purchase inputs, sell their products, bear the risks and distribute the surplus among themselves.

Experience of labour management in market economies have usually taken such a co-operative form; producer as well as consumer co-operatives have grown up in Scandinavian countries, the United Kingdom, West Germany, and Benelux, especially in the agricultural and service sectors. These co-operatives are often a reaction against the central state and dominant private firms. In France and Italy, collaboration with the state is important, but recently the autonomy of co-operatives has declined because of a reinforcement of public and private financial control.

Systems of worker participation have also evolved in socialist countries.

In Yugoslavia the first stage was a 'cogestion' system in which the state was the dominant partner, fixing the distribution quotas of profit, controlling prices, credit and investments.

Since 1965 state control has been reduced but the banking system has acquired an important influence. Today there is emphasis on building up labour-managed systems which retain the human and economic advantages of participation, such as the absence or reduction of alienation and incentive effects on productivity and effort and which at the same time minimise difficulties of the risk-bearing labour, hiring capital and financing conditions.

Models of a labour-managed firm

Developing the models of Ward[51] and Domar,[52] Vanek offers a general theory of a labour-managed economy.[53] The essential features of his system, not all equally important, are the following:

(i) the labour-managed economy is based on the principle of 'one man one vote' or a similar democratic system;

(ii) the participants in a labour-managed firm share the income of the enterprise, after having paid for costs of operation and having agreed upon various types of collective consumption and investment, and the increase of the reserve fund;

(iii) the workers have the right of 'usufructus', not of ownership, but there is no external control by capital lenders;

(iv) the labour-managed firm has an autonomous employment policy;

(v) the labour-managed economy is a market economy.

On this basis, various models could be constructed. Within the framework of an imperfect market structure, let us assume a monopolistic firm producing one good with one input, namely labour:

$$q = q(L), \quad \frac{dq}{dL} > 0, \quad \frac{d^2q}{dL^2} < 0,$$

where q = output, and L = labour.

The demand could be shifted by advertising expenditure:

$$p = p(q, s), \text{ with } \frac{\partial p}{\partial q} < 0, \frac{\partial p}{\partial s} > 0, \frac{\partial^2 p}{\partial q^2} \leqslant 0, \frac{\partial^2 p}{\partial q \partial s} = 0,$$

$$\frac{\partial^2 p}{\partial s^2} < 0.$$

where p = price, and, s = advertising expenditure. The capitalist firm is assumed to maximise profit:

$$\Pi = p(q, s)q(L) - w_0 L - s - T,$$

where w_0 is the market unitary wage and T is lump-sum tax. The first-order conditions for optimality are

$$\frac{\partial \Pi}{\partial L} = \frac{dq}{dL}\left(p + \frac{\partial p}{\partial q}q\right) - w_0 = 0, \tag{6.25}$$

which implies

$$\frac{dq}{dL}\left(p + \frac{\partial p}{\partial q}q\right) = w_0$$

and

$$\frac{\partial \Pi}{\partial s} = \frac{\partial p}{\partial s}q - 1 = 0 \tag{6.26}$$

According to equation (6.25), labour is hired until the wage rate equals the (positive) marginal-revenue product; and equation (6.26) tells us that the optimal level of advertising is such that its marginal product equals its marginal cost.

With a labour-managed firm, the argument of the objective function is different. The maximisation of income per worker (or value added per worker) is the new objective of the firm and shares in income or in value added replace salaries:

$$y = \frac{Y}{L} = \frac{1}{L}\{p(q, s)q - s - T\},$$

where Y is total income and y is income per worker. The first-order conditions are as follows:

$$\frac{\partial y}{\partial L} = \frac{1}{L^2}\left\{ L\left(\frac{\partial p}{\partial q}\frac{dq}{L}q + p\frac{dq}{dL}\right) - (pq - s - T) \right\} = 0, \tag{6.27}$$

which implies

$$L\frac{dq}{dL}\left(\frac{\partial p}{\partial q}q + p\right) = pq - s - T$$

$$\frac{\partial y}{\partial s} = \left(\frac{1}{L}\frac{\partial p}{\partial s}q - 1\right) = 0. \tag{6.28}$$

Condition (6.27) could be written:

$$\frac{dq}{dL}\left(\frac{\partial p}{\partial q}q + p\right) = \frac{pq - s - T}{L} = y, \tag{6.29}$$

that is labour is hired until the average income of firm members equals the (positive) marginal-revenue product.

Comparing conditions (6.25) and (6.29), it appears that the capitalist firm equates the marginal-revenue product with the fixed market wage rate, while the labour-managed firm equates the marginal-revenue product with average income per member of the firm. This does not imply that equilibrium marginal revenue will be identical in the two models, so that market wage would equal income per head; indeed, if this were true, profits would be zero for the capitalist firm. As there is a positive profit, we must have for a given s and T, $w_0 < y$, which requires a lower marginal-revenue product for the capitalist firm:

$$\left\{\frac{dq}{dL}\left(p + \frac{\partial p}{\partial q}q\right)\right\}_{\Pi} < \left\{\frac{dq}{dL}\left(p + \frac{\partial p}{\partial q}q\right)\right\}_{y}.$$

This implies that the number of workers employed, and so the output of the capitalist firm, will be greater than that of the labour-managed firm. This result is displayed in Figures 6.5 and 6.6. The amount of labour is measured along the horizontal axis, the total revenue of the firm on the vertical axis. As L increases, pq increases but at a diminishing rate. In Figure 6.5, the slope of the given line AB is the market wage rate, while in Figure 6.6 the adjustable line $A'B'$ is the net income per worker. For an identical level of advertising s and lump-sum tax T, the optimal point at which $A'B'$ is tangential to the pq curve corresponds to a lower level of L, that is OC', than the point of profit maximisation at which AB is tangential to the corresponding pq curve, once a positive profit is postulated in the case of the capitalist firm. Therefore, in conditions of monopolistic competition each labour-managed firm will tend to be of smaller size than the corresponding capitalist firm. *Ceteris paribus*, there would be more firms and thus a more competitive market structure in a labour-managed economy. The explanation of this result lies in the objective

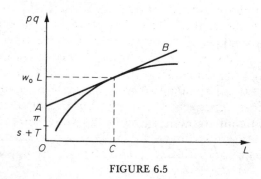

FIGURE 6.5

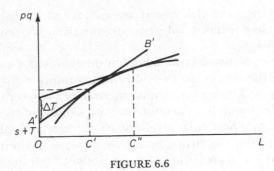

FIGURE 6.6

function: the labour-managed firm maximises net income *per worker* whereas a capitalist firm could have more incentive to increase size so as to maximise *total* profit.

Finally, defining $V = pq$, we can derive from (6.29):

$$\frac{dL}{dT} = \frac{\partial y}{\partial T} \Big/ \frac{\partial^2 V}{\partial L^2} = -\frac{1}{L(\partial^2 V/\partial L^2)} > 0.$$

Noting that $dp/dT = (dp/dq)(dq/dL)(dL/dT)$, it is clear that $dp/dT < 0$. By contrast with the case of the profit-maximising firm, where lump-sum taxes do not affect the short-run equilibrium, a positive lump-sum tax leads to an increase in employment and production and a reduction in prices for the labour-managed firm. This is illustrated in Figure 6.6, in which the labour-managed firm increases its employment and output from the level C' to the level C'' when tax increases; the lump-sum tax can then be spread over a larger number of employees, so that the average income is increased.[54]

The preceding model could be refined and enlarged. Atkinson shows that it is most likely that the initial scale of operation and growth rate of capitalist firms exceed those of labour-managed firms.[55] Meade compares the reaction of a capitalist monopolist and a labour-managed firm in the same initial equilibrium position to an increase in demand and concludes that the former will always expand more or contract less than the latter.[56] Litt, Steinherr and Thisse, using optimal control theory, compare optimal investment policies of neoclassical and of labour-managed firms;[57] the main result confirms that the output of the neoclassical firm making sufficient profit exceeds the output of the labour-managed firm. Dreze, using a general equilibrium approach, proves rigorously that workers' control and entrepreneurial management lead to the same Pareto optimal situation in the long run, provided that there is perfect mobility of factors and perfect competition.[58] This stresses the importance of labour mobility for efficiency.

The main interest of this recent research is to establish that such a socially appealing form of industrial organisation is compatible with economic efficiency.

Nevertheless, many questions remain unanswered. One of these is the choice of the *maximand*: simplifying assumption that the labour-managed firm will seek to maximise income per worker can be challenged. For example, Furubotn assumes that the *maximand* is a welfare index of a particular group of workers, namely the workers initially controlling the firm who try to preserve the best possible economic and social conditions for themselves.[59] It could also be assumed that the *maximand* combines several conflicting objectives, for example profit and income per head:

$$V = (1 - \gamma)\Pi + \gamma \left(\frac{Y}{L} \right),$$

where γ expresses the degree of participation, the pure capitalist case implying $\gamma = 0$.

Another important question, as emphasised by Meade, concerns risk: 'while property owners can spread their risks by putting small bits of their property into a large number of concerns, a worker cannot easily put small bits of his efforts into a large number of different jobs'.[60] Another difficulty relates to the financing conditions, since full external financing would imply changes in the conventional banking system.

At this stage, let us stress, in agreement with Vanek, that the promotion of worker participation in particular sectors or in the whole economy goes beyond the technicalities of economic analysis and meets the need for a new social state where men participate in the determination and decision-making of the activities in which they are directly involved.

CONCLUSION

To conclude, the system by which firms are run and their objectives determined in Europe seems to be financial and familial rather than managerial. This does not imply that the firm and its various participants are one and the same, or that they share the common goal of profit maximisation. Non-profit-maximisation behaviour is often apparent in European firms. Others aspects, such as security, financial autonomy or size, are plausible supplementary arguments of the objective function and will affect the firm's strategy, so that today we must accept the existence of a collection of theories of the firm rather than a single unified theory. One aspect of the enlargement of the theoretical framework that has become a major political issue in European countries is the question of the workers' participation in decision-making and income-sharing. As previously demonstrated, this redistribution of power could also influence the firm's policies.

All these considerations underline the danger of formulating direct links between market structure and economic performance, without considering the intermediate effects of conduct. On the contrary, future models in industrial organisation will increasingly have to incorporate the behavioural dimension if they are to have an effect on applied research and policy analysis.

This need is still clearer if the permanent interplay between the firm and its market (and non-market) environment is taken into account. Recent dynamic models based on optimal control theory constitute a first step in this direction. In European countries such an interplay is so important that there is a strong tendency towards planning agreement between industry and the state in order to avoid market uncertainties.

European Competition Policy: Goals and Means

When deciding what sorts of policy to adopt to ensure that the industrial economy functions efficiently the European authorities chose competition policy. But the choice of the most impersonal means of social control of the economy must be justified by showing that competition policy is a more efficient way of achieving given economic goals than the other types of policy. As the Economic Council of Canada has said: 'where competition is such as to promote the efficient use of manpower, capital and natural resources, it obviates or lessens the need for other forms of control such as more or less detailed public regulation or public ownership of industry'.[1] An analysis of the goals and methods of this way of controlling the working of the European market is the subject of this chapter.

GOALS OF EUROPEAN COMPETITION POLICY

A first eventual goal is the *diffusion of economic power* and the protection of individual freedom. This aspect, which was originally basic to anti-trust legislation, still occupies an important place, perhaps more at the level of public opinion than at government level.* To many people, freedom of competition is synonymous with equality of opportunity, the spirit of enterprise and responsibility. The use of competition policy increases the credibility of the system. Such a viewpoint implies a suspicion of bigness as such; big firms represent a concentration of power in private hands rather than in democratically chosen governments. Such private power can cross economic boundaries and poses the threat of an 'extra-market' power which can change the rules of the game in favour of the dominant corporations. In such a situation, where relationships between firms and their socio-economic environment

---

*In a recent book Sir Alec Cairncross *et al.* write: 'Our concern for the maintenance of effective competition extends beyond purely economic considerations. Competition is one of the foundations of an open society in which all member countries of the European Community have a substantial stake. . . . It is therefore necessary to weigh against the gains from industrial concentration the socio-political consequences of concentrations of private power, which could discredit property-owning democracy.'[2]

constitute a mixture of market and non-market bonds, the authorities aim at a dispersion of private power. Even if this entails some loss of economic efficiency, such a choice would not necessarily be 'irrational', because such costs may be outweighed by social or political advantages.

A second goal may be to protect the *economic freedom of market participants*, specifically of small and medium-sized firms. Here the protection of competitors takes precedence over the defence of the competitive process as such. In this case attention will be directed towards abusive practices, such as coercion, discrimination, refusal to sell, boycott, and so on, by which powerful firms might endanger the existence of weaker competitors. On the other hand, the safeguarding of behaviour leading to 'reasonable profits' would be part and parcel of such a policy. This type of approach is particularly in evidence in European countries; it not only attacks unfair competition but also emphasises legislation relating to freedom of contract of trade or of prices.

The third type of goal is dear to the heart of the economist. Competition policy has to assure the *efficient allocation of scarce resources*. According to the Pareto model, perfect competition brings about the optimal allocation; in the long run prices will be equal to average and marginal cost, which are at their lowest level and determine the optimal output of units producing at full capacity. According to some economists, the aim of anti-trust policy should be to bring about the maximum satisfaction of consumers which the perfectly competitive model ensures.

The existence of monopoly elements means that prices no longer indicate relative scarcities and the efficient utilisation of resources.

Several criticisms have been voiced against this point of view. Some of these have already been mentioned in the preceding chapters.

It is said that the development of technology and the accompanying economies of scale create a conflict between the competitive process, based on a multitude of small firms, and the productive efficiency, which requires large-scale firms which dominate and plan the market. According to Galbraith, the enemy of the market is not ideology but the engineer! But let us recall that technological economies of scale do not justify the size which some firms have already attained (Chapter 5), and that other types of scale economy (commercial, financial, managerial, and so on) have never rigorously been shown to exist. However, in some of our industries there may be a tendency towards 'natural' monopoly or oligopoly, as in railways or public utilities; or there may be high social costs, as in the energy sector, where the time

horizon of private firms is shorter than that of society as a whole.
In such cases more direct control might be justified: price control,
taxation, subsidisation, and/or public ownership might assure the
efficient operation of such industries provided that publicly owned
firms can themselves be efficiently managed.

The dynamic nature of our economy makes it necessary to view
efficiency from an evolving standpoint. The continual emergence of
new products, new firms, new industries, new methods of production and organisation, and the disappearance of outdated products
and processes, is closely bound up with research, technical progress
and innovation. However, we have seen that competitive conditions
appear to promote and not to retard this process of renewal (see
Chapter 5).

More fundamentally it has been argued that perfect competition
cannot be achieved because of a number of insurmountable
(technical and institutional) obstacles, and we have encountered
the 'theory of second best' (Chapter 5), which stated that the non-
realisation of one or more of the conditions for Pareto optimality
leaves it doubtful whether it is still worth while to meet the
remaining conditions.

Three principles seem to have inspired the European authorities
in this matter.

First, they seem to have adopted the view that the rules of
competition were not formulated to give protection to individual
competitors but to uphold the competitive process. Up to a point
both objectives can be reconciled, because a sufficient number of
competitors is essential for the maintenance of competition. On
the other hand, vigorous competition implies a continuous movement of entry and withdrawal from the market; the creation and
disappearance of firms are the basis of a market economy. Whereas
classical national legislations in Europe concerning unfair competition focus upon subjective elements and economic behaviour
(forbidding only practices contrary to honest commercial conduct
and inquiring into motives), the new European approach is mainly
interested in setting up and safeguarding certain objective market
conditions. In its First Report on *Competition Policy* the
Commission wrote:

> Competition is the best stimulant of economic activity since it
> guarantees the widest possible freedom of action to all. An
> active competition policy makes it easier for the supply and
> demand structures continually to adjust to technological
> development. Through the interplay of decentralized decision-
> making machinery, competition enables enterprises continuously
> to improve their efficiency which is the *sine qua non* for a

steady improvement in living standards. Such a policy encourages the best possible use of productive resources for the greatest possible benefit of the economy as a whole and for the benefit, in particular, of the consumer.[3]

But let us note that in the same report it is also stated that 'competition policy must ensure fair competition so that enterprises . . . can in general benefit from the same conditions of competition'. This is why the Commission also encourages co-operation between small and medium-sized companies to penetrate foreign markets, a goal which may not always be compatible with the first objective.

Second, the idea is not to strive after the realisation of perfect competition but to promote a 'workable competition', that is a process of rivalry under conditions of uncertainty. This would ensure mobility of resources, the provision of alternative choices for producers and consumers and the use of the best economic practices in production and distribution.

'Workable competition' does not have the same solid theoretical foundations as perfect-competition theory and implies a value judgement from the political authorities; it simply describes market structures in which new technologies, organisational forms, preferences or products can arise and be developed without public or private restrictions.

Finally, as we saw in the introduction, competition is not the exclusive means of achieving the Community's goals. Other instruments may have to be used in situations when competition in itself is not enough to obtain the required results without too much delay and intolerable social tension. The choice between the alternative policies available must be based on their relative efficiency.

APPLICATION OF COMPETITION RULES TO THE PUBLIC SECTOR

The Treaty of Rome (1957), instituting the European Economic Community, is clear about the role of competition.

In order to promote the goals mentioned in Article 2, namely a harmonious development of economic activities, a continuous and balanced expansion, an increase in stability, an accelerated raising of the standard of living and closer associations between the states belonging to it, the activity of the Community will establish a regime assuring that competition within the Common Market is not falsified (Article 3).

The third part of the Treaty (Title 1) is devoted to the common rules, and deals with competition rules in the first chapter. The

scope of their application appears to be very wide. Agreements
between firms, the abuse of dominant positions and public aid to
companies are all subject to supervision and control; the third
chapter stipulates that the Commission has to act against every
disparity, new or old, between the legislative or administrative
regulations of member states which could distort competition
(Articles 101 and 102). This broadly formulated point of view is
necessary because of differences in the economic organisation of
member states, which may range from public or private monopolies
to cartels, oligopolies or competitive structures, so that focusing
attacks on one organisational form would be discriminatory. It is
becoming especially necessary for the E.E.C. authorities to protect
the competitive process against nationalist interference. Since
nation states are no longer able to protect their firms and
industries by customs duties, they are more inclined to resort to
direct (industrial or regional) and indirect aid. The latter types
may be disguised as health or safety regulations or may claim to
maintain tax revenues or to stabilise markets. In fact they erect
new barriers to entry, penalise or exclude foreign products, close
national markets in the public sector or prevent the free establishment of foreign companies (see Chapter 4). The Treaty calls for
the competition rules to be applied to member states in so far as
such types of economic intervention create or threaten to create
specific distortions.

Two types of state activity are considered: (1) specific distortions which result from acts which affect persons or groups of
persons, whether favourably or unfavourably; and (2) general
distortions which are the result of differences between the
provisions laid down by law, regulation or administrative action in
member states. The former distortions are regulated by E.E.C.
competition rules and are prohibited, unless exempted by the
Commission, whereas the latter have to be eliminated through the
harmonisation of laws. They can, if necessary, be prohibited
through the issue of directives by the Council of Ministers. This
dichotomy implies that the Treaty provisions with respect to
distortions of competition can be divided according to the schema
shown in Figure 7.1.

We now review briefly the main specific distortions related to
member states or public enterprises and how they are dealt with
by competition policy.

Article 7 prohibits discrimination on the basis of nationality both
by persons and by states. Discrimination was defined by the
European Court as 'either treating similar situations differently or

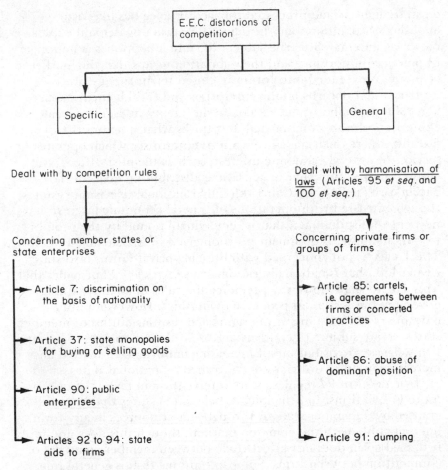

FIGURE 7.1

different situations in the same way'. An example would be if a
public enterprise showed preference for domestic products over
imports — which would affect trade between member states.

Article 37 concerns the monopoly powers of member states in the
buying or selling of goods (not services). Such powers may be
exercised directly or through state monopolies. Such state
monopolies need not be abolished, but the use made of their
exclusive rights is strictly limited. In particular, no hindrance to the
free movement of goods inside the Common Market is allowed; even
import licenses granted automatically are considered to infringe this
rule. For this reason, member states with extensive monopolies have
tended to abolish them, or are currently doing so: Italy has ended (or
is ending) state monopolies in salt, bananas, flints, cigarette paper,

cigarette lighters and processed tobacco; France has likewise abolished state monopolies in tobacco, potash powder and explosives, basic slag and matches. The subject of state monopolies is no longer of practical importance and their abolition means that the market economy is extended into formerly closed territory.

Article 90 concerns public enterprises and forbids them or their controlling member states to violate the Treaty rules. (The legal expression is more complicated, but this is what it amounts to.) Exceptions are only made in favour of enterprises which operate services of general economic interest, such as the post offices, still allowed to prevent other organisations distributing mail. In the Sacchi case (1974), the Court ruled that national television systems, though entrusted with operations of general economic interest, have no right to discriminate, that is they remain bound by the prohibition of an abuse of dominant position given in Article 86 (see below). The Treaty is not concerned with bringing private firms into state ownership, that is nationalisation, because Article 222 provides that 'this Treaty shall in no way prejudice the rules in member states governing the system of property ownership'. However, public enterprises shared some of the rights and responsibilities of member states, so are subject to controls on top of those applying to private firms. These provisions are of increasing importance now that an increasing number of firms are controlled by national states.

Articles 92 to 94 regulate state intervention in favour of one or more E.E.C. firms. In principle, Article 92(1) states that 'any aid granted by a member state or through state resources in any form' is 'incompatible with the common market', though this does not apply if the aid given does not affect trade between member countries or competition between firms. Some exceptions to this general rule are allowed since the full implementation of such a rule could result in social distress or prevent distress from being relieved with the required urgency. The most important exceptions concern regional development aid. (In recent years, environmental aid has also been taken into account.) Only the Commission is empowered to grant these exceptions, and member states are therefore obliged to inform the Commission of their plans to grant or alter aid two months in advance. If the Commission considers the proposed aid to be incompatible with the rules of the Common Market, it may prevent the member states from putting the measures into effect.

Deciding on whether to allow state aids for regional or industrial development involves wide discretionary powers for the Commission. How does it arrive at its decisions? One criterion is 'regional specificity': restrictions of competition are allowed in order to facilitate the development of certain regions. Consequently it must be established, first that the region concerned is in need of assistance as compared with other regions, and second that the proposed aids really do constitute an incentive to development. Thus the Commission gets more and more involved with the economic policies of member states. The criteria on which regional need is assessed include the number of jobs created or lost, the composition of the employed population, the rate of unemployment, the average income, the level of investment, and so on.

Aid which is meant to assist but not to 'develop' an area cannot be accepted. Article 9 of Italian law No. 464 provided for aid to firms which had to dismiss workers or put them on short time. Basically, the aid consisted of interest subsidies for a maximum period and a maximum amount. The Commission took the view that these proposed subsidies were concerned with keeping ailing firms alive and would not contribute to their rationalisation, and decided to act against the scheme under Article 93 (2). As a result the Italian government agreed to make the aid conditional upon reorganisation schemes submitted by the firms, to give priority to the Mezzogiorno (South) and other less-favoured areas, and finally to give prior notice of specific cases in other areas. Similar actions were undertaken earlier against Belgian general aid schemes and against French and Dutch development funds.

Systems of aid for the following specific industries have been reviewed: the shipbuilding industry in France, the wool industry in the United Kingdom, industrial research institutes in several Italian industries, similar research establishments in French industries, and so on.

In the latter cases, finance for the research activities was partly derived from a levy on sales of domestic products and imported products in the industry concerned. Although the Commission generally approves aid which facilitates the industrial development of small or medium-sized firms, the import levies could not be allowed because they affected trade and competition. If governments finance such expenditure from other, non-distorting sources, no further objections will be raised.

The point is clear from cases of aid given to encourage new technological developments. Many small and medium-sized firms promote worth-while research and development, but run into difficulties at the stage of industrial or commercial exploitation. In many cases where innovations have been made, these difficulties are of a financial nature because research and promotional expenditure has to be covered and current profits, though increasing, are still insufficient. The expansionary phase, moreover, requires large amounts of capital,

and the banking system does not always provide sufficient means
because it is wary of the hazardous nature of innovations. Consequently many promising ventures fall into the arms of large-scale
firms, bent on diversification. This tends to reduce competition from
new firms and (at the least) to promote over-all concentration.

In several nations, for example the United States, Japan and
Sweden, venture capital systems have been set up by banks, investment companies or industrial groups to make such capital available
to innovating firms. The Commission did not object when the
German government promoted such a scheme, the Venture Financing
Fund (V.F.G.), supported by the large banks, under which the
German government guaranteed to repay three-quarters of the losses
incurred by the Fund. Similar funds have been set up in recent years
in other member states, including France (the Sociétés Financières
d' Innovation). Such developments demonstrate that competition
policy can be used positively to stimulate competition as well as
negatively to end distortions.

POLICY WITH RESPECT TO PRIVATE RESTRICTION OF COMPETITION: CARTELS, CONCERTED PRACTICES AND DOMINANT POSITIONS

Principles

According to Article 85, '*agreements* between firms, decisions by
associations of firms and concerted practices which may affect trade
between member states and which have as their object the
prevention, restriction or distortion of competition within the
Common Market shall be prohibited as incompatible with the
Common Market'. Several examples of such agreements are then
given, for example price-fixing, restriction of production, market-
sharing, tying of sales, and so on. Such prohibited agreements or
practices are automatically void, but can be exempted under the
following conditions:

(i) if they contribute towards the improvement of the production
or distribution of goods or promote technical or economic progress;

(ii) if they allow consumers a fair share of the resulting benefits;

(iii) if the restriction is necessary for the attainment of the
objective; and

(iv) if the firms concerned are not enabled to eliminate competition in respect of a substantial part of the product in question.

Regulation 17, adopted by the Council of Ministers in 1962,
empowers the Commission exclusively to enforce its dispositions.
For this purpose, one of the Commissioners is given responsibility

for competition policy and he has a *Directorate-General* for competition under his command.

The Commission has established a system of negative clearances, so that firms which wish to continue an agreement without penalty can apply to the Commission for a declaration that their agreement is not prohibited by Article 85. If, on the other hand, the Commission finds fault with the agreement or practice, it can compel the firms to abandon the agreement or practice by issuing a formal decision. Before doing this the Commission may issue an informal recommendation to the firms concerned to voluntarily terminate the agreement or to adapt it to such an extent that it is no longer objectionable.

If the agreement or practice comes under the prohibition of Article 85(1), the Commission may exempt it from prohibition on the basis of Article 85(3), if the agreements have been notified by the parties concerned. Failure to notify does not condemn the agreement or practice but it cannot be exempted.

Furthermore, the Commission has been given power to exempt whole categories of agreements, for example those relating to standardisation, research and development and specialisation. Only the last-named type has so far been the subject of a block exemption. Decisons taken by the Commission are subject to litigation before the European Court of Justice.

Finally, the Commission and the Court of Justice have established that an agreement between enterprises is not prohibited under the terms of Article 85 if its effect on competition and trade between states is imperceptible. Quantitative criteria for insignificance were given in a notice on agreements of minor importance issued by the Commission in 1970; if firms participating in an agreement have a combined market share of less than 5 per cent of the product concerned, or an aggregate turnover no more than 15 million units of account (20 million to firms in the distributive sector), the agreement is considered insignificant.

Article 86 forbids the *abuse of a dominant position* in the Common Market or in a substantial part thereof if trade between member states is involved. Some examples of abusive practices are given: the imposition of unfair prices, the restriction of production, markets or technical developments, discriminatory practices and the tying of sales. There is no exemption from the prohibition of Article 86 parallel to that provided in Article 85(3). The Commission can order observed abuses to be ended, but again their decision can be contested before the Court.

There is no article in the Treaty which specifically deals with *merger* cases and *concentration* as such. However, in 1965 the

Commission issued a memorandum indicating that a merger which created a near-monopoly position could be considered an abuse of dominant position as prohibited by Article 86. This position, focusing on the structural effects of a merger, was subsequently found inadequate to deal with the numerous mergers which occurred in the late 1960s and early 1970s which might reduce competition without actually creating monopolies.

As we have seen in Chapters 2 and 3 over-all and market concentration within the Community has risen appreciably, and there has been a substantial reduction in the number of firms, so that in certain industries the four largest firms in the Common Market now control between 80 and 90 per cent of sales or production.

In July, 1970, the Commission sent to the Council a proposal for a regulation on the control of concentrations between enterprises, of which the main provisions are as follows:[4]

(i) mergers which result in the power to hinder effective competition are incompatible with the principles of the Common Market;

(ii) mergers indispensible to the attainment of general objectives of the Community (technological, social, regional, and so on) are not incompatible and may be exempted on the basis of a trade-off system weighing the mergers' advantages against its anti-competitive effects;

(iii) mergers involving firms with aggregate sales of 1000 million units of account have to be notified — the Commission has three months during which to initiate proceedings;

(iv) if proceedings are not instituted, the merger is deemed compatible with the principles of the Common Market — if proceedings are initiated, a final decision must be taken within nine months;

(v) the Commission has exclusive powers to enforce the prohibition mentioned under (i) and can order dissolution of the merger.

(vi) the obligation to notify under (iii) above does not apply if the acquired firm is small, that is, if its sales are less than 30 million units of account.

The Commission's proposal has already been approved (subject to minor amendments) by the European Parliament and the Social and Economic Council. At the time of writing it is under consideration by a special working party of experts from member states as a preliminary to the Council's decision.

Comparison of different approaches

Anti-trust legislation and policy may be considered (on the level of both diagnosis and cure) using the structure—conduct—

performance paradigm like any other topic in industrial organisation. Theoretically, this threefold division should be clear cut; in practice, things cannot be arranged so neatly, as we shall see. Some legislation puts the emphasis on the characteristics of *market structure*: level of concentration, growth or stagnation of the market, level of barriers to entry, and so on, and the policy solution chosen will be a structural measure such as breaking heavily concentrated markets, disentanglement of company structures, granting or supervision of compulsory licences.

Other types of legislation focus more on aspects of conduct. In this case it is some type of behaviour by a firm, such as the tying of sales and discrimination, which constitutes a restriction of competition, and the policy action takes the form of forbidding the firm to continue behaving in such anti-competitive ways.

In a third type of legislative systems the essential criterion is *performance*. Intervention here depends on the results achieved by the competing or colluding firms, such as level of profit margins or economic—technical progress and sanctions will aim to control performance characteristics. In reality legislative systems are mixed and will emphasise different criteria at different times. Thus U.S. policy has frequently used structural tests, although behavioural criteria have also been applied. For example, U.S. policy towards mergers and dominant firms between 1919 and 1951 were orientated towards the abuse principle, but since the early 1950s emphasis has increasingly shifted towards structural criteria.

In the United Kingdom several *Monopolies Commission* reports have shown concern for performance aspects, while in continental Europe a mixture of conduct and performance criteria has long prevailed. This is especially the case in France, with the *Commission techniques des ententes,* while the German system is closer to the American one.

It is difficult to go beyond such general indications of types of policy, because considerations, other than the search for economic efficiency, have influenced the authorities' policies. Among these have been bureaucratic traits such as the probability of achieving a success, the necessity to set a precedent, the political opportunity to press a case, the views of leading bureaucrats and the directions given from on high which may have personal motivations (recall some anti-trust settlements under ex-president Richard Nixon).

There is no doubt that since the Commission started to formulate and enforce competition policy at the European level, there has been a revival of national anti-trust policies, and increased attention has been devoted to economic considerations, contrasting with a legalistic approach.

Control of collusion*

Most industrial situations exhibit some degree of interdependence in the oligopolistic sense, so that the firms always have to choose between the opposing strategies of some kind of co-operation and competitive behaviour, in the sense of rivalry for the best positions or results, using whatever competitive parameters are available.

Collusive behaviour may be formal, that is based on written agreements, as in cartels, or informal, as with concerted practices. Article 85 of the E.E.C. Treaty considers and controls such types of behaviour. As we shall see later in this chapter, collusion based on the dominant position of a leading firm, surrounded by a set of minor companies, is dealt with by Article 86.

The typical cartel may fix prices, divide markets or regulate production by means of quotas. The classical static case is that in which the cartel strives after joint profit maximisation and behaves as a monopoly by setting a unique price (Figure 7.2). The market price and total output will be determined by the equality of total marginal cost and marginal revenue, derived from the given total demand curve. The contribution of each firm to total output will be determined according to the rule $MC_1 = MC_2 = MC_3 = MC_T$, and by definition $q_T = q_1 + q_2 + q_3$.

The total industry profit will then be divided between the firms in accordance with their negotiating powers. The main message of this simple model is that a 'perfect' cartel could lead to results identical to a monopoly.

In practice, however, cartels will assume various complex forms to cope with the uncertainty of changing supply and demand conditions. For example, an information-sharing system (open price agreements, basing-point systems, and so on) may be instituted to rule out surprise actions. And, despite all these arrangements, we have seen (Chapter 2, pp. 74–5) that cartels are rarely 'perfect' and always unstable. It is highly opportune to keep this in mind when discussing European competition policies.

The Commission has taken a broad view of collusive behaviour, which covers five main types of agreement or practice. We shall discuss the first four of these categories in more detail below:

(i) vertical agreements between firms in successive stages of production or distribution of goods or services;

(ii) horizontal agreements between companies in the same stage of producing and/or distributing goods or services;

*In the following sections, some parts follow the lines given in our contributions to K. George and C. Joll (eds), *Competition Policy in the U.K. and E.E.C.* (Cambridge University Press, 1975).

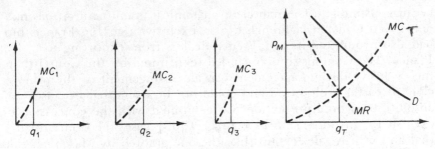

FIGURE 7.2

(iii) concerted practices between firms, that is co-ordinated
market behaviour not founded on explicit agreements and open
price systems;

(iv) exclusive rights — patents, trademarks, copyrights, know-
how and so on — creating monopoly positions on the basis of
agreements;

(v) various particular forms of co-operation dealing with trading
practices not normally in direct conflict with competition rules but
which may indirectly affect them, such as fairs and exhibitions,
joint publicity, use of common labels, and so on.

Vertical agreements. Exclusive dealing has occupied a prominent
place in E.E.C. competition policy from the outset. Such agreements may stimulate market penetration but they may also create
obstacles to market integration if the dealer is granted territorial
protection, that is if parallel imports from dealers outside the
protected territory are prevented because the manufacturer will not
supply dealers without an export prohibition, and the protected
dealer has no right to sell in another exclusive dealer's territory.
The aim of such exclusive dealing agreements is of course to split
up markets, create barriers to entry (see Chapters 2 and 4),
practice price discrimination and reap profits by means of pricing
according to the competitive situation in each of the sub-markets.
The Commission has therefore stood out against these practices.
Exclusive dealing is only objectionable, however, if agreements
between independent trading partners contain such export
prohibitions. In December 1962 it was announced that exclusive
agency contracts made with dependent commercial agents do not
come under Article 85(1). The decisive test for independence is
whether the agent assumes the risk arising from the transaction. In
the leading case, *Grundig v. Consten* [1964] (with a ruling from
the Court of Justice in 1966), it was found that price levels in
France and West Germany differed by between 20 and 50 per cent

because Grundig, a German electro-chemical manufacturer, has not only given Consten, a French dealer, exclusive rights in France, but had also prohibited its non-French dealers from exporting to France. The Commission concluded (confirmed by the Court) that the exclusive dealing agreement was an infringement of the principle of cartel prohibition and could not be exempted because absolute territorial protection was combined with the concession of exclusivity. In the *S.T.M. v. M.B.U.* [1966] case, the Court ruled that an exclusive dealership (like the one granted by Maschinenbau Ulm to Société Technique Minière) was not an infringement as such to Article 85. In accordance with the view that the legality of an agreement depends partly on its significance, an unimportant exclusive contract (but one which is liable to be imitated on a mass scale) which would create barriers to entry into the market by foreign producers was found illegal while an exclusive dealership contract containing territorial protection (*Völk v. Vervaecke* [1966] was upheld because the matter was so unimportant.

In the meantime, the Commission issued a block exemption, authorising bilateral exclusive dealing agreements which satisfied certain conditions, especially that stipulating that parallel imports shall not be prevented. Thus export prohibitions, *de factor* or *de jure*, are not allowed, and in recent years the Commission has succeeded in removing most of them. Of the 30,000 cases concerning exclusive dealing arrangements initially notified, 4500 of which contained export prohibitions, only 1500 were still pending at the beginning of 1972.

The *Trans-Ocean Marine Paint Association Decision* of 1967 (renewed in 1972), which allowed a group of smaller European paint manufacturers with a limited market share to co-operate to the extent of dividing markets between them, confirms the principle that temporary territorial protection may be allowed if it enables the penetration of new markets. Thus in the light of these rulings, the legality of exclusive dealing agreements seems to depend on whether the agreement is indispensable for creating new competition, as well as on whether its anti-competitive effect is significant.

On the other hand, the *W.E.A.—Filipacchi Music S.A.* was fined in 1972 because it had forbidden its dealers in France to export light-music records to West Germany, so that the price differential of 50 per cent between these markets could be maintained. Similarly, *Pittsburgh Corning Europe*, selling cellular glass from Belgium throughout the Common Market, through concessionaires tried to prevent parallel imports into West Germany, where prices were maintained some 40 per cent higher than in Benelux, by

means of according substantial rebates to Benelux dealers who did
not export this insulating material

The Commission has been very strict against collective exclusive
dealing agreements concluded between groups of manufacturers/
importers and distributors. The Commission has always refused
exemption on the grounds that such agreements seal off national
markets and thereby restrain or regulate Community trade.
Aggregated rebate cartels of all types have found no grace. If
producers in a member state grant buyers in that state a rebate
related to total purchases made during a particular period, the
buyers will have an incentive to make all their purchases from
domestic producers. Foreign sellers are barred from access to
distribution chains even if they offer more favourable terms. The
impact of such cartels depends on the market shares of producers/
importers and distributors, but as a rule they tend to cover a large
number of national firms. In its Third Report on *Competition
Policy*, the Commission says that many Common Market firms are
members of such cartels.[5] For example, according to the Belgian
hot-water boilers and geysers agreement concluded between three
producers and two importers with more than 70 per cent of total
market sales between them, imposed aggregate rebates on these
suppliers are to be given on all (not only their own) deliveries to
associated dealers. As these distributors brought 94 per cent of
their requirements from the cartel members and had 75 per cent
of national sales, this erected a barrier to the entry of foreign
suppliers.

Two other types of vertical agreements are resale price maintenance and selective distribution. Individual resale price
maintenance falls outside the E.E.C. competition-policy rules,
provided buyers remain free to purchase wherever they want. This,
of course, undermines the national resale price maintenance system,
as the German record and photographic producers have discovered.
Low priced records, films and photographic equipment simply
entered the national market by circulating through France and
Benelux.

Selective distribution was dealt with in the *Omega* (November
1970) and *Kodak* (July 1970) cases. Manufacturers appoint only a
limited number of dealers selling high-quality wares for each area
depending on estimated demand. They make them sign standard
sales agreements providing, *inter alia*, for costly after-sales service
and guarantees. In return the dealer is given protection against
others who might reduce his sales. Such agreements may be
exempted, on condition that the price-equalising force of parallel
imports is allowed to work.

On this occasion, the Commission stated an important rule, later confirmed by the Court, regarding relations between the *parent company* and its completely controlled subsidiaries. Restrictions imposed on the subsidiary company by the parent could be considered as 'a division of tasks within the economic organisation of the group as a whole'.[6] They cannot be considered as agreements or restrictive practices, as defined in Article 85. However, in the Commission's view, 'this does not exempt from the prohibition in Article 85(1) agreements concluded within a corporate group if they have wider implications, for instance agreements which restrict the scope for non-member undertakings to penetrate a given market'.[7]

Horizontal agreements. The main types of horizontal agreement may be divided into national and international cartel agreements. The latter are so flatly in conflict with the prohibition of Article 85(1) that there is no chance of their being legally valid and they can only survive by failing to notify the Commission. If such a cartel is subsequently detected it will be heavily fined. Table 7.1 gives a survey of E.E.C. policy with respect to horizontal agreements and practices up to the end of 1975. The agreements have been divided into five groups: (i) those relating to price-fixing and the stipulation of other sales conditions; (ii) those containing outright export bans or delivery refusals; (iii) those fixing quotas, import or export levels or delivery agreements; (iv) agreements and practices containing investment prohibitions or bans on participation in foreign companies; and finally (v) joint sales agencies or syndicates. The last column indicates how the Commission dealt with these agreements: whether they were approved and obtained a negative clearance (N.C.), often after intervention by the Commission (I.), or whether they could not be exempted (N.A.). In some further cases, especially in later years (1974–5), it is known that agreements were subsequently dissolved by the parties concerned after Commission intervention (informal cartel policy). The survey of Table 7.1 is therefore not exhaustive, but representative with respect to the policies pursued.

Table 7.1 shows that out of fifty-nine cases which came up for examination, only seven obtained negative clearance; both Alliance Machine Outils and S.A.F.C.O. were associations of small French producers, not able to restrain competition in the Common Market because of their limited market share, the wide range of products competing in both quality and price and (in the first case) the possibility for association members to fix their own selling prices. On the other hand, S.A.F.C.O. was the first syndicate granted a negative clearance without the attachment of conditions. Inter-group S.F.M.P.

TABLE 7.1

Horizontal cartel agreements or practices, 1964—75
(excluding specialisation agreements)

	P	B	Q	I	S	
V.V.V.F.	x					I. 1965, 1969, 1975
Cleaning products		x				Dissolved 1966
Construction equipment		x	x			Dissolved 1967
Semi-finished metallic products		x				Dissolved 1967
Laminated steel agencies, West Germany					x	I. 1967
Cobelaz					x	I. 1968
Alliance Machine Outils					x	N.C. 1963
International Cables	x	x		x		Dissolved 1969
Quinine	x	x				N.A. 1969
Dyestuffs	x					N.A. 1969
S.E.I.F.A.					x	I. 1969
Sheet glass	x		x			N.A. 1970
Noordwyks Cement agreement	x					Dissolved 1970
A.S.P.A.	x		x			I. 1970
Julien/Van Katwijk		x	x			Dissolved 1970
German scrap iron	x		x			N.A. 1970
S.U.P.E.X.I.E.					x	I. 1970
Belgaphos					x	Dissolved 1970
N.C.H.	x				x	N.A. 1971
V.C.H.	x					N.A. 1971
C.I.M. France					x	I. 1971
S.A.F.C.O.					x	N.C. 1971
C.R.N.			x	x		N.A. 1972
Cimbel	x		x			N.A. 1972
Polyester fibres				x		N.A. 1972
Gisa	x		x			N.A. 1972
Laminated steel agencies, West Germany					x	N.A. 1972
Asybel	x				x	Dissolved 1973
N.V.C.P.		x			x	I. 1973
Sugar	x	x	x			N.A. 1973
S.C.P.A.—Kali und Salz	x		x		x	N.A. 1973
Kali und Salz					x	N.A. 1973
Ilor—Lancomé	x		x			N.A. 1974
Glass container manufacturers	x					N.A. 1974
Belgian wall paper manufacturers	x					N.A. 1974
F.R.U.R.D.		x				N.A. 1974
Zwarte Kip		x				N.A. 1974
French—Japanese ball bearings	x		x			N.A. 1974
Dutch records	x					N.A. 1974
Belgian and Dutch electrodes	x					N.A. 1974
Flat glass, West Germany	x					N.A. 1974
Rank/Sopelem	x	x	x			N.A. 1974
Nuclear fuels				x	x	I. 1974
S.H.V.—Chevron					x	N.C. 1975
Sirdar—Phildar		x				I. 1974
Maarden—en Kachelbureau	x		x			N.A. 1975
Intergroup	x					N.A. 1975
Kabel metal—Luchaire		x				N.C. 1975
Crude Aluminium	x					I. 1975

TABLE 7.1 *(continued)*

	P	B	Q	I	S	
U.N.F.D.E.	x			x		N.A. 1975
S.F.M.P.					x	N.C. 1975
A.O.D.P. — Beyrard			x	x		N.C. 1975
Bomée	x					N.A. 1975
Gutehofmunghülte—Wreland—						
Frefumetanx	x					N.A. 1975
Instituent Industriele Formgoing				x		N.A. 1975
Linoleum Manufacturers Export						
Convention	x					N.A. 1975
Chain manufacturers	x	x				N.A. 1975
Sicaworms—Givon					x	N.C. 1975
Belgian Wood Panels	x					N.A. 1975
TOTAL 59	32	15	16	6	17	

P = price fixing and alignment of sales or purchase conditions; B = import/export ban or delivery refusals; Q = quotas, frozen import or export levels or delivery agreements; I = investment or participation bans; S = joint sales or purchase agency or syndicate.
N.A. = not accepted by the Commission for exemption or fined.
N.C. = approved or given negative clearance by the Commission.
I. = adapted after intervention by the Commission.
'Dissolved' means that the agreement was ended after intervention.

Source: based on the Commission's four *Competition Policy* reports and E.E.C. bulletins.

and Sicaworms—Givon relate to joint purchasing activities, not eliminating competition and U.N.F.D.E. concerned trade-exhibition activities, which was approved conditionally.

The rest of the agreements were either dissolved, amended or not accepted at all, and sometimes the companies concerned were fined. The heavy preponderance of price restrictions in this sample of cartels is clear; there were thirty-two price agreements or concerted practices, and thirty quantity restrictions. The majority of these were found to be unacceptable and had to be withdrawn or amended.

The evidence therefore confirms that market-sharing agreements, price-fixing and quantity restrictions are hardly ever exempted. This general rule also holds for purely national cartels which affect trade flows, as such cartels may easily raise 'thresholds' against intra-E.E.C. trade by means of international price or output alignments, or through the connection of horizontal agreements with vertical cartels (for example collective exclusive-dealing contracts or aggregated rebate systems).

Joint sales agencies were initially treated differently. Of the fourteen cases decided up to the end of 1973, two obtained immediate negative clearance, six were adapted and accepted and six

were found unacceptable and had to dissolve. Nearly all these
syndicates operated in producer-goods sectors: laminated steel,
fertilisers, cement, sulphuric acid, that is homogeneous products in
which price-cutting may be fierce. Such syndicates try to restrain
price competition by means of their exclusive sales policy, the allocation of delivery quotas among producers and the fixing of uniform
prices and other terms of sales. But it turned out subsequently that
the syndicates' behaviour did not justify favourable treatment; they
often encouraged the alignment of prices at the highest level of costs
and did not demonstrate much flexibility in adapting to demand
changes.

One of the West German steel syndicates threatened to eliminate
by price discrimination a small outsider who could only be saved by an
appeal to Brussels. Research has shown that the cement and fertiliser
syndicates which were authorised did not achieve worth-while cost
reductions from rationalisation (rarely more than 5 per cent on an ex-
works price) and did not benefit the consumer. Such developments,
plus some criticism of the aforementioned syndicate decisions, have
prompted the Commission to change its attitude. Consequently, the
decisions taken in 1972 and 1973 with respect to syndicates were
negative; the laminated steel groupings were ordered to dissolve;
Asybel, the sulphuric acid sales agency of the Belgium non-ferrous
metal producers, and the Belgian—German, kalium-salt syndicates
were likewise stopped.

Thus the rule with respect to formal cartel agreements is now
clear: horizontal cartels will only be allowed in those cases where
their market share is unimportant.

Specialisation agreements between small and medium-sized firms
are more favourably looked upon. On 20 December 1972 a block
exemption regulation was issued for such agreements, on the grounds
that they improve production (by securing economies of scale and
rationalisation) and strengthen the competitive position of small
companies. If effective competition is not jeopardised, the
specialisation agreements will have beneficial effects. Two conditions
were therefore laid down in the exemption regulation: (1) the
market share of the participating firms should not exceed 10 per cent
(for this purpose the market is defined as the national market); and
(2) total turnover of all firms involved should not exceed 150 million
units of account. Specialisation is allowed only in the manufacture of
goods. Experience of distribution and service trades was considered
too limited for the granting of block exemptions. Specialisation
agreements, as covered by the block exemption, may include
reciprocal obligations not to produce certain items, but the commitment can refer only to the nature and not to the quantity of the

goods produced. Price regulations restraining competition will not be
approved. In general, restrictions functionally related to increasing
specialisation are accepted, but those in excess of this are frowned
upon.

Concerted practices. Collusion without formal agreement may be
expected to increase when cartel agreements are forbidden. A
celebrated initial case was the *Dyestuffs Manufacturers'* price
collusion in the years 1964–7. In the two ensuing cases, *Pittsburgh
Corning Europe* and the *sugar producers*, concerted practices were
also in evidence; the former concerned price discrimination between
the German and Benelux markets, operated by the exclusive agents
of P.C.E. in Benelux who aligned their export prices to those
prevailing in the West German market. The second case related to
concerted market sharing; the Commission reproached the sugar
manufacturers for respecting each other's markets by means of
export limitations, export price alignments and pressure on traders to
follow these policies. In its ruling of December 1975, however, the
Court reduced or removed altogether the fines previously imposed on
the six companies involved, blaming the absence of the free competition mainly on the way in which the sugar market had been organised
by member states themselves.

The concept of concerted practices emerges most clearly in the
dyestuffs case. In 1964, some ten producers sent telexes to their
subsidiaries at almost exactly the same time, telling them to raise the
prices of particular dyestuffs by a uniform rate of 14 per cent in
Italy and in Benelux. In January 1965 the increase was applied to
West Germany. For other dyestuffs, a general round of price
increases amounting to 10 per cent took place on the same day.

In August 1967 a meeting of dyestuffs' manufacturers was held in
Basle, Switzerland. One of them announced his intention of raising
prices by 8 per cent in October. The other firms reacted by stating
that the proposal would be considered. At the end of August, Geigy
informed its agents and customers in several countries that prices
would be raised. Other companies followed in September.

The accused companies defended themselves by stating that the
parallel action was not concerted, but was based on the compelling
force of the prevailing oligopolistic situation. In other words, the
argument was that the companies could not have behaved otherwise
because of the structure of the market. Price cuts were made secretly
and price rises were announced beforehand, thereby increasing
market transparency with respect to price in order to protect the
initiating firm's market share (Figure 7.3). The defence claimed that
a firm which abstained from raising its price could not have improved

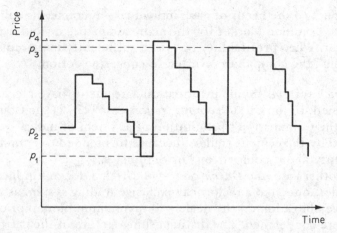

FIGURE 7.3 *Pricing in the dyestuffs market*

its market position because its competitors would have withdrawn
their announced increases, and the profitability of all would have
been impaired. However, both the Commission and the Court
pointed out that concertation of action had been in evidence; in
1964 telex messages in similar terms had stipulated equal price
increases at exactly the same time. In 1965 and again in 1967 the
facts belied the manufacturers' contention, and indicated gradual
progressive co-operation between the firms concerned. After the
experience of 1964, when announcement and price increases
occurred simultaneously, behaviour in later years was based on a
time interval between them in order to give the firms a chance to
observe reactions and behave accordingly. This, it was concluded,
constituted action as such behaviour was intended to eliminate the
uncertainty of market actions with respect to the percentage, date
and place of the price increases and products affected. Concerted
behaviour can therefore be deduced from direct or circumstantial
evidence relating to number and size of firms, the market (growth
and size) behaviour, and so on. What about the contention that an
oligopolistic market structure compels firms to behave similarly? In
the dynamic and uncertain conditions of real markets, this is not at
all obviously true. In the dyestuffs' case there were several factors
promoting intermittently competitive behaviour, such as the inter-
changeability of the standard colours, the different cost structure of
manufacturers and the growing over-all demand for dyestuffs. These
account for the stepwise price declines which occurred (Figure 7.3).
Other factors, such as the small part of the final price of the product
made up of the price of aniline colours, the technical adaptation of

the product to the needs of each individual buyer and the splitting up of the Common Market for the main companies make for parallel behaviour. When profitability had been sufficiently impaired by price 'chiselling', the companies reverted to concerted action.

Open price systems. Some information agreements have recently been condemned. In the *Dutch cement traders* case (1972) the Court upheld the Commission's prohibition of a system of indicative prices practised by the cement traders, because this tended to eliminate uncertainty about competitors' price policies.

In another case, the *Dutch cartridge* cartel, a dozen suppliers and 150 dealers operated a reciprocal exclusive trading system as well as a collective obligation on the dealers to maintain minimum prices. Both were condemned. The distinguishing feature of the cartridge cartel was the open price system, which obliged suppliers to register their individually fixed prices with a suppliers committee, which circulated the information. This, the Commission held, hampered competition by reducing individual price flexibility and discouraging collective price changes.

The most interesting case of an information agreement relates to the *European glass packages manufacturers* (1974). A group of twenty-six producers in West Germany, Benelux, France and Italy operated a 'fair competition rules' agreement supervised by the International Fair Trade Practices Rules Administration (IFTRA) at Liechtenstein. The rules stipulated that sales at below cost price, intended to undermine competitors or to establish a monopoly, systematic selling below a competitor's price, discrimination and other practices were unfair. Manufacturers therefore had to inform each other immediately about price changes, while foreign competitors were obliged to align their price quotations for exports to those of the 'natural price leader' in the national markets.

This price leader was whichever national manufacturer raised his price first after an increase in costs. The structure of the glass-container industry (bottles, jars and flasks) facilitated the open price system and was as shown in Table 7.2.

In recent years demand has grown relatively fast because of the shift by consumers toward disposable bottles and the development of the market for glass packages in the pharmaceutical, cosmetic and food industries. National or individual productive capacity was sometimes insufficient to cope with this growth in demand, and trade flows within the Common Market increased.

Increased uncertainty during the 1960s led to the establishment of national information offices to centralise information concerning price lists, rebates and conditions. Such information was exchanged nationally and internationally and facilitated the detection of price-cutters. A further step was the introduction of an international scheme for cost-price calculations in the second half of the 1960's. A system of carriage-paid uniform delivery prices was also operated in order to counter the growing tendency of bottlers to shop around for the lowest ex-works price. The system was supervised by IFTRA and held together by the threat of a fine for trespassers of at least 30 per cent of sales in the sector where the infringement occurred. Naturally the Commission held the system illegal and pointed out that such an 'information agreement', ostensibly meant to promote fair competition, did in fact eliminate price competition. In 1975, a similar agreement based on IFTRA rules, concluded between the leading European aluminium producers, was likewise condemned.

TABLE 7.2

Structure of the European glass-packages market

	Number of producers	Degree of concentration*	Controlled by or liaisons with firms in area
West Germany	13	4 had 88%	—
Belgium	3	2 had 100%	4
Netherlands	1	1 had more than 90%	4
France	5	2 had 90—100%	—
Italy	4	3 had 40%	4
TOTAL	26		

*Of total market in bottles, demijohns, jars and flasks

Industrial and commercial property rights. Rights to industrial and commercial property, such as trademarks, patents, copyrights, and so on, and the licences which can be given for such rights, are limited to the national states in which they are issued. The resulting separation of markets may permit the owners of such rights, who are mostly firms, to pursue an oligopolistic or monopolistic pricing policy both within and between national territories. An unrestricted use of such rights would tend to hamper or even eliminate altogether the free flow of trade. On the other hand, by giving priority to the principle of free international trade, such exclusive rights might lose much or all of their economic value. How has this conflict been resolved?

A series of rulings by the Court of Justice has clarified this matter sufficiently, at least from an economic point of view:

(i) In the *Grundig–Consten* case (1966), the sole dealership of
Consten in France for the products of Grundig was supported by the
trademark G(rundig)INT(ernational). The mark 'GINT' was chosen
by Grundig because it had found out in the Netherlands that its
trademark 'Grundig' could not protect it from parallel imports
deriving from its own production in West Germany. The Court ruled
in this case that the trademark agreement constituted an infringement
of competition, because Consten used the 'GINT' mark to prevent
parallel imports.

(ii) In the *Parke-Davis* case (1968) a Dutch Court wanted to know
whether a patent issued in the Netherlands for a pharmaceutical
product could be upheld against imports from independent firms in
Italy, where there is no patent protection for such products, and
whether the answer would depend on the price differential between
the two countries. The Court ruled that the exercise of the patent
right with this aim did not infringe on Articles 85 and 86, moreover
that the price differential did not matter.

(iii) In the *Sirena* case (1971) the issue was different. Before the
Second World War an American firm granted the exclusive right to its
trademark to an Italian firm for Italy and a German firm for West
Germany. The Italian firm complained about imports with the same
trademark coming from West Germany and sought to stop these. It
was told that its behaviour was in conflict with the prohibition of
Article 85. Licence agreements between firms or with third parties
may not be used to stop parallel imports. Note that whereas in the
Grundig–Consten case the abuse of the trademark was condemned,
in the *Sirena* case the effect of market closure was held to be
contrary to the rules of competition.

(iv) In the case of *Deutsche Grammophon Gesellschaft* (D.G.G.)
(1971) a joint subsidiary of Philips (Holland) and Siemens (West
Germany), producing and selling records in E.E.C. countries, the
Court ruled that D.G.G. had no right to invoke the German copyright
law in order to stop parallel imports. D.G.G. had sold records to its
subsidiary Polydor S.A. in France under an exclusive licence. Now,
D.G.G. exercised resale price maintenance in West Germany, but
Polydor was unable to do so in France, as the practice is forbidden in
that country. The price differential for records in the two countries
was used by a Hamburg dealer to sell D.G.G. records in West
Germany below the fixed resale price. Polydor, the subsidiary, then
cut off sales to the Hamburg dealer, but the latter was able to get
supplies from a Hamburg wholesaler, who bought the records from a
Swiss firm supplied by Polydor France. And so the circuit was

closed again. While the European Court denied recourse to paragraph 85 of the German copyright law, resale price maintenance in West Germany crumbled and record prices fell.

(v) The last case in this field is *Kaffee H.A.G.* (1974). Due to post-war expropriation of the trademark, H.A.G., a Belgian company, became the distributor of this type of decaffeinated coffee for Belgium and Luxembourg on behalf of the Belgian producer who had bought both the producing company and the trademark H.A.G. from the sequestrator. Encouraged by the former rulings of the Court, the German firm Kaffee H.A.G., originator of the trademark and pre-war owner of the Belgian subsidiary, to which the trade-mark was assigned, started selling this coffee in Belgium. The Luxembourg Court then posed the question to the European Court whether a trademark-infringement would be barred by E.E.C. law and the Court replied affirmatively.

The important economic implications of these rulings seem to be as follows:

(1) No firm can use industrial property rights to restrain competition. In case of conflict, the competition rules prevail over nationally granted property rights.

(2) If no infringement (of Article 85(1)) is ascertainable, it has to be decided whether there is a conflict with other Treaty rules. This might be the case with Article 36, which leaves open the possibility of deviation from unrestricted free trade inside the Community by means of an appeal on industrial and commercial property rights *inter alia*. However, restraints may not be used to discriminate or to secretly hamper competition. This means that the existence of property rights will have to be distinguished from their use, which will have to be considered case by case.

(3) Property rights cannot be used for anything beyond their basic purpose. In the case of patents, for example, no tying agreements are allowed; the function of a trademark is to inform and guarantee the consumer of the origin and quality of the good.

(4) It makes a difference whether the owner or licencee(s) of a property right circulate the goods inside the Common Market (D.G.G. or Sirena), or whether independent firms sell the protected good on the licencee's market. In the latter case the protection given by the property right will be honoured; in the former the owner is not obliged to grant an unlimited number of licences, but, on the other hand, he is not entitled to restrain competition if and when he gives licences.

In conclusion, it follows that the European authorities have been rather realistic in their assessment of the concept of agreements.

On the one hand, they have covered both horizontal and vertical, explicit and implicit agreements. On the other hand, they have excluded minor agreements from the rules of competition policy. This does not suggest that there is no longer a cartel problem in Europe, given the possibly large number of agreements which have not been notified, but that the Commission's policy has become an efficient tool.

Exemptions and the general-interest criterion

The powers of the Commission have become clearly visible in Article 85(3), which deals with suspensions (individual cases) and exemptions (in group cases) from the prohibition of Article 85(1). As already mentioned, only the Commission is entitled to apply such dispensation and it is limited by the conditions laid down in Article 85(3).

The Treaty thus acknowledges that some agreements may have such beneficial effects of an objective economic nature that they can be approved. In American anti-trust law this is not possible. Does Article 85(3) allow anti-competitive agreements to slip through the general prohibition?

First, let us review the economic theory pertaining to this matter and second, let us see how the Commission has approached this task.

Williamson's model deals with an industrial sector which is monopolised (by a cartel or a merger, for example).[8] The monopoly, moreover, brings with it a reduction in the cost per unit of output. In Figure 7.4, the competitive price p_c is equal to the constant marginal cost MC_1 prevailing before monopolisation. Afterwards, the cost falls to MC_2, while the profit-maximising price is p_M. In order to appreciate whether the monopolisation is in the general interest, it is sufficient to compare areas A and B. Triangle A corresponds to the 'deadweight loss' (see Chapter 5), that is the loss of consumer welfare, not otherwise compensated for, and rectangle B corresponds to the savings in resources which become available for alternative use.

However, this simple cost—benefit analysis contains several recognised weaknesses:

(i) the analysis deals only with changes in price and output and neglects changes in product quality, range or durability;
(ii) the analysis is static and ignores the fact that in the evolutionary course of time an immediate advantage may be more than compensated for by lasting welfare losses;
(iii) the analysis is partial, ignoring relationships with other sectors;

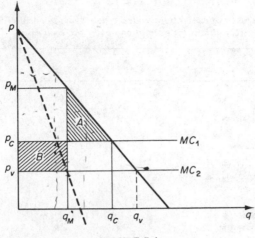

FIGURE 7.4

(iv) the analysis is in terms of certainty, neglecting the effects of risk or risk aversion;

(v) finally, the analysis supposes that the welfare gain can be obtained only by the restrictive action, while a still better outcome might be achieved by exerting public control over the monopoly— in this case, quantity q_v could be supplied, at price p_v which is a better solution than the market one.

Thus, in the present state of the theory, it can be argued that welfare economics cannot give an adequate solution to the welfare trade-off between competition and efficiency.

It is therefore interesting to see how the Commission has approached the job. Both approvals and rejections of applications for dispensation are instructive. Table 7.3 shows the Commission's refusals: in fifteen out of twenty-one cases no appreciable 'objective' advantages could be found, while in seven cases the restrictions imposed were not considered to be indispensable to the attainment of the stated objectives.

In the *Julien—Van Katwijk* case (1970) it was held that improve-ments in production or distribution or technical and economic progress cannot be promoted if competition is eliminated; in *Central Heating* (1972) similar claims advanced on behalf of an exclusive collective purchasing agreement were disposed of by the argument that the advantages were hardly discernible, while international trade was artificially curtailed; in the four cement cases, V.C.H. (1971), *Cement Agreement Nederland* (1972), N.C.H. (1971), *Cimbel* (1972), improvements were considered as possibly present (ranging

TABLE 7.3

Refusals of exemptions under Article 85(3) to end 1975
(conditions for exemption not met in each case)

	A	B	C	D
Grundig—Consten		x	x	x
Julien—Van Katwijk	x			x
German tile manufacturers	x			x
V.C.H.	x			x
N.C.H.	x	x	x	x
Central Heating	x			x
Pittsburgh Corning	x		x	x
Cement agreement Nederlands			x	x
Cimbel	x		x	x
Cut polyester fibres	x		x	x
S.C.P.A.—Kali und Salz				x
Kali und Salz/Kali—Chemie	x			x
Hot water boilers and geysers	x			x
Belgian wallpaper		x		x
G.G.G.—Wieland—Trefimétaux				x
Linoleum manufacturers	x	x		
Beyrard—A.O.I.P.	x			
Bomé	x			x
Aluminium	x			x
Haarden—en Kachelbureau			x	x
Sirdar—Phildar	x	x		x
TOTAL	15	6	7	19

A = improvement of production or distribution or the promotion of technical or economic progress.
B = fair share of the resulting benefit for customers.
C = no imposition of restrictions which are not indispensable.
D = no elimination of substantial amount of competition.

from 'extremely doubtful' to 'some improvements') but could not outweigh the effects of the restraint on competition which were clearly visible. Co-ordination of investments in order to avoid excess capacity was not allowed in the *Cimbel* case or in the *cut polyester fibre* case—the cartel was not considered to be better able than competition to solve the problem. Likewise, price and quota agreements and reciprocal exclusive dealing arrangements have hardly qualified for exemption so far. In the G.H.H.—Wielaud—*Trefimétaux* case (1975), which was unofficially terminated, the Commission stated that to allow the agreement was to invite uncontrollable consequences for competition. In the *Bomé* case (1975) the first condition was held not to be met, whereas the aim of the agreement was also to eliminate competition in the main brands of the cosmetics and toiletry industry.

On the positive side, a specialisation agreement between French cigarette-paper manufacturers, with a market share of 80 per cent in France and 70 per cent in Benelux, was exempted because the Commission found real competition from West German and Italian producers and potential competition from third countries' producers. Moreover, the agreed specialisation was not irreversible so that competition between the contracting partners could be revived. Countervailing power was also found to exist in the form of the tobacco monopolies and other large cigarette producers. In the *Henkel–Colgate* decision (1971), the argument was that the agreement could be exempted because the companies did not have a dominant position in the products concerned, even though they had important market shares in several countries. In view of the tight oligopolistic market structure, the Commission was of the opinion that developments had to be watched, and both companies were therefore obliged to inform it of all licence agreements concluded by the joint venture as well as interlocking directorates and shareholdings between the two groups.

The *Man–Saviem* case (1972) and the *A.C.E.C.–Berliet* case (1968) are also related essentially to agreements for joint research and development. Although the Commission was satisfied that the first condition of Article 85(3) would be met it was in doubt as to whether consumers would get a fair share of the benefits. In *A.C.E.C. –Berliet* the companies had only reached the manning stage so no benefit to consumers was yet discernible. In *Man–Saviem* the Commission maintained that consumer choice was reduced. In both cases the Commission relied on the forces of competition to look after the fulfilment of the exemption requirements.

From one point of view one might question the extent to which the Commission has really decided whether to grant or refine exemption on the basis of economic analysis or has more probably followed an 'impressionistic' approach influenced by the wording of agreements. Yet it could also be argued that the Commission has been able to more or less avoid the pitfalls of the public-interest criterion by relying heavily upon the fourth condition, that competition must not be eliminated for a substantial amount of the product concerned. Thus significant agreements which cannot be exempted as unimportant, and do have valuable economic or social effects, still cannot altogether escape the golden rule that competition must be maintained. The first clauses of Article 85(3) have no independent existence and depend on the fulfilment of the last clause, as the cases cited above demonstrate: the Latin saying *in cauda venenum* applies here.

Control of dominant positions

Article 86 of the Rome Treaty does not prohibit the creation or existence of a dominant position, but it does prohibit the abuse of that position. We shall examine this Article from the point of view of structure, conduct and performance.

A *dominant position* is not easy to describe in general terms. The simplest case is that in which a firm, by virtue of its market share, dominates the rest of the industry, which is composed of a fringe of small competitors unable to influence price. The dominant firm can then impose its price to be followed by the others. In Figure 7.5, total market demand is represented by DD'; the supply of the competitive fringe of firms at the price chosen by the dominant firm is SS'.

At a price OS', this supply is zero, because the price is lower than the minimum average variable cost of these firms and the dominant firm will supply the whole market demand. As the price rises, the output and sales of the fringe of firms will increase, being determined by the equality of price and (rising) marginal costs.

At price OG, the competitive fringe supplies the whole market demand and the dominant firm sells nothing. In between, it is possible to determine the demand supplied by the dominant firm by subtracting from total demand the fraction supplied by the fringe of firms. The demand curve facing the dominant firm is represented by the curve GBD, which has a marginal revenue curve MR.

Profit maximisation is achieved at a price Op at which $Oq = Z$ is sold by the dominant firm, while the fringe of firms sells $ZA = pT$.

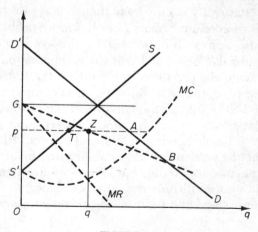

FIGURE 7.5

The total market is in equilibrium at quantities supplied and demanded at $pA = pZ + ZA$, and price will be appreciably higher than the competitive price.

But this price-leadership model suffers from several weaknesses:

(i) it supposes a knowledge of the supply of the competitive firms;

(ii) it does not make clear under what conditions a firm achieves or loses the price-leadership position; and

(iii) in essence it is static and does not take into account long-run profit maximisation.

Previously we have analysed dynamic models in which the dominant firm, by charging a high price, induces new firms to enter its industry (Chapter 6, p. 187). The conclusion was that a dominant firm, relying solely on its price policy without lower absolute costs, will lose its leading position in the long run, whether market demand is static or dynamic. And if uncertainty is introduced, the importance of barriers to entry for the dominant firm's position is reinforced. Then, to hold its leading place, the firm will have to use several strategies (including non-price behaviour) and to have a favourable cost structure. Simply having an important market share will not do.

The European authorities entrusted with competition policy have seen this too. The existence of a dominant position implies more than a preponderant market share linked with the power to influence market prices to some extent—it means market control: having the ability to exercise a major influence, without necessarily having a monopoly. A broad analysis is necessary, covering the level of barriers to entry, product differentiation, industry growth, and so on, as well as market share. Such a 'structural balance-sheet' was made effectively in the *Continental Can* case, which can be considered as a landmark anti-trust decision because of its emphasis on market structure.

Continental Can, the world's largest producer of metal cans and one of the most important producers of plastic and paper packagings, as well as of packaging machinery, created Europemballage—a wholly owned holding company—in 1970. Europemballage acquired an 85 per cent shareholding in Schmalbach Lubeca-Werke (S.L.W.), a German company, born of a previous merger between the two largest German producers of metal cans. S.L.W. is the leading continental European producer and has a share in the German market of between 70 and 90 per cent depending on the exact product and date specified. Europemballage made a public bid for the shares of Thomassen and Drijver-Verblifd (T.D.V.), the leading Benelux can producer (itself the result of an earlier merger between T.D.V. of Holland and Sobemi of Belgium), and acquired 80 per cent of these

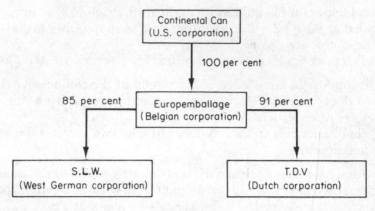

FIGURE 7.6

in addition to the 11 per cent it already held. (See Figure 7.6 for the presentation of this schematically).

The E.E.C. Commission condemned Continental Can and its European subsidiary on the basis of Article 86 for an abuse of their dominant position. In making this charge, the Commission took into account, the following points as well as market shares:

(i) the technologically advanced position of Continental Can, its patents and expert knowledge;

(ii) the broad assortment of products and wide geographical spread of its plants and depots;

(iii) the fact that it is a leading producer of machinery for making and filling cans;

(iv) the possibility of having recourse to international capital markets;

(v) the distances and transport costs facing the remaining West German producers as potential competitors for T.D.V.

Thus an over-all test integrating various structural features was made to support the charges levelled at the dominant American firm.

In this case, the principal difficulty was probably that of defining the market. Definition of the *product market* is rendered difficult, as we have seen (Chapter 3), by product differentiation and diversification, and this is borne out by the Continental Can case. In *The United States* v. *Continental Can Co.* [1964] the company argued that the purpose of its merger with Hazel—Atlas was to diversify into the glass-container field. The Supreme Court rejected the idea that a conglomerate merger was involved which would not distort competition and stated that although metal containers and glass containers were separate industries, the inter-industry competition between the manufacturers of these two types of containers meant that, for the purpose of judging the merger, metal and glass containers constituted a single product market. On the contrary, before the European Court of Justice, Continental Can (maybe convinced by the judgement of the U.S. Supreme Court) put forward the idea that the metal-container and the glass-container markets do not constitute separate lines of commerce: 'it would be notably inaccurate to say that the contents of metal containers can be sterilised or pasteurised more rapidly, after closure, than glass containers'.

The Commission lost its case against Continental Can because the Court decided that the Commission had underestimated competition from substitute products. However, the Court agreed that in principle Article 86 could be applied to mergers.

From the product-market point of view, it is also worth while noting that the law could be applied to *conglomerate firms*. The various criteria used for determining a dominant position make this perfectly clear, and the Commission has, in its proposal for the regulation of concentrations, explicitly stated that conglomerate operations will be covered by the rule.

The second aspect of definition of the market is *geographical*. Article 86 requires a dominant position 'inside the common market or a substantial part thereof'. In the decisions relating to G.E.M.A. (1971), and *Continental Can*, the Commission established that a single country (West Germany) may constitute a substantial part. But the difficulty is to establish in each case the extent of the market within which competition really makes itself felt. This means, in effect, that market delineation in the geographical sense has to be an *ad hoc* affair; sometimes market boundaries will be found to lie within a country, sometimes they may extend to the Common Market as a whole, while in other cases the world market will have to be taken into account. This is all that can be said in general, for in economic analysis there is no sense in automatically equating market boundaries with national frontiers. A market's limits may be as erratic as the lines on a contour map.

The Commission seems to go beyond the purely structural characteristics of a market to determine the existence of a dominant position. In its memorandum on concentration, it stated that a dominant position cannot be uniquely defined by referring to the market share of a firm or to other *quantifiable elements of market structure.*[9] It asserted that 'market domination is primarily a matter of economic potency, or the ability to exert on the operation of the market an influence that is substantial and also in principle foreseeable for the dominant enterprise'. According to this line of reasoning, the ultimate test of a dominant position is based upon the firm's ability to behave persistently in a manner which would be impossible in a competitive market, and not upon the characteristics of market structure. The concept of a separate conduct test of dominant position is much more controversial. In the Continental Can case the plaintiff (C.C.) argued before the Court that the existence of such independent conduct — possibly in the form of overpricing, scarcity of goods or deterioration of quality — was not proved anywhere in the decision of the Commission. The Commission replied that the proof of dominant position in this case did not depend on demonstrating the existence of the types of conduct mentioned by the plaintiffs, since such types of conduct represent the 'abuse of a dominant position'. But after saying this the Commission does not specify what types of conduct could show the existence of a dominant position without constituting an abuse.

In fact, either market conduct is not anti-competitive, and then it is not possible to infer the existence of a dominant position, or it is anti-competitive, in which case it cannot be distinguished from an abuse.

The concept of abuse. Clearly the concept of abuse needs to be analysed further. This concept was interpreted in the 1965 memorandum on concentration as follows: an abuse exists if the dominant firm exploits its ability to acquire advantages which it would not be able to get under effective competition. Some examples are given in Article 86 itself: the imposition of inequitable prices, the restrictions of output, discrimination or tying sales. One of the first applications of Article 86 was in the *G.E.M.A.* case (1971). This corporation deals with the author's rights with regard to musical works and has a virtual monopoly in the German market. G.E.M.A.'s members were, to all intents and purposes, tied for life to the society and were prevented from granting the use of their rights to any other society. Furthermore, various forms of discriminatory practice were exercised against citizens of other member states.

Among other things, the Commission's decision gave each member of G.E.M.A. the right to resign at the end of each year and recover his full rights and to divide these rights according to country and the different media involved (for example general performing rights, broadcasting rights and so on) so that each member could freely choose which society to grant his rights to in accordance with the royalties offered by each. Similar decisions were taken in 1974 against *S.A.C.E.M.* and *S.A.B.A.M.*, corporations with monopolies in authors' rights with regard to musical works in France and Belgium respectively.

Not all practices are so obviously abusive and it is not always easy to classify an observed trade practice as abusive, even if it is among those mentioned in Article 86. Sometimes a given practice is not only compatible with competition but may actually enhance it; for instance, the more successful the price discrimination, the greater is the incentive towards increased output. The final result of effective price discrimination might be a total output that falls not far short of the competitive level. Thus monopoly that cannot discriminate may lead to a more serious misallocation of economic resources than one that can. [10] In its first application of Article 86 to a price-discrimination case, Chiquita (December 1975), the Commission's decision illustrates the difficulties of such an analysis.

Where a dominant position exists, it may even be hard to determine whether a specific practice exploits the position and promotes inefficient performance, or in fact reduces inefficiency to a greater or lesser extent.

It can at least be said that once a dominant firm, defined by a broad set of structural features, exists, whatever its origin, there is a very strong probability that there will be some market conduct showing market power and resulting in some form of resource misallocation.

It is only by assuming that the firm will not exploit its position, and will behave 'as if' there were effective competition, that the distinction between a dominant position and its abuse holds. But to ensure such 'good' behaviour would require the exercise of much more direct public interference than that usually implied by anti-trust policy.

This is why it may be argued that it is more important to attack the conduct which creates or consolidates a dominant position than that which exploits it. Here we find the origin of a controversy which has been crucial for the future of European anti-trust policy.

Many lawyers consider that Article 86 is not concerned with maintaining competitive market structure, because it permits the existence of dominant positions. It prohibits certain forms of direct misuse of power which would damage customers' interests without going into the structural phenomena of the creation or growth of the dominant position.

The second paragraph of Article 86 lists the various types of conduct by enterprises that are considered abuses. . . . From this listing it can be inferred that practices of the type referred to in Article 86 are those having a direct effect on the market. The express reference to the prejudicial effects which the practices referred to would have for consumers, shows that the conduct concerned cannot be just an enterprise's internal structural conduct (plaintiffs in the Continental Can Case).

This position is supported by Joliet, who writes: 'Article 86 is not concerned with the manner in which domination is acquired, maintained or increased whether by coercive or exclusionary unilateral practices or by mergers. Its goal is not to preseve competitive processes but to ensure that market domination is not actually exploited to the detriment of utilisers'.[11]

Economically, this approach to anti-trust policy can be criticised for taking a static view of the relationship between market structure, market conduct and market performance. As we have seen in Chapter 6, a dynamic approach takes into account the feedback effect of market conduct, which affects market structure and in time changes the competitive situation.

Horizontal and vertical mergers, pooling of patents and extensive advertising may be dangerous, not so much as means of exploiting the actual market power of the firm at a moment in time, but as means of increasing such power through changes in the market structure. For example, it would be very short-sighted to prohibit a price policy which harms the consumer directly but at the same time to ignore the creation of monopoly positions, which by their nature transform the conditions of supply and demand in a way that, in the end (whether by the prices charged, quantities produced or various forms of expenditure), will harm consumers' welfare. Once an anti-competitive structure is built up, there are always alternative means to realise the same end: 'as soon as one specific set of collusive practices is found illegal and enjoined, another set may be invented, not nominally violating the first injunction, to accomplish the original purpose'.[12]

It could be argued therefore that anti-trust policy should apply to practices (within the market or outside it) which are the result of monopoly power as long as they cause harm to consumers, directly or indirectly. Such a view is supported by several lawyers. According to Canellos and Silber, 'impropriety of exploitation' must be judged in the light of the general goals of the Community and the basic mechanisms relied upon to achieve those goals.[13] Thus Article 86 may be used against mergers which involve the consolidation or extension of a dominant position, and such transactions are forbidden as 'improper' if, by eliminating effective competition, they prevent competition from performing the role assigned to it in the Treaty.

Analysing the examples of abusive behaviour provided in Article 86 itself, Cardon and Herbert show that predatory and exclusionary practices typically tend to create and preserve a more concentrated market structure than would otherwise exist, and to raise barriers to the entry of new sellers into the market.[14] Even if the actual prices

and qualities of the goods concerned are fair, such practices are
abusive because they tend to create and perpetuate an anti-
competitive market structure.

This is the line of reasoning followed by the Commission. In the
Continental Can case, it stated that since the concept of abuse is not
defined more precisely in Article 86, the Community's objectives set
out in the Treaty of Rome must be considered before the examples
of abuse given in Article 86 itself. An abuse is present where an
enterprise conducts itself in a way that is 'objectively' wrong in
relation to the goals of the Treaty:

> It is not, for example, a question of whether plaintiffs . . . as they
> claim . . . paid a fair price to TDV shareholders; what is important
> is whether plaintiffs through this acquisition virtually eliminated
> the actual or at least potential, competition in these products
> between TDV and SLW prior to the acquisition.

Thus the Commission considers that the market structure as such
has to be protected: a change in the supply structure which virtually
eliminates the alternative sources of supply to the consumer appears
to be an abuse in itself. Although the Court annulled the Commission's decision in the *Continental Can* case — mainly because the
relevant market was not adequately defined — it very clearly confirmed the soundness of its interpretation: Article 86 may be
applied to mergers. A similar decision, again confirmed by the
European Court (1974), was taken in the *Z.O.J.A.* case where an
American firm (C.S.C.) and its Italian subsidiary (I.C.I.), holding a
monopoly *de facto* for an intermediate product, withheld supply
from a firm which competed with I.C.I. in the market to a drug made
from the intermediate product (see Chapter 2, p. 64).

However, ambiguities remain. According to the Court, it can be
considered an abuse if an enterprise extends a dominant position to
the point where the objectives of the Treaty are threatened through a
substantial alteration of the supply situation, so that the consumer's
freedom of action on the market is seriously jeopardised. Hence, to
be condemned, the extension must amount to a substantial alteration
of the market structure. This implies that the criterion for 'abuse' is
in fact quantitative.

Even if the alteration of market structure is substantial, it could
besides be argued, in line with Section 2 of the *Sherman Act*, that the
abuse of a dominant position also requires that the consolidation of
the dominant position be wilful rather than the consequence of a
superior product, business acumen, or historic accident leading to
internal growth.

The Court, however, has stated that a company in a dominant position cannot improve it by any means whatever: 'the strengthening of the position held by the enterprise can be an abuse and prohibited under Article 86 of the Treaty regardless of the methods or means used to attain it', if the degree of dominance affects competition.

Does this imply that a firm has the right to acquire a dominant position through internal growth and that any consolidation of that position once it exists, whether by internal growth or by acquisition or merger, could be condemned? The Commission does not clarify this difficult point in its draft regulation on concentration, which states:

> the proposed regulation only covers concentrations which bring previously independent undertakings under the same control. External growth . . . frequently takes place independently of the competitive capacity of the undertakings concerned. Internal growth, on the other hand, which does not fall under this regulation is as such not subject to any restriction in any antitrust legislation.

There appears to be some inconsistency between this statement and that of the Court quoted above, but the Commission's position seems now to prevail.

The general-interest criterion. Article 86, unlike Article 85, makes no provision for an exemption based on a public-interest criterion. It could be argued, however, that activities which promote technical or economic progress or improve production or distribution are not likely to be considered abusive.

Thus it would be through the interpretation of the concept of 'abusive' or 'improper' advantage that a public-interest criterion could be developed in the application of Article 86, although so far there has been no guidance concerning public-interest criteria.

The draft regulation on concentration contains no further guidance on this matter. According to Article 1, para. 3, exemption from the general prohibition of paragraph (1) may be granted to mergers 'which are indispensable to the attainment of an objective which is given priority treatment in the common interest of the Community'. The general philosophy underlying this exemption rule could indicate some scepticism about whether competition will lead to optimum economic performance, but again no precise definition of the preferred objective is proposed.

As we have seen in Chapter 5, and in presenting Williamson's model, it is not easy to interpret the economic meaning of observed performance, to find systematic links between market structure or firms' characteristics and macroeconomic or microeconomic targets, and to take into account the multidimensional nature of consumers' welfare.

For example, high monopolistic profits are not always readily distinguished from the results of efficient management or of highly risky activities or low profits due to competitive pressure from poor performance produced by X-inefficiency (see Chapter 5). There is no scientific criterion to determine whether, on balance, allocating a greater percentage of resources than under more competitive conditions to activities such as research outweighs the welfare losses resulting from the static inefficiencies of the reduced competition.

In the same way, it was shown (in Chapter 5) that the main consequence of larger size is to reduce the variability of profit rates and hence the firm's exposure to risk. But the existing literature in welfare economics offers almost no assistance in answering the operational questions of policy raised by the risk-avoidance behaviour of large firms. And indeed the possible welfare effects of these forms of risk-avoidance are various; some reduce the rate of economic progress, some increase welfare through the pooling of risks and some have primarily redistributive effects.

These illustrations confirm the fact that using a 'common interest' of the Community's criterion requires the Commission and the Court to make a political choice. In trying to judge cases on the basis of their contribution to macro or microperformance, the European authorities make competition policy a part of their over-all economic and industrial policy.

Our own point of view is that in so far as the intention is to preserve a role for competition policy in Europe, it would be better to delimit clearly the function of each policy instrument. The job of the anti-trust authorities would then be to examine mergers or agreements on the basis that, to escape the prohibition of the law, they must not significantly reduce competition. The premise of this policy is that competition is the best way to serve the public interest and that the legality of market conduct depends on the extent of its anti-competitive effect. It must of course be possible to question such a premise but this should be done at a different level of public policy, leaving the enforcement of competition law to an independent institution in order to safeguard against political pressures and bureaucratic compromises.

APPLICATION OF ARTICLES 85 AND 86 TO FOREIGN FIRMS

The impressive rise of foreign direct investment in Europe during the past decade has taken several forms, such as the expansion of existing operations and the creation of new European subsidiaries and affiliates, but most frequently it has involved the acquisition of interest in companies domiciled in the E.E.C. or entry into joint ventures with E.E.C. enterprises. As shown in Chapter 3, the competitive effects of foreign investment vary, so that the application of strict anti-trust policy to foreign firms remains a necessity. Such a policy is *a priori* the least discriminatory for foreign business and is more likely to improve the welfare of the Community than piecemeal nationalist measures.

Still, the implementation of an appropriate and purposeful European policy on competition which extends to enterprises from non-member countries on a fair basis is not an easy task, because it may require a delicate trade-off between the effectiveness of the policy and the limits imposed by international law.[15]

Article 85

Several decisions of the Commission and the Court of Justice have clarified the issue somewhat, but uncertainties remain. Concerning *restrictive agreements,* the text of Article 85, para. 1, is quite clear; it prohibits agreements and concerted practices which are likely to affect trade between member states and which have the *objective effect of preventing, restraining, or distorting competition within the Common Market.* This rule seems to have a double implication. On the one hand, agreements occurring outside the Community or initiated by foreign enterprises which have effects within the Community are subject to the application of Article 85; while on the other hand agreements occurring inside the Common Market but which have external effects only are not affected.

The Court, in its judgement on 25 November 1971 (*Beguelin Import Co.*), confirms that 'the fact, for one of the undertakings involved in the agreement, that it is located in a non-member country, is no obstacle to the application of Article 85 where the agreement has effects within the Common Market'. However, there is a vast difference between the statement of broad principle and their proper application to the complexities of the real world.

The imputation of the effects is an important problem for foreign enterprise. The simplest situation is of course one in which the foreign firm has a formal corporate presence in the Common Market, such as a branch, in which case the application of Article 85 is straightforward. The solution is not so evident when a subsidiary is involved.

In the already mentioned *Dyestuffs* cases (1972), the Court of Justice, commenting on the arguments presented by three appellant firms whose head offices were outside the Community, held that:

(1) the price increases related to competition between producers operating in the Common Market; and (2) the appellants had compulsorily determined prices and other sales conditions for their subsidiaries in the Community. Its conclusion was that 'even if undertakings from non-member countries act in the Community through legally separate subsidiaries, the legal separateness of such companies cannot be adduced as evidence that their behavior on the market, for the purposes of the application of the rules of competition, is not uniform'. Hence foreign companies may violate the Treaty without having a formal presence in Europe, to the extent that the conduct of their subsidiaries is attributable to the parent company. An important aspect of this opinion is that neither the Court nor the Commission requires that the subsidiary be wholly owned by the parent company; they require only that the latter be able to exercise a determinant influence on the policies of the subsidiary.

Finally, one should consider the case of foreign companies without branches, subsidiaries or affiliates in the Common Market which have merely an export association selling to Common Market buyers. It seems that such conduct might be interpreted as violating Article 85. A recent opinion of the Commission regarding the practice of restraining imports of Japanese products into the Community stated a principle expressing this broad extra-territorial reach. This opinion states that arrangements between firms or associations of firms curtailing imports on the Community market of items from non-member countries, or controlling these imports (for example in terms of quantity or price), may be prohibited under Article 85, para. 1.[16]

This broad application of the concept of 'effects' reaches the limits of jurisdiction. Indeed, by relying on this concept, it would be possible to argue that the E.E.C. authorities have the right to order a foreign enterprise to sell to the Community, or to forbid foreign producers to discourage the purchase of European-made automobiles under a 'Buy-American' or 'Buy-Japanese' programme.

Article 86

As far as the application of Article 86 condemning abuses of dominant positions to foreign firms is concerned, the Commission has adopted the same attitude as for Article 85. In 1972, in an action against the United States, *Commercial Solvents Corporation* (C.S.C.) and its Italian subsidiary *Istituto Chemioterapica Italiano* (I.C.I.), previously analysed, the Commission found that C.S.C. had a *de facto* world monopoly for the manufacture and sale of the relevant raw material. In this case the Commission took into account not

merely the firm's position in the E.E.C. but its power at the world
level in determining the existence of a dominant position in the
Common Market. This implies that the activities and the importance
of a firm outside the Common Market might well be relevant for
implementing Article 86.

Second, the Commission ruled that the ownership of 50 per cent
of the corporate capital of I.C.I. by C.S.C. and the existence of
interlocking directorships between I.C.I. and C.S.C. showed that
C.S.C. had exercised the power of control over I.C.I. For the
implementation of Article 86, the two companies were therefore to
be regarded as constituting only one economic unit.

The Court confirmed this opinion in the *Continental Can* case,
saying that 'the fact that Continental does not have its seat in the
territory of one of the Member States is not sufficient to remove this
enterprise from the application of Community Law'.

Hence the Commission has a strong basis for controlling the
industrial combination movement in the Common Market and the
possible related abuses from foreign firms. It is well known that
firms from non-member countries have more operations involving
two or more member countries in the E.E.C. than firms originating
in member countries themselves (see Chapter 2), and that it is mainly
through wholly owned subsidiaries, shareholdings and joint ventures
that these foreign firms penetrate the Common Market. Once the
Commission and the Court consider that a transaction, which
directly or indirectly affects the Common Market, could be
submitted to Article 86, the strategies of companies from non-
member countries will be more directly examined. This situation is
reinforced by automatically holding a foreign parent company
responsible for the conduct of its subsidiaries.

A further step in this line of thought would be to speculate that
the Commission could instigate action against foreign firms which
have no European subsidiaries but which occupy a dominant
position and compete in the Common Market. This view, which
would generally be considered as an improper extension of the
territorial principle of jurisdiction, could be taken by the Commission in the light of its attitude towards export agreements. Nevertheless, so far the European Court has required not only an effect
within the Common Market but also that the conduct being
investigated itself occurred in the market through a subsidiary.

The draft 'Regulation on the Control of Concentrations Between
Undertakings' takes the same approach; its basic provision states that

> any transaction which has the direct or indirect effect of bringing
> about a concentration between undertakings or groups of under-
> takings, *at least one of which is established in the Common*

Market, whereby they acquire or enhance the power to hinder
effective competition in the Common Market or in a substantial
part thereof, is incompatible with the Common Market insofar as
the concentration may affect trade between Member States
(Article 1).

To conclude, with respect to Article 85, the activities of foreign,
especially U.S. firms in the E.E.C. were largely unaffected because of
two special circumstances. First, the *Sherman Act* has a broader
scope than Article 85 in that it is applicable to *all* restraints of
competition affecting American commerce. Further, U.S. law, in
contrast to Article 85(3), makes no distinction between so-called
'good' and 'bad' cartels. The severity of the American law, then, may
have been the primary factor preventing U.S. firms from joining local
cartel arrangements. Second, American-controlled enterprises
operating in the E.E.C. are linked with other affiliates outside the
Common Market and are usually strong enough to remain outside
cartels. The strategy of entering and expanding in the Common
Market through alternative forms of business maneouvres, such as
acquisitions, mergers, and joint ventures, was more or less safe
during this time because of the non-application of Article 86.

However, the *Continental Can* case and the tenor of the
Commission's draft regulation on concentration suggest that, to the
extent that foreign firms usually act within the Common Market by
means of acquisitions tending to increase concentration, there will be
stricter control by the European authorities in future.

Competition policy towards foreign firms has wider implications
because of the growing interdependence of national economies
through multinational corporations and their subsidiaries. The
behaviour of the large foreign firm operating on an international
scale will increasingly affect the Common Market, at least indirectly.
If the European authorities are determined to implement an effective
anti-trust policy along the lines previously discussed, they are in real
danger of transgressing the limits of European jurisdiction under
international law and of creating international conflict in which the
companies will be caught in the middle.

It appears then that this situation calls for some sort of international collaboration beyond the Common Market. In fact the
Commission, like the member states, has associated itself with the
work undertaken by the O.E.C.D., which has drafted a code of good
competitive conduct for multinational enterprise and of building up
international co-operation to control their behaviour.

CONCLUSION

The philosophy on which the E.E.C. anti-trust policy has been
developed is that competition is a basic stimulant to economic

activity. The way in which the European legislation is enforced in practice confirms the determination to prohibit any form of substantial restriction to competition, whether it be cartels, abuses of dominant positions or concentrations of industry, either by public or private restrictions, by European or non-European firms.

Until recently the greatest success has been in enforcing competition policy in the field of restrictive agreements, while Article 86, in effect, remained an empty threat. The most radical attacks have been made against market-sharing, price-fixing and the allocation of quotas, practices for which, to this date, there has not been a single case where exemptions have been granted. Since 1971, with the Continental Can case and from the tenor of the Commission's draft regulation on concentration, a new situation has emerged: the control of market power and of its undesirable consequences has become a central question for European policy.

All this does not mean that the European approach is becoming similar to the American attitude. It could be argued that in the United States, for cultural and political as well as economic reasons, competition is regarded as a 'way of life' or an end in itself. In the E.E.C., on the other hand, competition is not seen as an end and even not as the only way of achieving the fundamental purposes of the Community. Other instruments may be used in situations where competition in itself is not enough to obtain the required results without too much delay and intolerable social tension. Clear examples of the concept are found in Article 85 (section 3) of the Treaty, where a distinction is drawn between good and bad cartels from a public-interest point of view and in the draft regulation on concentrations, which accepts concentrations substantially reducing effective competition, but which help the attainment of important objectives of the Community. This is an expression of the emphasis given in Europe to values such as stability, social security, quality of work and equality in development, even at the expense of allocative efficiency. The anti-trust policy is consequently compromised by these other economic policies orientated towards achieving these other goals.

In order to safeguard the principal role of anti-trust policy in the Common Market, it is therefore necessary to achieve a clearer delineation of functions and to establish a more autonomous agency concerned with competition policy, leaving the role of promoting regional expansion, full employment, price stability and similar goals to other more suitable policy weapons.

8

Roles of Industrial Policy

Many firms will, as we have seen, try to replace the uncertainties of the competitive process by co-operation or concerted conduct. The large firm is inclined to control its environment by means of some kind of private planning, assuring it more predictable market structure and performance. The public authorities, confronted with these tendencies, adopt two types of policies: on the one hand, they use anti-trust policy to maintain market uncertainty and competitive pressure; on the other hand, they have recourse to industrial policy inspired by sectoral or regional considerations which often results in some form of planning agreement between industry and the state. It is the object of the present chapter to examine the contents of such a policy, its relationship with anti-trust policy and implications for the Community as a whole.

There are several reasons why industrial policy in Europe merits attention and discussion. First, some aspects of an industrial policy were already present in the Coal and Steel Treaty, covering two relatively homogeneous sectors of industry. In comparison, the E.E.C. industrial structures are much more heterogeneous, which prevents the Commission from simply copying the policies of the previous High Authority, which moreover had supra-national powers. Thus the coal crisis of 1958 was solved by means of a systematic reconversion of the activities of the old mine-working regions, when the competitive solution would have generated large-scale social strife. Policy towards the steel industry has tried to dampen the effects of cyclical fluctuations, to promote modernisation and restructuring of firms and to control the self-imposed export restriction of international producers.

Second, new technological developments have become important since the Treaty was signed in 1956, and it seems that the requirements for participation in some of the newer sectors are so heavy — both technologically and financially — that public intervention is unavoidable — which raises the problem of to whom and under what conditions such aid should be given.

Third, industrial policy has acquired prominence because of the ending of the fast and spontaneous expansion which characterised the 1950s and 1960s. Several sectors of industry are shifting into lower gear, or have even gone into decline, and so the social and economic problems of restructuring industry have attracted attention.

Finally, there is the long-standing regional imbalance between centre and periphery within the Community: the inability of the mainly agricultural areas to attract industrial establishment into these areas, coupled with the low value of welfare indicators, such as *per capita* income, employment prospects, health and medical care, housing, and so on.

These various reasons, taken together, indicate that the *main problems in the industrial field are of a regional and sectoral nature.*

GOALS OF EUROPEAN INDUSTRIAL POLICY

The first manifestations of industrial policy in the E.E.C. context go back to 1964, when the concept of a medium-term economic policy was introduced. The Commission insisted on the necessity for public intervention in order to improve the Community's industrial structure. It created a *Directorate for Industrial Policy* with the task of formulating the goals of a common industrial policy and co-ordinating the intervention of member states. Also, sectoral discussions were held with industrialists, trade-union representatives and national experts in various industries such as aircraft construction, shipbuilding, data-processing, paper and textiles.

In about 1970 the need to define a general policy with respect to industry became widely felt and such a policy was laid down in the *Memorandum on Industrial Policy* (also called the Colonna Memorandum, 1970) sent by the Commission to the Council. It stated that, as the transitional stage had ended, the goal of the next phase of industrial policy should be to permit industry to draw maximum benefit from the existence and size of the Common Market. This broad goal was narrowed down by some negative statements:

(i) it was not envisaged that all industrial development problems should be regulated at the Community level, but rather that industrial dynamism should be freed from remaining obstacles;

(ii) it was not considered necessary to retard industrial growth in the most industrialised sectors and countries, but to achieve a compromise between the interests of member states;

(iii) it was not thought to be opportune to choose between a horizontal policy dealing with a wide range of different industries on the one hand, and a more interventionist sectoral policy concentrating on a few sectors on the other hand — instead it seemed more important to stimulate progress and innovation in all sectors, while admitting that particular industries (whether emerging or declining) would need special treatment.

The main specific goals were given as follows:

(i) improvement in working conditions to prevent ordinary
workers from turning their backs on the industrial system;

(ii) more active participation of employees in the definition of
the goals and actions of firms;

(iii) protection of the natural environment in order to locate
industrial development so as to take account of the costs of regional
concentration;

(iv) more harmonious division of the world's wealth, including
a transfer of industrial activities towards developing nations.

Among the means mentioned of achieving these goals were the
completion of the Common Market through the elimination of
technical obstacles, the opening of Markets for public activities, the
abolition of fiscal frontiers, unification of the legal, fiscal and
financial frameworks, the restructuring of firms so that transnational
European firms could be formed, new policies to ease the redistribution of employments, the exploitation of innovations and the
improvement of business management.

Despite its good point, the *Memorandum* made a not wholly
satisfactory impression. There was a sharp contrast between the
detailed information about the position of industry in the Common
Market and the vagueness of the proposed policies.

In the *Declaration of Paris* (October 1972) the heads of national
governments subscribed to such an industrial and technological
policy which was once again expressed in rather general terms, apart
from the desire to co-ordinate policies at the Community level and
to have a precise timetable and finance settled before 1 January
1974. Moreover, the slow progress towards a joint statement of
principle is understandable in view of the enlargement of the
Community, the diverging views of the old member states (neo-
liberalism in West Germany, interventionism in France and Italy) and
the projects undertaken outside of the Common Market context
(Concorde, Airbus, and so on). On the basis of the *Declaration of
Paris*, the Commission drew up the *Spinelli Report*, a programme for
industrial and technological policy. A number of topics were
mentioned which it was considered that the Council and member
states should adopt; accordingly, a timetable was proposed for the
years up to 1977:

(1) Several proposals for directives to eliminate technical
obstacles to trade and to harmonise national regulations were
advanced. The achievement of important qualitative goals concerning
public health and environmental protection was also foreseen.

(2) The Commission asked the national states to promote a greater transparency of national markets for public-sector purchasing. Rules for the publication of public contracts in the *Official Journal of the Communities* were established.

(3) A group of regulations governing the establishment of European transnational firms, able to compete effectively and secure economies of scale, were proposed. Harmonsation of company law, as well as the appearance of new legal forms, such as the European company, the European group of co-operating firms and the joint enterprise (reserved previously to the nuclear domain), figured prominently among the proposals. For small and medium-sized firms development contracts on the Common Market level were proposed which would serve to sustain and promote co-operation between firms belonging to different member states.

(4) Special problems were recognised to exist in technologically advanced industries and in structurally weak sectors. The Commission was especially concerned about the heavy investment-goods sector, in which the long-term provision with raw materials, energy and key products must be assured. This problem is currently being investigated.

(5) The necessity to bring about coherence with other policies was also recognised, but no concrete proposals were made, apart from the institution of a European Social Fund.

In summary, the main characteristics of an industrial policy based upon the above view is that it has to specify and solve the problems of structural change in the economy. Such structural problems are primarily sectoral or regional; consequently, industrial policy will have to operate somewhere between the micro and macro levels of economic activity. Its task is to create conditions such that the necessary structural transformations can be carried out optimally. The need for transformation arises from changes occurring in the process of industrial development: technological changes, shifts in demand, maturing and declining industries, and so on. The required adaptations take time, so that industrial policy is essentially long term.

Against this background a structural policy has a double function. First, it expresses the view that a market economy is more than the functioning of a competitive process. Competition, for all its positive values, sometimes has undesirable social and economic repercussions, while on the other hand a number of essential new avenues can only be opened up by the market mechanism.

Second, if cost—benefit analysis indicates that policy interventions can be advantageously made in some cases, it would be unwise to abstain for dogmatic reasons alone. The essential prerequisite is of course that either the analysis can be quantitatively convincing — which is rare — or that there is democratic agreement on the political choice made.

It is from the above point of view that we will discuss the relationship between competition policy and industrial policy.

INDUSTRIAL POLICY AS A COMPLEMENT TO ANTI-TRUST POLICY

According to the liberal point of view, the range of a policy of structural transformation can only be determined by admitting the primary responsibility of entrepreneurs to take decisions in a market economy. This approach to the problem means that a Common Market industrial policy is a mixed bag of studies and measures to change competitive conditions so as to make competition more effective.

At a first stage this involves *the promotion of conditions which favour competition.* The diffusion throughout the Common Market of technological, economic and statistical *information*, the dissemination on a general scale of what is known only on a partial basis (for example by means of building up adequate industrial statistics, firm comparisons, technological information, and so on), eases competitive forces and accelerates adaptations.

In the same sense obstacles to the free and rapid *mobility* of factors of production must be spotted and dealt with. Professional education, and re-education, the transferability of unemployment benefits and pensions are some examples.

On the level of the industries themselves the structure—conduct—performance scheme can be used as a guide. Policy should aim at the elimination of artificial or institutional *barriers to trade,* such as diverging technical, safety or health standards, discriminatory fiscal charges, closed public markets or state or banking regulations which distort conditions for the acquisition of financial means by private firms.

As regards *concentration*, industrial policy means the promotion of regroupings or the promotion of co-operation between small firms where this is necessary to achieve effective competition. Firms may be too small to achieve the necessary economies of scale or to carry out desired innovations. It is not always true that spontaneous forces will lead to optimal outcomes, at least not in some European countries. Large outsider firms (that is those coming in from other industries) will sometimes set in motion a concentration process to 'rationalise' an industry so that small firms are forced out of the field. But it must be emphasised that in this view public policy will

be needed to restructure industry in only a limited number of cases
and must always be used with caution. Otherwise, as we shall see
later in this chapter, a conflict between competition and industrial
policies will emerge, as was the case in the United Kingdom in the
late 1960s (when the Industrial Organisation Corporation, whose job
was to encourage mergers, co-existed with the Monopolies Commission, which was meant to control mergers and monopolies operating
against the public interest). Industrial intervention here is only
sensible if it sustains competition and does not push it into the
background.

At a second stage, an industrial policy has to get around competitive *market failures or deviations from market mechanisms*. It is
basically useful in three cases:

(1) Where competition does not work or cannot be made
workable. Such cases concern *monopolies or tight oligopolies, which
are based on technological or organisational considerations*. A change
in the structure of the industry would then imply a less optimal
situation, and society has to choose between greater efficiency with
monopoly and less efficiency with competition. National states have
often solved this dilemma by means of regulation or nationalisation
of the monopolistic firms. But nationalisation at the level of the
Common Market is not a feasible solution, so regulation is the only
answer. The firm's conduct will then be influenced by regulations
about pricing, investment, employment, and so on.

An additional advantage of such regulatory types of policies is
that they can be changed or withdrawn according to the circumstances. The monopoly position may be undermined by shifts in
market demand or by technological development or by firms
entering the Common Market from abroad.

On the other hand, in contrast to the French experience, U.S.
experience is not at all favourable as to whether such monopolised
industries can be efficiently regulated. Very often the question
becomes 'who regulates whom?' and regulating boards may be turned
from industry supervisors into industry spokesmen.

(2) The second deviation from the market mechanism occurs
when the process of adapting a *structurally declining industry* would
be accelerated with socially or regionally devastating effects. Social
tensions will then develop and the market economy will be dis-
credited. Moreover, the argument of so-called 'hardline' free-traders,
that competition should be left to do its work, is hardly acceptable.
For such wholesale destructions often have a habit of generating
protectionism, financial handouts from governments, minimum-price
cartels and other measures which prevent adaptation. The cumula-

tion of irrational and mistaken measures may virtually paralyse the industry and make the final outcome still less desirable. Also, accelerated decline may bring vertically or horizontally related industries into difficulties and endanger otherwise sound firms. The prevention of these consequences may promote welfare as much as the elimination of untenable activities would. From such examples — which are not at all unreal — it follows that industrial policy should aim at the optimal rate of transformation of industrial structure.

The necessity for co-ordinated and harmonised Community policy is essential in these types of deviation. Socio-political pressure in member states and the relative ease with which aid, protection and restrictions can be given and applied mean that national disparities can easily evolve. If national measures are to be severely limited, the Community must offer a coherent policy of its own in replacement.

The main question then, is what the criteria for an effective industrial policy for declining sectors should be. First, the difficulties should relate to the whole industry or region and should have a decisive adverse effect.

Second, aid or protection should be given only if reorganisation or improvement can be achieved within a reasonable time period and with a reasonable probability of success.

Third, if no such prospects exist, the aid or protection should only be given to assure an orderly retreat, that is to prevent cumulative negative effects; otherwise the aid or protection is wasted.

Only if the above criteria are strictly applied can an industrial policy be recommended as a systematic way of dealing with the above deviations from the market mechanism.

(3) The third type of deviation from the market mechanism is related to *technologically induced innovations* on such a scale that private industry cannot shoulder the costs. The structural problem here is the acceleration of the adaptation process, or the reduction or elimination of the obstacles which prevent the industry from anticipating the dynamics of future structures. Such decisions relate to the future and so cannot be guided by objective evidence (as with the other types). The choice of activities to be stimulated, the amount required and the question of what firms should be entrusted with the pioneering tools are largely arbitrary. A centralised Common Market approach offers the advantage that costly and prestigious duplications may be avoided, and that larger jobs may be dealt with by pooling resources, but also multiplies the danger of misguided actions or the creation of big 'white elephants'. Clearly this type of deviation can only be treated as a problem of a Common Market industrial policy if its solution is recognised as involving the availability of sufficient objective information about technological

processes and a political decision to be accounted for in a democratically elected European Parliament which has the power to turn down the Commission's proposals.

INDUSTRIAL POLICY: CONFLICT WITH ANTI-TRUST POLICY?

According to a more interventionist conception, industrial policy is any means or method used by the public authorities to direct industrial activity within the context of a general economic programme for the attainment of a number of previously fixed goals. In this perspective contradictions may arise between the finding of competitive solutions and the advancement of socio-political aims.

Such contradictions may appear at two different levels. On the one hand, the authorities may try to achieve certain *nationally defined objectives,* although the forces of international competition would satisfy customers better. In the same way, the European authorities might be tempted to promote strictly European initiatives, while third parties might be able to offer proposals better suited to existing needs. The conflict would therefore be situated at the national (or European) level. On the other hand, industrial policy may be opposed to competition policy independent of national or international considerations, but simply because its *goals cannot always be achieved by competition.* This means that competition and competition policy are regarded as only one means among others, to be adopted or dropped according to their ability to realise certain desirable goals, within acceptable time limits and without intolerable social tensions. Let us examine these two levels.

As we have already seen in the previous chapter, European states, which are no longer able to protect their industrial economies by means of customs systems, still try to support their leading firms and to strengthen cartels or mergers against foreign competitors, European or otherwise. The report on the French Sixth Plan, says:

> that it is necessary to conserve the French character of industries essential for our development, by means of consolidation of the international positions achieved by French firms and the restructuring of particular sectors which are endangered. . . . This will be reached in particular through fiscal incentives for mergers and partial asset take-over.

National authorities also erect barriers to foreign competition by means of the various measures enumerated earlier (technical specifications, safety standards, closure of public markets, and so on).

Attitudes towards foreign direct investments are more varied. In certain European countries there are regulations which control investment interfering with national interests. The French regulations of 27 January 1967, of 24 November 1968 and of 22 February 1971 amount to the following:

(i) all direct investment operations coming from or going to residents of non-E.E.C. countries have to be declared to the Ministry of Finance, which may hold up the operation;

(ii) all direct investments which involve capital movements have to be authorised by the Ministry of Economics and Finance under the exchange-control system;

(iii) operations with E.E.C. residents which do not involve capital movements have to be declared for statistical purposes only; and

(iv) the power to suspend transactions applies to those made with residents of third countries.

Moreover, a specific control relating to transactions concerning industrial property rights and those relevant to scientific or technical aid has been adopted. Likewise, under the Belgian Law of 11 July 1972, all purchases of quoted Belgian equities by natural or legal persons residing outside E.E.C. countries have to be authorised in advance by the Ministry of Finance. This type of regulation focuses primarily on the transfer of trade marks or customers to an existing firm rather than on the creation of new firms.

Contrasting with such controls there exists a whole panoply of regulations, ranging from reduced interest rates to tax exemptions and infrastructural advantages, intended to locate foreign investments in particular areas. Many of these aids go far beyond the compensation necessary for the inconvenience experienced by the foreign firm at its desired location.

If national industrial policies are justified, because no European policy is available, they may nevertheless be ineffective. As Stoleru wrote: 'a French spacecraft, alongside Luna and Apollo, what an ambition! A purely French nuclear fission to compete with Westinghouse and General Electric, what an error! A purely French computer facing IBM and ICL, what an illusion.'[1]

Beyond the nationalism of the member states, there is the question of European nationalism. Through European mergers and the constitution of 'Eurogiants', the idea is to limit intra-European competitive forces and to unite European competitive strength to fend off foreign giants and penetrate foreign shores. Concern has been expressed in the United States and in Japan, for example, that when the European Community does set about agreeing on a common industrial policy, it may go to protectionist excesses against external interests.

Several points can be made about this policy:

(1) We have established, by a review of the relevant evidence, that the benefits of regrouping and mergers are exaggerated and that performance does not improve with size. However, some large-scale common projects may be worth while.

(2) Although European unification is desirable and even necessary, this should not be exalted into a European nationalism striving after a position of power in the world which does not promote the much broader goal of world economic solidarity. A large state cannot do without power, but a responsible state should use its economic resources to promote world integration.

(3) A purely European industrial policy is probably already out of date now that, as we have seen (Chapter 3), multinational firms, whether of American, European or other origin, transcend continental regions. The policy of concertation with European private firms becomes increasingly illusory.

It seems to us far preferable that the large industrialised states in the world should co-ordinate their efforts to control multinational corporations by jointly agreed rules and policies. As already mentioned in Chapter 7, some kind of co-operation between national competition-policy authorities is already developing through the O.E.C.D., to which information is exchanged and policies are compared. The institution of an 'International Control Commission' is envisaged. Instead of lessening the impact of European competition policy it should be strengthened so that a data bank could be set up, international studies undertaken and a minimum of mutually agreed policies carried out.

A more fundamental challenge to competition as a means of attaining a number of socially important objectives is provided by the various shortcomings of the market mechanism. As already mentioned, the free operation of market forces does not guarantee full employment or regional balance, or job satisfaction. For example, in the absence of pollution control firms will adopt the cheaper method of production even if this pollutes the environment. But if laws or regulations prohibiting or reducing pollution differ between countries, competitive forces will lead firms to set up in the countries where control is weakest. The effect will be the operation of a kind of Gresham's law: bad practice drives out good practice.

These considerations inspire the thought that a regulatory Community industrial policy, which is not confined to making or restoring effective competition, is necessary. A number of goals should be fixed for private and public sectors. This is in line with the aims already given in the Commission's *Memorandum on Industrial Policy* and the *Declaration of Paris*.

The fundamental danger of such a policy is that it could be executed by various agencies of the Commission without any democratic control.

We have underlined that it is not the task of competition-policy authorities to look for a better regional distribution of industry within the Common Market or for a 'humanisation' of working conditions (safety regulations, job rotation, codetermination, and so on). Their role is to watch market structure and firms' conduct and restrictions and abuses, but other policies carried out by other authorities, entrusted with industrial, social and regional policies, might well reduce competition.

Then alternative aims, methods and costs will have to be compared and conflicts will have to be solved. If both types of policies are forced into the straitjacket of internal negotiations between the agencies, power conflicts and inefficiency will be the inevitable results and solutions will become more and more technocratically orientated. Compromises will be reached without democratic discussion of the alternatives and large-scale alienation will result.

On the contrary, all the parties concerned, and not just the Commission's civil servants, should be consulted in the process of goal formulation, and final control should be vested in the European Parliament. The idea that Europe's economy can be run as a technocratic organisation should be fully exposed and stamped as illusory. Industrial, regional and social policies affect the lives of ordinary citizens and must be debated publicly, with full knowledge of all the details, in a democratic industrial society.

CONCLUSION

To conclude, the main instrument for organising Europe's industrial economy remains the competitive process, which guarantees freedom of individual choice, the exercise of responsibilities and free scope for initiative. This requires the application of a strict and rigorous competition policy to safeguard the essential virtues of the system.

But at the same time industrial society is increasingly beset by problems. The economy seems less and less capable of spontaneously realising the goals which individual citizens value. We produce and consume more, but the environment in which we live and work deteriorates, from spoiled beaches to fumes destroying our ancient monuments. We become richer, while disasters hit our neighbouring fellows in nearby continents. Our dogs eat more than the average

individual diet of an inhabitant of India, the Sunday edition of the
New York Times alone consumes twenty hectares of Canadian forest
every week, the oil refineries of Porto Marghera are destroying
Venice, and tranquilisers are the best-selling drugs. The economy
shows its fragility by becoming more and more dependent upon
exhaustible reserves of energy and raw materials.

The response to these anxieties cannot be found in a total over-
throw of the system. Nationalisation of the means of production and
State planning of the economy do not lead to better performance
and ensure that the economy functions in the interest of the
overwhelming majority of the population; rather they bring about a
concentration of economic power, far above the existing level which
has been discussed in this book. The response will have to be found
by making social and political decisions at an international level. The
first task of Europe today is not to find a technological or even an
industrial identity but to focus on the contours of a new society, and
this requires continuing debate followed by democratic decision.

In ancient Athens, the *agora*, or market-place, was also the arena
for public debate. This is symbolic: to build a European society,
economics and democracy can and should be merged.

References

CHAPTER ONE

1. See J. Schumpeter, *Capitalism, Socialism and Democracy* (New York: Harper & Row, 1942).
2. See, for example, E. S. Mason, 'Price and Production Policies of Large-Scale Enterprise, *American Economic Review* (March 1939); J. Bain, *Industrial Organization* (New York: Wiley, 1959). Among the important exceptions would be O. E. Williamson, *Corporate Control and Business Behaviour* (Englewood Cliffs, N.J.: Prentice-Hall, 1970); F. M. Scherer, *Industrial Market Structure and Economic Performance* (Chicago: Rand McNally, 1971); A. Philips, *Market Structure, Organization and Performance* (Harvard University Press, 1962).
3. For a synthesis of these attempts, see J. and G. Papanek (eds.), *Industrial Organization and Economic Development*, in honour of E. S. Mason (Boston: Houghton Mifflin, 1971); and L. Weiss, 'Quantitative Studies of Industrial Organization', in *Frontiers of Quantitative Economics*, ed. M. D. Intriligator (Amsterdam: North-Holland, 1971).
4. See especially P. W. S. Andrews, *On Competition in Economic Theory* (London: Macmillan, 1964); R. Marris and A. Wood, *The Corporate Economy* (Harvard University Press, 1971); J. Houssiaux, *Le pouvoir de monopole* (Sirey, 1958); F. Perroux, *L'économie du XXème siècle* (Paris: P.U.F., 1964); A. Cotta, *Les choix économiques de la grande entreprise* (Paris: Dunod, 1970); H. Arndt, *Die Konzentration der Wirtschaft* (Berlin: Duncker & Humblot, 1971); A. Jacquemin, *L'enterprise et son pouvoir de marché* (Paris and Librairie Universitaire, Louvain: P.U.F., 1967) and *Economie Industrielle Européenne* (Paris: Dunod, 1975); H. de Jong, *Dynamische Concentratie theorie* (Leiden, Stenfert-Kroese, 1972); E. Penrose, *The Theory of the Growth of the Firm* (Oxford: Blackwell, 1959); P. Sylos-Labini, *Oligopolio e Progresso Tecnico* (Einaudi: Piccola Biblioteca, 1967).
5. L. H. Dupriez, *Philosophie des conjonctures* (Nauwelaerts: Louvain, 1959).
6. E.E.C. Commission, *Competition Policy*, 1st Report (April 1972) p. 17.
7. E.E.C. Commission, *Competition Policy*, 2nd Report (April 1973) p. 76.
8. See, for instance, United Nations, *The Growth of World Industry*, vol. 1.

CHAPTER TWO

1. K. Marx, *Capital* (1867); see also P. Sweezy (ed.), *Karl Marx and the Close of his Systems* (New York: Kelley, 1949).
2. P. Florence, *Ownership, Control and Success of Large Companies* (London: Sweet & Maxwell, 1961).
3. N. Baloff, 'The Learning Curve, Some Controversial Issues', *Journal of Industrial Economics*, no. 3 (July 1966).
4. J. Blair, *Economic Concentration* (New York: Harcourt, 1972) pp. 114–52.

5. H. Leibenstein, 'Allocative Efficiency vs. "X-Efficiency" ', *American Economic Review* (June 1966).

6. See, for example, R. Polli and V. Cook, 'Validity of the Product Life Cycle', *Journal of Business*, vol. 4 (1969).

7. S. Marglin, 'What do Bosses Do, Origins and Functions of Hierarchy in Capitalist Production', Working Paper (Harvard University, 1970).

8. G. Stigler, 'A Theory of Oligopoly', *Journal of Political Economy*, LXXII, no. 1 (February 1964) pp. 44–61.

9. See the now classical article of G. Debreu and H. Scarf, 'A Limit Theorem on the Core of an Economy', *International Economic Review* (September 1963).

10. K. George, *Industrial Organization* (London: Allen & Unwin, 1971) p. 89.

11. W. Adams and W. J. Adams, 'The Military–Industrial Complex: A Market Structure Analysis', *American Economic Review* (May 1972) pp. 279 ff.

12. See, for example, M. Hall and N. Tideman, 'Measure of Concentration', *American Statistical Association Journal*, no. 62 (March 1967); W. Hildebrand and H. Paschen, 'Ein Axiomatisch Begründetes Konzentrationsmas', *Statistische Informationen*, no. 5 (1964); C. Marfels, 'Absolute and Relative Measures of Concentration Reconsidered', *Kyklos*, vol. XXIV (1971).

13. For France, see Y. Morvan, *La concentration dans l'industrie française* (Paris: A. Colin, 1972) p. 177; and for the United Kingdom, see H. Leak and A. A. Maizels, 'The Structure of British Industry', *Journal of the Royal Statistical Society* (1945) pp. 142–200.

14. See Stigler, 'A Theory of Oligopoly', and K. Cowling, 'Price, Quality and Market Share', *Journal of Political Economy* (November–December 1970).

15. Henry de Jong, *Hearings on Economic Concentration*, 7, Senate Sub-Committee on Antitrust and Monopoly, Washington D.C. (1968).

16. For a full discussion, see E. Malinvaud, *Méthodes statistiques de l'économétrie* (Paris: Dunod, 1964).

17. See also F. L. Pryor, 'An International Comparison of Concentration Ratios', *Review of Economics and Statistics*, no. 2 (May 1972).

18. See E.E.C., *Memorandum on Industrial Policy* (1970) p. 103; and J. P. Nioche, 'Taille des établissements industriels dans sept pays développés', *Entreprises*, Collection de l'I.N.S.E.E., series E, no. 1 (1969) pp. 3–109.

19. The source for this is A. P. Weber and F. Jenny, *Concentration et politique des structures industrielles*, La Documentation Français (Paris, 1974).

20. J. Müller and R. Hochreiter, *Stand, Entwicklung und Konsequenzen der Unternehmenskonzentration in der Bundesrepublik* (Berlin: International Institute of Management, 1975) pp. 62 and 67. For a previous period, see H. Arndt (ed.), *Die Konzentration der Wirtschaft* (Berlin: Duncker & Humblot, 1971).

21. H. de Jong, *Ondernemingsconcentratie* (Leiden: Stenfert-Kroese, 1971).

22. Report of the Commission, *Competition Policy*, 3rd Report, pp. 122–4; figure from p. 125.

23. I. Horowitz, 'Employment and Concentration in the Common Market', *Journal of the Royal Statistical Society*, series A, 133, 3 (1970).

24. K. Arrow, *Essays in the Theory of Risk-Bearing* (Amsterdam: North-Holland, 1970).

25. M. Adelman, 'Concept and Statistical Measurement of Vertical Integration', in National Bureau of Economic Research, *Business Concentration and Price Policy* (Princeton University Press, 1955) p. 282.

26. I. Barnes, in National Bureau of Economic Research, *Business Concentration and Price Policy* (Princeton University Press, 1955).

27. R. Mazzolini, *European Transnational Concentrations* (New York: McGraw-Hill, 1974).

28. That is what recent studies have brought out for West Germany (see J. Müller, *The First IIM Conference on Economics of Industrial Structure* (Berlin, 1974); for France, see A. P. Weber and F. Jenny, 'Concentration et politique des structures industrielles', *Document de travail* (January 1974); for the Netherlands, see de Jong, 'Theory and Evidence Concerning Mergers: An International Comparison; in Jacquemin and de Jong (eds.), *Markets, Corporate Behaviour and the State* (The Hague: Nijhoff, 1976); for the United Kingdom, see L. Hannah and J. A. Kay, *Mergers and Concentration in the U.K., 1919– 1969*, Working Paper (April 1974), and P. Hart, M. A. Utton and G. Walshe, *Mergers and Concentration in British Industry* (Cambridge University Press, 1973) and the papers in *Markets, Corporate Behaviour and the State*, ed. Jacquemin and de Jong.

29. See R. Liefmann, *Kartelle, Handwörkerbuch der Staatswissenschaften*, H. Anflage, 5 Bard (Jena 1923) pp. 611–30.

30. See F. Segelmann, 'Wettbewerb und Rationalisierung unter Berücksichtigung der Syndikate und Spezialisierungskartelle', in *Zehn Jahre Bundeskartelamt* (Köln: Heymanns Verlag, 1968).

31. *Official Journal*, C14 (15 February 1974).

32. See T. Saving, 'Concentration Ratios and the Degree of Monopoly', *International Economic Review*, vol. 11 (February 1970), on which this simplified presentation is based.

CHAPTER THREE

1. J. Houssiaux, *Le pouvoir de monopole* (Paris: Sirey, 1958).

2. K. Arrow, *Essays in the Theory of Risk-Bearing* (Amsterdam: North-Holland, 1970) p. 235.

3. E. T. Penrose, *The Theory of the Growth of the Firm* (Oxford: Blackwell, 1959).

4. H. de Jong, *Dynamische Concentratie-theorie* (Leiden: Stenfert-Kroese, 1972).

5. For the case of the United Kingdom, see M. A. Utton, 'Aggregate versus Market Concentration', *Economic Journal* (1974) pp. 150–5.

6. See F. Edwards, 'Tie-in Sales in Banking and One Bank Holding Companies', *Antitrust Bulletin* (Autumn 1969).

7. See R. S. Markovits, 'Tic-ins, Reciprocity and the Leverage Theory', *Yale Law Journal*, no. 7 (1967).

8. For a general discussion see J. Hirshleifer, *Investment, Interest and Capital* (Englewood Cliffs N.J.: Prentice-Hall, 1970) pp. 278–84.

9. See H. M. Markowitz, *Portfolio Selection – Efficient Diversification of Investments* (New York: Wiley, 1959).

10. W. G. Lewellen, 'A Pure Financial Rationale for the Conglomerate Merger', *Journal of Finance* (May 1971).

11. W. J. Adams, 'Corporate Power and Profitability in the North Atlantic Community', Ph.D. Unpublished thesis (Harvard University, August 1973) p. 22.

12. D. E. Logue and P. A. Naert, 'A Theory of Conglomerate Mergers', *Quarterly Journal of Economics* (November 1969).

13. J. Kitching, 'Why do Mergers Miscarry?', *Harvard Business Review* (November–December 1967).

14. C. Kaysen, 'The Corporation, How Much Power? What Scope?', in *The Corporation in Modern Society* (New York: Atheneum, 1969) p. 100.

15. A. Kaplan, *Big Enterprise in a Competitive System* (Washington D.C.: Brookings Institution, 1964).

16. L. Engwall, *Models of Industrial Structure* (New York: Lexington Books, 1973).

17. See A. Jacquemin and M. Cardon, 'Size Structure, Stability and Performance of the Largest British and E.E.C. Firms', *European Economic Review*, no. 4 (1973).

18. C. Berry, 'Corporate Growth and Diversification', *Journal of Law and Economics* (October 1971).

19. J. D. Gribbin, 'The Conglomerate Merger', *Applied Economics*, no. 8 (1975).

20. A. M. Kumps, *Le conglomérat* (Brussels: La Renaissance du Livre, 1974).

21. D. Schwarz, 'Zum Stand der Wirtschaftskonzentration im Gemeinsamen Market', *Der Bürger im Staat*, no. 4 (1973).

22. E. T. Penrose, *The Theory of the Growth of the Firm* (Oxford: Blackwell, 1966).

23. A. Jacquemin, 'Une mesure entropique de la diversification', *Revue economique* (September 1975).

24. See J. H. Dunning, *La croissance de la grande firme multinationale* (Paris: C.N.R.S., 1973).

25. R. Vernon, 'International Investment and International Trade in the Product Cycle', *Quarterly Journal of Economics* (February 1967); L. Wells, *The Product Life Cycle and International Trade* (Harvard Business School, 1972).

26. The source for the figure is R. Vernon, *The Economic Environment of International Business* (Englewood Cliffs, N.J.: Prentice-Hall, 1972).

27. R. Caves, 'International Corporations, The Industrial Economics of Foreign Investment', *Economica* (February 1971); see also S. Hymer and R. Rowthorn, *International Big Business*, Occasional Papers, no. 24 (Cambridge University Press, 1971).

28. European Commission, *Competition Policy*, 3rd Report, p. 145. These data are only indicative as they mix establishment and acquisition of sales as well as manufacturing operations.

29. L. Franko, 'The Growth, Organizational Structure and Allocative Efficiency of European Multinational Firms', in *La croissance de la grande firme multinationale*, p. 337.

CHAPTER FOUR

1. R. Stonebraker, 'Corporate Profits and Risk of Entry', *Review of Economics and Statistics* (February 1976).

2. K. Lancaster, 'A New Approach to Consumer Theory', *Journal of Political Economy* (April 1966).

3. See Z. Griliches, 'Hedonic Price Indexes for Automobiles: An Econometric Analysis of Quality Change', in *Readings in Economic Statistics and Econometrics*, ed. A. Zellner (1968); J. Triplett, 'Automobiles and Hedonic Quality Measurement', *Journal of Political Economy* (1969); and D. Chif, 'Recherche d'un indice de la variation de qualité pour les voitures automobiles sur le marché belge, 1966 à 1970', *Recherches économiques de Louvain*, no. 2 (May 1971).

4. Thus K. Cowling, 'Price, Quality and Market Share', *Journal of Political Economy* (November–December 1970) has shown that variable quality has a very significant positive statistical effect on the market shares of firms in the agricultural-tractor business.

5. See K. Lancaster, 'Socially Optimal Product Differentiation', *American Economic Review* (September 1975).

6. See R. Caves and R. Jones, *World Trade and Payments* (Boston: Little, Brown & Co. 1973) pp. 216—17.

7. J. J. Lambin, *Advertising, Competition and Market Structure in Oligopoly over Time* (Amsterdam: North-Holland, 1976).

8. See P. Sylos-Labini, *Oligopolio e Progresso Tecnico* (Ennandi: Piccola Biblioteca, 1967); J. Bain, 'Relation of Profit Rate to Industry Concentration: American Manufacturing 1936—1940', *Quarterly Journal of Economics* (August 1951); F. Modigliani, 'New Developments on the Oligopoly Front', *Journal of Political Economy*, no. 2 (June 1958); and P. W. S. Andrews, *Manufacturing Business* (London: Macmillan, 1949).

9. P. Pashigian, 'Limit Price and the Market Share of the Leading Firm', *Journal of Industrial Economics* (July 1968).

10. A. C. Johnson and P. Helmberger, 'Price Elasticity of Demand and Market Structure', *American Economic Review*, no. 5 (December 1967).

11. See K. Cowling, 'On the Theoretical Specification of Industrial Structure — Performance Relationships', *European Economic Review*, no. 1 (June 1976).

CHAPTER FIVE

1. See the survey by L. Weiss, 'Quantitative Studies of Industrial Organisation', in *Frontiers of Quantitative Economics*, ed. M. D. Intriligator (Amsterdam: North-Holland, 1971).

2. H. Leibenstein, 'Allocative Efficiency vs. "X-Efficiency" ', *American Economic Review* (June 1966).

3. H. Levin and J. Müller, *The Meaning of Technical Efficiency* (Berlin: International Institute of Management, October 1973).

4. See R. Posner, *Economic Analysis of the Law* (Boston: Little, Brown & Co., 1972).

5. J. Tinbergen, *Economic Policy and Design* (Amsterdam: North-Holland, 1965).

6. C. Ferguson, *A Macroeconomic Theory of Workable Competition* (Duke University Press, 1964).

7. E.E.C., *Competition Policy*, 1st Report (Brussels, April 1972) p. 12.

8. F. Jenny and A. P. Weber, 'Taux de profit et variables structurelles dans l'industrie manufacturière française', *Revue économique* (November 1974).

9. J. Khalilzadeh-Shirazi, 'Market Structure and Price—Cost Margins in United Kingdom Manufacturing Industries', *Review of Economics and Statistics* (February 1974).

10. W. Shepherd, 'Structure and Behavior in British Industries with U.S. Comparisons', *Journal of Industrial Economics* (November 1972).

11. I. Horowitz, 'An International Comparison of the International Effects of Concentration on Industry Wages, Investments and Sales', *Journal of Industrial Economics*, no. 2 (1971).

12. L. Phlips, *Effects of Industrial Concentration* (Amsterdam: North-Holland, 1971).

13. See F. Jenny and A. P. Weber, 'Concentration, syndicalisation et rémunération salariale', *Revue économique* (July 1975).

14. See M. Blair (ed.), *The Roots of Inflation* (London: Wilton, 1975).

15. H. Demsetz, *The Market Concentration Doctrine* (Washington, D.C.: American Institute for Public Policy Research, 1973).

16. A. Kahn, in *The Roots of Inflation*, ed. Blair, p. 261.

17. S. Ross and M. Wachter, 'Wage Determination, Inflation, and the Industrial Structure', *American Economic Review* (September 1973).

18. See the various contributions in *The Roots of Inflation*.

19. Kahn, in *The Roots of Inflation*, ed. Blair.

20. G. Stigler and J. Kindahl, *The Behaviour of Industrial Prices* (Columbia University Press, 1970).

21. See H. N. Ross, 'Illusions in Testing for Administered Prices', *Journal of Industrial Economics*, no. 2 (April 1973); and the reply by L. Phlips, 'Illusions in Testing for Administered Prices: A Reply', *Journal of Industrial Economics*, no. 2 (April 1973).

23. P. Finet, 'Déterminants de la Recherche—Développement Industrielle en Belgique', *Recherches Economiques de Louvain*, no. 1 (1975).

24. W. J. Adams, 'Firm Size and Research Activity, France and the United States', *Quarterly Journal of Economics* (August 1970).

25. J. J. Servan-Schreiber, *Le Défi-Americain* (Paris: Denöel, 1967).

26. W. Baumol, *Business Behaviour, Value, and Growth* (London: Macmillan, 1959).

27. A. Jacquemin and W. Saëz, *Compared Performances of the Largest European and Japanese Industrial Firms, Oxford Economic Papers* (July 1976).

28. F. Jenny and A. P. Weber, 'Profit Rates and Structural Variables in the French Manufacturing Sector', *European Economic Review* (January 1976).

29. Y. Morvan, *La concentration de l'industrie en France* (Paris: Colin, 1972).

30. J. Samuels and D. J. Smyth, 'Profits, Variability of Profits and Firm Size', *Economica* (May 1968).

31. Weiss, 'Quantitative Studies of Industrial Organisation'.

32. A. Singh and G. Whittington, *Growth, Profitability and Valuation* (Cambridge University Press, 1968).

33. R. Caves, 'International Corporations: The Industrial Economics and Foreign Investment', *Economica* (February 1971).

34. Morvan, *La concentration de l'industrie en France*.

35. J. C. Morand, 'Taille et croissance des entreprises', *Revue d'économie politique*, no. 77 (1967).

36. P. Hart and S. J. Prais, 'The Analysis of Business Concentration: A Statistical Approach', *Journal of the Royal Statistical Association* (1956); Singh and Whittington, *Growth, Profitability and Valuation*; and J. Samuels and A. Chester, 'Growth, Survival and the Size of Companies, 1960—1969', in *Market Structure and Corporate Behaviour*, ed. K. Cowling (London: Gray-Mills, 1972).

37. L. Engwall, *Models of Industrial Structure* (New York: Lexington Books, 1973).

38. Adams, 'Firm Size and Research Activity'.

39. J. P. Biname and A. Jacquemin, 'Structures industrielles des régions belges et grandes entreprises: quelques éléments d'analyse', *Recherches économiques de Louvain*, no. 4 (December 1973).

40. J. Defay, *Recherche et croissance économique*, no. 3 (Brussels: S.P.P.S., 1973).

41. P. Finet, 'Déterminants de la recherche-développement industrielle en Belgique', *Recherches économiques de Louvain*, no. 1 (March 1975).

42. See F. M. Scherer, *Research and Development Return to Scale and the Schumpeterian Hypothesis: Comment* (Berlin: International Institute of Management, July 1973).

43. J. C. Morand, 'La recherche et le développement selon la dimension des entreprises', *Le progrès scientifique*, no. 122 (September 1968).

44. B. Johanisson and C. Lindstrom, 'Firm Size and Inventive Activity', *Swedish Journal of Economics* (December 1971).

45. Weiss, Quantitative Studies of Industrial Organization'.

46. C. Freeman, 'The Role of Small Firms in Innovation in the U.K. since 1965', Committee of Inquiry on Small Firms, *Research Report*, no. 6 (London: H.M.S.O., 1971).

47. D. J. Smyth, J. Samuels and Tzoanos, 'Patents, Profitability, Liquidity and Firm Size', *Applied Economics* (June 1972).

48. C. Kennedy and A. P. Thirwall, 'Surveys in Applied Economics, Technical Progress', *Economic Journal* (March 1972).

49. For a complete discussion of these difficulties, see E. Malinvand, *Statistical Methods of Econometrics* (Amsterdam: North-Holland, 1966), or H. Theil, *Principles of Econometrics* (Amsterdam: North-Holland, 1971).

CHAPTER SIX

1. E. Mason, *The Corporation in Modern Society* (New York: Atheneum, 1966).

2. R. Larner, 'Ownership and Control in the 200 Largest Non-Financial Corporations, 1929 and 1963', *American Economic Review* (September 1966).

3. See also J. M. Chevalier, *La structure financière de l'industrie américaine et le problème du contrôle dans les grandes sociétés américaines* (Paris: Cujas, 1970). He uses the criterion of 5 per cent, below which he considers that there is a managerial control. He concludes that it is the case of 40 per cent of the largest U.S. corporations.

4. O. E. Williamson, *Corporate Control and Business Behaviour* (Englewood Cliffs, N.J.: Prentice-Hall, 1970) p. 129.

5. Ibid.

6. *Patman Report* (1968) p. 5.

7. P. S. Florence, *Ownership, Control and Success of Large Companies* (London: Sweet & Maxwell, 1961).

8. H. K. Radice, 'Control Type, Profitability and Growth in Large Firms: An Empirical Study', *Economic Journal* (September 1971).

9. P. Holl, 'Effect of Control Type on the Performance of the Firm in the U.K.', *Journal of Industrial Economics* (June 1975).

10. H. Daems, *The Holding Company and Corporate Control* (Leiden: Nijhoff, 1977).

11. See ibid.

12. R. Marris, *The Economic Theory of 'Managerial Capitalism'* (London: Macmillan, 1964).

13. O. E. Williamson, 'Managerial Discretion and Business Behaviour', *American Economic Review* (December 1963).

14. W. Baumol, *Business Behaviour, Value and Growth* (London: Macmillan, 1959).

15. See mainly R. Monsen, J. Chiu and D. Cooley, 'The Effects of Separation of Ownership and Control on the Performance of the Large Firm', *Quarterly Journal of Economics* (August 1968); R. Larner, *Management Control and the Large Corporation* (New York: Dunellen, 1970); and D. Kamerschen, 'Ownership and Control and Profit Rates', *American Economic Review* (June 1968).

16. J. Palmer, 'The Profit-Performance Effects on the Separation of Ownership from Control in Large U.S. Industrial Corporations', *Bell Journal of Economics and Management Science*, vol. 4, no. 1 (1973).

17. Radice, 'Control Type, Profitability and Growth in Large Firms'.

18. Holl, 'Effect of Control Type on the Performance of the Firm in the U.K.

19. A. Jacquemin and E. de Ghellinck, 'Propriété, Contrôle et Profitabilité des Grandes Entreprises Françaises,' *Revue d'Economie Politique* (1977).

20. G. Yarrow, 'Executive Compensation and the Objectives of the Firm', in *Market Structure and Corporate Profitability*, ed. K. Cowling (London: Gray-Mills, 1972).

21. G. Meeks and G. Whittington, 'Directors' Pay, Growth and Profitability', *Journal of Industrial Economics* (September 1975).

22. Marris, *The Economic Theory of 'Managerial Capitalism'*.

23. J. Williamson, 'Profit, Growth and Sales Maximisation', *Economica* (February 1966).

24. G. M. Heal and A. Silberston, 'Alternative Managerial Objectives, An Exploratory Note', *Oxford Economic Papers* (June 1972).

25. F. Seton, 'The Geometry of Managerial Objective, A Supplementary Note', *Oxford Economic Papers* (June 1972).

26. H. Leland, 'The Dynamics of a Revenue Maximising Firm', *International Economic Review*, no. 2 (June 1972).

27. See M. Intriligator, *Mathematical Optimization and Economic Theory* (Englewood Cliffs, N.J.: Prentice-Hall, 1971) ch. 14.

28. N. Chamberlain, *The Firm: Micro-Economic Planning and Action* (New York: McGraw-Hill, 1962) p. 375.

29. See E. Latham in *The Corporation in Modern Society*, ed. E. Mason (New York: Atheneum, 1966).

30. J. K. Galbraith, *The New Industrial State* (London: Hamish Hamilton, 1967).

31. R. M. Cyert and J. G. March, *A Behavioral Theory of the Firm* (Englewood-Cliffs, N.J.: Prentice-Hall, 1963) p. 112.

32. A. Shonfield, *Modern Capitalism, the Changing Balance of Public and Private Power* (Oxford University Press, 1965).

33. P. W. S. Andrews, *On Competition in Economic Theory* (London: Macmillan, 1964).

34. The mathematical tools used in the following pages are clearly described in Intriligator, *Mathematical Optimization and Economic Theory*.

35. A. Jacquemin, 'Market Structure and the Firm's Market Power', *Journal of Industrial Economics*, no. 2 (April 1972).

36. V. K. Chetty, 'Necessary and Sufficient Conditions for Optimal Path for a Class of Dynamic Models with Infinite Time Horizon', *CORE Discussion Paper*, 7209 (Louvain, 1972).

37. For a general overview, see A. Jacquemin and J. Thisse, 'Strategy of the Firm and Market Structure: An Application of Optimal Control Theory', in *Market Structure and Corporate Behaviour*, ed. K. Cowling (London: Gray-Mills, 1972).

38. See R. Dorfman and P. O. Steiner, 'Optimal Advertising Policy and Optimal Quality', *American Economic Review*, no. 5 (1964).

39. See M. Nerlove and K. Arrow, 'Optimal Advertising Policy under Dynamic Conditions', *Economica* (1962).

40. P. Dehez and A. Jacquemin, 'A Note on Advertising Policy Under Uncertainty and Dynamic Conditions', *Journal of Industrial Economics*, no. 1 (September 1975).

41. J. K. Gaskins, 'Dynamic Limit Pricing: Optimal Pricing under Threat of Entry', *Journal of Economic Theory*, no. 3 (1971).

42. N. Ireland, 'Concentration and the Growth of Market Demand: A Comment on Gaskins' Limit Pricing Model', *Journal of Economic Theory*, no. 5 (1972).

43. Jacquemin and Thisse, 'Strategy of the Firm and Market Structure'.

44. M. I. Kamien and N. L. Schwartz, 'Cournot Oligopoly with Uncertain Entry', *Review of Economic Studies*, vol. 42 (1975).

45. R. de Bondt, *On the Effects of Retarded Entry*, Working Paper (Catholic University of Louvain: Department of Applied Economics, November 1975).

46. M. I. Kamien and N. L. Schwartz, 'Theory of the Firm with Induced Technical Change: *Metroeconomica* (September—December 1971).

47. See, for example, L. Ruff, 'Research and Technological Progress in a Cournot Economy', *Journal of Economic Theory*, no. 1 (1969).

48. E. Hochman and O. Hochman, 'On the Relation between Demand Creation and Growth in a Monopolistic Firm', *European Economic Review*, no. 4 (1973).

49. J. Schumpeter, *Capitalism, Socialism and Democracy* (New York: Harper & Row, 1942).

50. For a model developing the economic implications of the French system of participation, see G. Koenig, 'Politique de la firme et système français de la participation aux résultats', *Revue économique*, no. 2 (March 1975).

51. B. Ward, 'The Firm in Illyria: Market Syndicalism', *American Economic Review* (September 1953).

52. E. Domar, 'The Soviet Collective Farm', *American Economic Review*, no. 56 (1966).

53. J. Vanek, *The General Theory of Labor-Managed Market Economies* (Cornell University Press, 1970) and *The Participatory Economy* (Cornell University Press, 1971).

54. For a general analysis of the impact of different tax systems upon the main market conducts of the labour-managed firm, see A. Jacquemin and A. Steinherr, *A Note on the Effects of Taxation Assuming Different Objectives for the Firm*, Working Paper 75—39 (Brussels: European Institute for Advanced Studies in Management, November 1975).

55. A. B. Atkinson, 'Worker Management and the Modern Industrial Enterprise', *Quarterly Journal of Economics* (August 1973).

56. J. Meade, 'Labour-Managed Firms in Conditions of Imperfect Condition', *Economic Journal* (December 1974).

57. F. X. Litt, A. Steinherr and J. F. Thisse, *Investment Decisions in Profit-Maximising and Labor-Managed Enterprises: A Dynamic Comparative Analysis* (Berlin: International Institute of Management, August 1975).

58. J. Dreze, *The Pure Theory of Labor-Managed and Participatory Economies* (Louvain: CORE, 1974) pt. I, 'Certainty'.

59. E. Furubotn, 'The Long-Run Analysis of the LM firm: An Alternative Interpretation', *American Economic Review* (March 1976).

60. J. Meade, 'The Theory of Labour-Managed Firms and of Profit Sharing', *Economic Journal*, supplement (March 1972).

CHAPTER SEVEN

1. Economic Council of Canada, *Interim Report on Competition Policy* (Ottawa, 1969) p. 5.

2. A. Cairncross *et al.*, *Economic Policy for the European Community* (London: Macmillan, 1974) p. 143.

3. European Economic Commission, *Competition Policy*, 1st Report (Brussels, April 1972) pp. 11–12.

4. European Economic Commission, *Memorandum on Industrial Policy* (Brussels, 1970).

5. European Economic Commission, *Competition Policy*, 3rd Report.

6. European Economic Commission, *Competition Policy*, 1st Report.

7. European Economic Commission, *Competition Policy*, 4th Report (Brussels, 1975) p. 34.

8. O. E. Williamson, 'Economies as an Antitrust Defense – The Welfare Tradeoff', *American Economic Review* (March 1968).

9. European Economic Commission, *La concentration des entreprises dans le Marché Commun* (Brussels, December 1965).

10. L. Telser, 'Abusive Trade Practices: An Economic Analysis', *Law and Contemporary Problems*, no. 3 (1965).

11. R. Joliet, *Monopolization and Abuse of Dominant Position* (The Hague: Nijhoff, 1970) p. 293.

12. J. Bain, *Industrial Organization* (New York: Wiley, 1959) p. 495.

13. P. Canellos and H. Silber, 'Concentration in the Common Market', *Common Market Law Review*, vol. 7, no. 2 (April 1970).

14. M. Cardon and F. Herbert, *Evolution récente de la notion d'abus de position dominante*, Document de travail CRIDE, no. 719 (Louvain, 1971).

15. For a general analysis, see A. Jacquemin, 'Recent Applications of European rules on Competition to Foreign Firms', *Antitrust Bulletin*, vol. 19, no. 1 (1974).

16. European Economic Commission, *Competition Policy*, 2nd Report (Brussels, April 1973).

CHAPTER EIGHT

1. L. Stoleru, *L'impératif industriel* (Paris: Seuil, 1969).

Index

269